VOTES FOR WOMEN

North Wales Suffragists' Campaign
1907-1914

First published in 2015

© Barbara Lawson-Reay

© Gwasg Carreg Gwalch 2015

ISBN: 978-1-84527-550-1

Published with the financial support
of the Welsh Books Council

Cover Design: Eleri Owen

Published by Gwasg Carreg Gwalch,
12 Iard yr Orsaf, Llanrwst, Conwy, LL26 0EH.
Tel: 01492 642031 Fax: 01492 641502
e-mail: books@carreg-gwalch.com
internet: www.carreg-gwalch.com

VOTES FOR WOMEN

NORTH WALES SUFFRAGISTS' CAMPAIGN
1907-1914

Barbara Lawson-Reay

Early in July 1913, people from all over England and Wales set out from their hamlets, villages, towns and cities on a National Union of Women's Suffrage Societies (NUWSS) Pilgrimage to walk just a few miles, or all the way to London. For the 70,000 who reached the capital there was a rally in Hyde Park on 26 July.

The north Wales contingent left Bangor on 2 July and was joined by further supporters en route to Prestatyn, their chosen destination. But at least four of the women walked all the way to London, two of whom were Secretaries of their local societies – Mrs Charlotte Price White of Bangor and Miss Mildred Spencer of Colwyn Bay.

This book is written to commemorate Mrs Price White and Miss Spencer and all the other named and unnamed women – and men – who supported the NUWSS in Rhyl, Colwyn Bay, Llandudno, Penmaenmawr, Bangor, Bethesda, Caernarfon and Llŷn, walking 'shoulder to shoulder and friend to friend'.

They deserve to be remembered.

This book is also for Mrs Ruth Short,
English Mistress,
West Kirby County Grammar School for Girls, Wirral,
late 1950's – early 1960's
After more than fifty years
I still remember her with gratitude and affection.

Barbara Lawson-Reay

Contents

Notes   8

Chapter 1   **1907**
**The Formation of the First Women's Suffrage
Society in north Wales at Llandudno**   10

Chapter 2   **1908**
Membership of the Llandudno Cell reaches 120   16

Chapter 3   **1909**
Rhyl, Colwyn Bay and Bangor Societies formed   23

Chapter 4   **1910**
**Welsh Women Liberals give up political work to
support the National Union of Women's Suffrage
Societies (NUWSS)**   50

Chapter 5   **1911**
Penmaenmawr Society formed   64

Chapter 6   **1912**
Welsh-speaking women join the campaign   92

Chapter 7   **1913**
The year of 'The Pilgrimage'   123

Chapter 8   **1914**
The end of an era   163

Chapter 9
The War and afterwards   181

Appendix A
Visiting Dignitaries – Who was Who   186

The following Appendices list Officers, Committee Members and Supporters:

Appendix B
Llandudno   216

Appendix C
Rhyl and Abergele   227

Appendix D
Colwyn Bay   233

Appendix E
Bangor   248

Appendix F
Penmaenmawr   259

Appendix G
Caernarfon, Bethesda, Cricieth and Pwllheli   261

Postscript   265

Acknowledgments   266

Photographic Credits   267

Bibliography   268

Index   269

Notes

Double-barrelled surnames:
In the Appendices, double-barrelled names (including St ...) will be found under the second name

Frequently used abbreviations:

ILP	Independent Labour Party
NUWSS	National Union of Women's Suffrage Societies (non-militant Suffragists)
WFL	Women's Freedom League (refused to pay taxes and complete government forms, e.g. Censuses, but non-violent)
WSPU	Women's Social and Political Union (militant Suffragettes)

Conversion rates:

£	1910	1920
£1	£43	£21
£5	£285	£106
£10	£570	£212
£25	£1,426	£530
£50	£2,853	£1,060
£100	£5,706	£2,121
£1,000	£57,060	£21,210

Many Suffragette postcards were produced – those not issued by the Suffragettes themselves were invariably derogatory. The card on the cover is unusual in that she is wearing both the Suffragists' red and the Suffragettes' purple, white and green.

Chapter 1

1907

The formation of the first Women's Suffrage Society in north Wales, at Llandudno

Most locals and many visitors to Llandudno will be aware of the Cocoa House restaurant situated in George Street at the side of the Town Hall. If they pause to read the framed newspaper articles on their way downstairs, they will learn that they are entering the building where the first cell of the National Union of Women's Suffrage Societies (NUWSS) in Wales, was formed on 23 January 1907. Today's restaurant would have been the cellar of the original building which opened directly onto Mostyn Street.

At that time the Cocoa House was part of a chain of Temperance Restaurants and Hotels (Chester had four) where working men, their wives and families, met to eat pies and cakes, drink cocoa and coffee and sing – nothing indecent allowed! Penny dinners were served to the poor and from 1884 the Workmen's Blue Ribbon Club was set up there to reform drunkards. Imbibers 'Signed the Pledge' to spurn drink for twelve months, donate 3d per week to the Temperance Society and pay a fine of 2/6d if caught drinking alcohol – this was a huge amount in 1907, with wages for many standing at around £1 per week.

The Llandudno Cocoa House was run by Sarah Annie Reeves Hughes and her husband Hugh. It's probable that the Llandudno Ladies' Temperance Society met there and a formidable bunch they look! It's also probable that at least

*Llandudno Cocoa House – 1st NUWSS cell in Wales formed here on
23 January, 1907*

some of the members of the Temperance Society became
Suffragists, as the British Women's Temperance
Association, to which their society would have been
affiliated, actively supported women's suffrage.

NUWSS members were Suffragists – dignified and law-
abiding – as befitted Victorian and Edwardian 'ladies', as
opposed to the militant and sometimes violent Suffragettes
– 'the shrieking sisterhood'. It's understandable that
Suffragettes considered the Suffragists ineffectual – so little
progress had been made over a period of more than fifty
years. The Suffragettes thought the campaign needed to be
higher profile and if that meant chaining themselves to
railings, or damaging property in order to get publicity for
'The Cause' – then so be it! 'Deeds not Words' was their
motto.

Early in 1907 a circular was sent to a number of Llandudno

Llandudno Ladies' Temperance Society

ladies as follows: 'On Wednesday 23rd January at 2.30 p.m. a ladies' meeting by invitation will be held at the Cocoa House by kind permission of Mrs Reeves-Hughes, to discuss the question of women's suffrage. You are cordially invited to attend. No press and no men admitted. Kindly bring this card with you'.

The Welsh Coast Pioneer reported that the meeting was chaired by Mrs Annie Walton-Evans, wife of David Evans, the Archdeacon of St Asaph. She said that women's suffrage had become so important that the women of Llandudno felt it behoved them, as intelligent women, to discuss the matter and decide as to their attitude towards it. She declared herself to be strongly in favour of women's suffrage on the same terms as it was, or may be later, granted to men.

Mrs Mary Gooddy, a surgeon's wife, based her support on the fact that laws needed to be updated or new ones made, particularly with regard to marriage and inheritance; indirect taxation – which greatly affected working women of the lower classes and the registration and hours of labour of sick nurses. She believed women to be as capable of legislating on these matters as men.

A Mrs Edgell (whom I haven't been able to trace) spoke about the proper position of women in the world, pleading that if women would only take their rightful place, men would speedily recognise women's perfect suitability to be consulted on the framing of laws affecting the well-being of the nation.

Miss Marie-Louise Eakin, owner of a private girl's school, spoke on behalf of teachers and university women.

Miss (Susan) Edith Champneys stated

*Miss (Susan) Edith Champneys,
in the uniform of Chief Inspector,
Women's Auxilliary Police WW1*

that once women were given the parliamentary vote they would be able to vastly improve social conditions, pointing out that their advice on over-crowding, housing, sanitation, education, infirmaries, inebriate's homes and lunatic asylums would be invaluable.

After discussion it was decided to form the Llandudno Cell of the NUWSS with the object of obtaining the parliamentary franchise for women on the same grounds as it was, or may be, granted to men. Mrs Walton-Evans was the first President, Miss Lucy Champneys, Secretary and Mrs Gooddy, Treasurer.

Mrs Gooddy, Miss Walton-Evans, Miss Florence Wright and Dr Edith Guest followed Miss Champneys as Secretary. I believe Miss Walton-Evans to have been Annie Beatrice, but she is always referred to as Miss Walton-Evans. From 1910 Mr Alfred Pugh, Chartered Accountant and Estate Agent, became Treasurer.

The *North Wales Weekly News* did not see fit to report on the inaugural meeting, only to publish an obsequious

Mrs Millicent Garrett Fawcett, National President NUWSS

editorial stating that whilst it was an honour for Llandudno to be the home of the first women's suffrage organisation in north Wales, it was hoped that members would not feel it necessary to go to gaol as 'martyrs for The Cause', nor follow the violent examples of the Pankhursts and Mary Gawthorpe.

The only other Llandudno meeting reported in 1907 was a visit in March by Mrs Millicent Garrett Fawcett, NUWSS President, to a reception at the Craig y Don Boarding Establishment. Whether there weren't any further meetings – or more likely, the newspapers failed to report on them isn't known.

Possibly news of the newly formed Llandudno Cell reached Bangor, because the Rev. T. Wheldon of Tabernacl Chapel took it upon himself to advise the ladies of his Literary Society at their April Tea, not to become involved with 'The Movement'! In May Bangor youths, seeing the Women's Movement as something to be ridiculed, dressed as females and played a burlesque football match on Bangor City ground.

During 1907, three members of the WSPU, unhappy at Mrs Pankhurst's domination of the organisation, broke away and formed the Women's Freedom League (WFL), the Liverpool branch of which was active in north Wales. Members of the WFL were militant in that they refused to pay taxes and complete government forms, e.g. censuses, but they were non-violent.

Chapter 2
1908

Membership of the Llandudno Cell reaches 120

January

The Llandudno Cell's first AGM was chaired by Mr Harold Rathbone (founder of the Della Robia Pottery, Birkenhead), who said it was gratifying that they had started out with twenty members and now had 120. He said it was very important that women should attend meetings where their own interests were concerned. There had recently been a meeting to decide whether Llandudno should continue as an Urban District Council or become a Borough, which would affect lodging-house keepers – many of whom were women – but the audience had been mainly men. 'Married women should use their influence with their husbands, with due patience and avoidance of irritation, of course, to widen their husband's views with respect to female claims'.

Mr Rathbone continued that no sane person would deny that women should have equal rights with men. Women couldn't be excluded without a gigantic loss to society – where would art, drama, literature and music be without women? Women, he said, had only recently awakened to the fact that their right to be equal should not be dependent upon the goodwill or whim of men, so women had set out to prove that intelligence and perseverance were not the prerogative of men.

Miss Barker and Mrs Wilson were elected vice-presidents. (I haven't been able to identify either of them due to lack of initials and partial addresses and there were large numbers of both names in the Llandudno Directory, published circa 1912).

Miss Edith Champneys then proposed putting forward a woman candidate for the forthcoming Llandudno UDC election. Mrs Elsie Marks pointed out that only single women would be eligible. Councillor Ernest Bone responded that he was not in favour of the NUWSS nominating a candidate since the NUWSS was supposed to be independent; but if an NUWSS member wished to put herself forward just as a woman interested in local affairs, rather than representing the NUWSS, then he would have no objection. (No woman actually stood for the March Election).

February
The Llandudno Cell met at the Cambridge Restaurant, the meeting being chaired by Councillor Bone.

Mrs Elsie Marks gave an account of the quarterly Council Meeting in London and said how impressed she had been with the businesslike way in which it had been conducted and the high standard of discussion. She said that she had left with an even deeper conviction that women should have the vote.

Miss Florence Wright, Secretary, reported on the NUWSS Reception she had attended at the opulently decorated blue and gold Grand Hall of the Criterion Restaurant, London, and commented that what particularly impressed her was the total absence of vulgarly overdressed cartoon Suffragettes. This venue was frequently used for meetings of the Actresses' Franchise League.

A Miss Edwards then addressed the meeting and explained how, for fifty years, the NUWSS had worked on constitutional lines. Just one appeal to the House of

Commons had cost £700. Some people asked why they didn't employ cheaper methods, e.g. petitions, but petitions had proved ineffective – once they reached the House of Commons they were never heard of again.

Referring to the Suffragettes Miss Edwards said she felt it was better to show some energy than be satisfied with a sluggish cause – the NUWSS should either make progress, or cease to trouble the world with its existence. Mr Asquith (Prime Minister, 1908-16) had said they still had to prove that the majority of women wanted the vote and they should make every effort to demonstrate that they did. [applause]

Councillor Bone said that he was in favour of the bill shortly coming before parliament to give women the vote and moved that the House of Commons be petitioned to pass the Women's Franchise Bill during this session. Mr William Brookes seconded the resolution, but added that he thought the NUWSS would gain more sympathy from men and have greater success, if it could align itself with another

Mrs Edith Rigby

movement for women – particularly working women, e.g. a Trades Union for women employed in factories. The resolution was carried unanimously.

Also in February 1908, an ex-Penrhos College student, Edith Rigby (nee Rayner), played a leading role in 'The Pantechnicon Incident'. After the King's speech once again failed to mention women's enfranchisement, Mrs Rigby hired two furniture vans, filled them with Suffragettes and arranged for them to be parked directly outside the House of Commons to give the women chance to enter the lobbies. (The previous year the Suffragettes had tried to march to parliament but only fifteen out of 400 succeeded in getting past the police on 'Black Friday'.)

May

The *North Wales Weekly News* (Llandudno) May Day report was headlined: 'Suffragettes overawed by Police Inspector' and went on to explain: 'the presence of Police Inspector Victor Turnpenny in the Procession was an innovation and suggested itself to the May Day Committee in view of the possibility of a disturbance by Suffragettes'. They added that: 'it is only fair to say that his professional services were not called upon'.

Mrs Walton-Evans came over from St Asaph to preside at the Llandudno Cell's meeting and spoke about the great Suffrage Procession which was to be held in London on 13 June. She said that by going to London they would prove that women did indeed want the vote. (The main objection to women having the vote was the popular misconception that most of them didn't want it.) The NUWSS went in strongly for constitutional policy and it had occurred to the heads of the organisation that by arranging a demonstration, the argument against women having the vote would be removed. She said she knew some women had a dislike of being put in a public position, but it was marvellous the way they lost their self-consciousness when they got together with other women.

The London and North Western Railway had refused to offer NUWSS members concessionary fares, despite the fact that a few weeks earlier they had run a special excursion from Llandudno to London for the Cup Final for 11/- ... obviously it was more important for men to be able to watch football than for women to get the vote!

Mrs Walton-Evans urged them all to travel to London on the 13th to join the procession, as it was the last opportunity to impress upon men that women really wanted the vote, before the Conciliation Bill was debated in parliament.

October

Miss Walton-Evans held an 'At Home' at 4 Abbey Road, Llandudno attended by a large number of fashionably-attired ladies.

Councillor James Marks presided and introduced Miss Eleanor Rathbone (daughter of the late William Rathbone MP), Liverpool's first female Councillor and Secretary of Liverpool NUWSS, who stood on a chair in the drawing room to deliver her speech. She said that every fair-minded person must think that whatever may be said against the WSPU, they had brought women's suffrage before the

Miss Eleanor Rathbone

public and made it a real question of practical politics. Those who spoke harshly of the unladylike or undignified conduct of certain women, should ask themselves whether any good cause in the world had been successfully advocated without some undesirable demonstrations of honest zeal? Surely women wouldn't be subjected to the restraint and discomfort of imprisonment just for the sake of seeing their names in the newspapers? To date moderate methods had failed and WSPU methods had injured the lives, physical well-being and comfort of no one except the Suffragettes themselves.

When parliament took it upon itself to regulate every minute detail of women's lives – e.g. when and for how long they could take meal breaks in factories and shops and, as had recently been proposed by Mr David Shackleton, MP for Clitheroe, solving the unemployment problem by restricting the hours of work of married women, then it was time for women to have their say. Mr Shackleton should remember, said Miss Rathbone, that his salary in his official capacity with the Trades Union was paid by the sixpences of the very women whose hours he wanted to restrict! Indeed, women's suffrage was now a matter for the masses of working women rather than just the wealthy and leisured. Miss Rathbone then moved a resolution to Mr Asquith to consider women's suffrage in the next session, which was seconded by Dr Edward Gooddy and carried unanimously.

Archdeacon Evans in his thanks to Miss Rathbone mentioned what a true benefactor her father had been to Caernarfonshire, especially in the field of education. He said that one of his own daughters (Annie Beatrice Walton-Evans) was now the youngest Lady Guardian in England and Wales, serving on the St Asaph Board of Guardians. After only three years she had been appointed HM Inspector of the Boarding-Out of Children and if she hadn't first been given the opportunity to serve as a guardian, she would never have been able to prove that she had the qualities necessary for the post of inspector. But, he added as a cautionary note, he didn't believe that the end ever justified the means where Suffragettes' attacks upon property were concerned.

November

Early in the month the *North Wales Weekly News* reported that an Anti-Suffrage League was in the process of being formed in Llandudno and developments were awaited with interest.

At the end of the month the newspaper reported that much comment had been made upon the fact that no members of the Anti-Suffrage League had accepted the challenge of Miss Walton-Evans on behalf of the local Suffragists, to debate upon their respective positions. Miss Walton-Evans had done all she could to bring about a meeting of the opposing sides, but up to the time of writing, without success.

Chapter 3
1909

Rhyl, Colwyn Bay and Bangor Societies formed

January

On New Year's Day Llandudno launched 'The Llandudno Suffrage News' and took care to point out on the title page that the NUWSS was non-party and non-militant.

In her letter to subscribers, the editor, Miss Walton-Evans, urged each of them to convert one person to women's suffrage each quarter. 'So let us all take up this work in this new year, that in years to come we may be able to say that we helped to get the vote for women' she wrote.

February

The Llandudno Cell held its AGM at the Craig y Don Boarding Establishment, courtesy of Miss Edith Middleton.

Dr Edward Gooddy chaired the meeting and opened by saying that several MP's were in favour of women's suffrage but the present government wasn't. The Home Office was treating women who interrupted meetings as common criminals, not political prisoners – it was ridiculous. Mr David Lloyd George (Chancellor 1908-1915, Prime Minister 1916-22) had said that interrupting meetings was a disgrace – but Dr Gooddy considered it merely a breach of good manners.

He then appealed for more subscriptions, saying Llandudno ought to be able to send more than £30 per year to NUWSS Head Office.

Mrs Gooddy, Treasurer, reported that they had started the year with £1 17 8d in hand, had collected £18 13 6d from 170 members and now had £6 19 10d in hand.

Several unspecified alterations to their rules were proposed by Mrs Elsie Marks and seconded. Miss Walton-Evans' sister, Ana Decima, was elected to serve on the committee.

In the same month, Rhyl ladies held a meeting at the Town Hall to discuss whether to form a branch of the NUWSS. They persuaded gentlemen to act as stewards wearing sashes in the NUWSS colours – red, white and green.

Dr Wycliffe Goodwin presided and the platform party included Miss Margaret Ashton from Manchester, Miss Champneys, Mr J. Roger Dawson, Miss Eakin, Dr Edward and Mrs Mary Gooddy, Mr Harold Rathbone and Miss Florence Wright from Llandudno and Rev. Verrier Jones, Miss Florence Perks, Mrs Annie de Rance and Mr Henry Tilby from Rhyl.

Dr Goodwin said he was in favour of some women getting the vote, but if all women got the vote it would be a catastrophe – just as it would be if all men got the vote. As soon as women were educated to the same level as men, women should get the vote. Women didn't reason like men but when they had been educated to reason, they would be a power to be reckoned with.

Miss Ashton then said all they wanted was for women who qualified by having the same responsibilities as men, to have the same rights as men. Men had nothing to fear from women having the vote, because for every woman there would still be five men with the vote. In countries where women already had the vote there hadn't been any revolutions and although when women first got the vote more of them tended to use it than men, once men realised this, more men voted as well. MP's shouldn't be representing only half the population and it was robbery to take taxes from women when they didn't have any say in how those taxes were spent.

At this point a cat walked down the length of the centre aisle, surveyed the stage and jumped onto a gentleman's knee, where it settled itself comfortably and dozed for the rest of the meeting.

Miss Ashton continued that she wasn't saying all men were bad, but some were and women wanted to be able to protect themselves from bad men. Women's enfranchisement wouldn't affect men who were doing their duty by women, but it would help women who had bad husbands or bad employers. [cheers]

From Rhyl, the Rev. Verrier Jones said he supported 'The Cause' because it was just.

Mr Henry Tilby said he supported women's suffrage because it would be for the national good, but he didn't think MP's or men in general were ungenerous to women. Women must convince their own sex of the importance of the vote before 'The Movement' would have the success it deserved. He said women were as educated, intelligent and moral as men and where women were responsible for household finances, no government could justify with-holding the vote from them. He said that with every past government's extension of the franchise it had been feared that the country would go to the dogs, but it hadn't and this government was as good as any other. [prolonged cheers]

From Llandudno Dr Gooddy said there were many questions only women could deal with and many men preferred talking about cup ties and horse-racing, rather than politics.

Miss Wright said only ignorant and selfish men opposed women getting the vote.

Mr Rathbone said it was unfair to keep women down and if he had his way every little boy would be taught to sew buttons on!

Dr Goodwin concluded that he thought women had been apathetic about politics and urged them to take practical action to support the NUWSS.

Lady Laura McLaren of Bodnant was invited to be Rhyl Society's President.

May

The Llandudno Cell held a meeting at the Aberconwy Temperance Hotel with the aim of forming a branch in Conwy (but that doesn't appear to have come about). The meeting room was adorned with a banner stating 'England (not Wales) loves fair play'.

Llandudno's Treasurer, Mr Alfred Pugh, praised the work of the Llandudno Cell and stressed that members belonged to no political party – or rather to all political parties, embracing as they did people of various political opinions, who nevertheless agreed as to the justice of 'The Cause' of women's suffrage.

Mr Pugh said that so long as women, as at present, discharged their obligations as citizens, there was no reason why they should be debarred from the citizen's right to take an active and decisive part in the government of their own country. Parliament was becoming more and more a machine for social legislation and administration and he would welcome the participation of women voters, because he believed legislation would become more altruistic and therefore more sympathetic in dealing with those questions which had become so pressing that they could not be ignored by this or any future government – questions of unemployment, poverty, drunkenness and depravity.

Miss Spencer from Colwyn Bay said that the formation

of the Anti-Suffrage League was a good thing, because it meant people were thinking about women's suffrage and apathy, not outright opposition, was the hardest thing to overcome. She continued that people had come to the point where they wanted the opportunity to hear both sides of the argument, but it was difficult to lure the opposition into debate because their position was indefensible. The Suffragists had the facts and logical argument on their side, whereas the Anti-Suffragists had merely inertia, prejudice and tradition.

Miss Spencer continued that she had read the report of the recent Anti-Suffragists' meeting in Rhyl – it had been described as 'quite a fashionable gathering with a considerable proportion of the county families from Denbighshire and Flintshire represented'. She thought it very unfortunate that one speaker had chosen to quote Queen Victoria's comment: 'We women are not made for government and if we are good women we must dislike these masculine occupations', when everyone knew that Queen Victoria had been an excellent ruler and made her influence felt not only throughout Britain, but in every corner of the Empire.

Miss Spencer said the Anti-Suffragists' Chairman had claimed that 'poets, scientists, statesmen and theologians – the aristocracy of intellect – had, to a man, been against women's suffrage'. She went on to refute this with her own list of men eminent in their fields – but still supporters of votes for women. She added that if the Anti-Suffragists' Chairman's speech was the best they had to offer, she didn't think the Suffragists had anything to fear.

Miss Spencer concluded that when justice was done, good always resulted and only good could come from women having the vote.

The reporter who summarised the meeting said that

Miss Spencer's speech was peppered with apt sayings, but he had space to include only one example: 'I have my own definition of 'a woman's sphere' – it is any place where a woman can be of use'.

Mrs Walton-Evans was next to take the floor and opened by explaining that they were not asking for a vote for every woman (because not all men had the vote), but if the woman of the house paid the rates and taxes and supported the home financially, then she should be the one able to vote. She referred to the sweated labour of women in workshops and factories. There were at that time 1¼ million more women than men in Britain who had to work to live.

The cotton trade was said to be the best paid, with an average wage for a woman of 14/- per week. But there were thousands of women who could not hope to earn more than half of that for their whole lives.

Concluding, she appealed to women who had not yet joined a suffrage society to do so, for their less fortunate sisters' sakes if not for their own and also to men to support them.

Dr Helena Jones, Birmingham Schools Medical Officer

June

In the summer of 1909 Miss Mary Gawthorpe was persuaded by her friend, Dr Helena Jones to pay her first visit to north Wales. Dr Jones arranged for Conwy Town Hall to be booked for Miss Gawthorpe to address a meeting there on 28 June. But Miss Gawthorpe's visit to

Conwy was only nine days after Suffragettes had disrupted the Eisteddfod being held in London's Albert Hall. Prime Minister, Mr Asquith (no doubt persuaded by Mr Lloyd George) had agreed to attend the Ceremony of the Crowning of the Bard, but as soon as he stepped onto the platform, banners were unfurled accompanied by cries of '*Pleidlaisiau i Fenywod*' (Votes for Women). These were largely drowned out by the choir singing '*Hen Wlad fy Nhadau*' (Land of my Fathers – the Welsh National Anthem), but Mr Asquith's address was continually interrupted and a number of Suffragettes were forcibly ejected from the hall.

VOTES FOR WOMEN.

Photo. by Schmidt, Manchester.

Miss MARY E. GAWTHORPE,
Organiser, National Women's Social and Political Union,
4, Clement's Inn, Strand, W.C.

Miss Mary Gawthorpe

For good measure Mrs Emmeline Pethick-Lawrence chained herself to a seat and it took a considerable time to extricate her. This caused a good deal of ill feeling towards the Suffragettes.

The main reason there were sufficient Welsh-speakers in London to be able to organise their own Eisteddfod, was because in the mid-1800's a huge number of dairymen, experiencing very difficult times in Wales, had moved themselves and their dairy herds to London and opened 'milk shops'. By 1900 it is estimated that half the dairies in London were owned by Welshmen and 700 were still in existence in 1950. It's thought the last one closed as late as 2001.

Mrs Edith Mansell-Moullin, a member of the WSPU, formed the Cymric Union in London and this group regularly handed out suffrage literature at Welsh chapels and milk shops in the capital.

For some days before the Conwy meeting, handbills announced that Miss Gawthorpe was coming. When the *North Wales Weekly News* reporter spoke to her prior to the meeting Miss Gawthorpe was undaunted by the hostility. She was holding a 'Votes for Women' banner and was eagerly anticipating the excitement to follow. Miss Gawthorpe was described as 'a little lady with a waxen complexion, bright dancing eyes and keen determination, quick at perception, smart at repartee and fearless – no-one could deny her pluck.'

When the day arrived, Conwy Town Hall was packed with young men. When the Chairman, Sir Henry Lewis from Bangor stood up to open the meeting the youths burst into '*Hen Wlad fy Nhadau*', followed by three cheers for Mr Lloyd George! Miss Gawthorpe, after being greeted with a hearty rendition of 'Mary had a little lamb' gamely tried for an hour to give her speech, but was completely drowned out by rattles, horns, penny-trumpets, squeakers, whistles, catcalls and singing. She invited those who wanted to hear what she had to say to come to the front, but it was the hecklers who surged towards the stage. She said quiet meetings were never reported, but accounts of this meeting would be broadcast throughout the length and breadth of England and Wales.

By 8.15 p.m. the Chairman was so concerned for Miss

Conwy Town Hall

Gawthorpe's safety and that of the audience, that he asked her to close the meeting, saying it was obvious that an accident could occur at any second and he could not be held responsible.

But Miss Gawthorpe shouted above the din: 'We have nothing to fear – I am going on!' And further, turned her attention to the Rev. Hubbard who was standing at the end of the stage and shouted at him that she believed he was encouraging the rioters. He dissented but added 'She's got some spirit.'

At this point Miss Gawthorpe realised that someone was about to throw a chair and shouted 'Put it down!'

A woman close to the stage remarked 'She's got good lungs.'

When a man actually climbed onto the stage Miss Gawthorpe asked why the police didn't arrest him like they arrested Suffragettes?

Suddenly the crowd tried to turn over the reporter's table and the Rev. Hubbard appealed to them to refrain from horseplay, at which point the Chairman stood up, said the meeting was closed and walked out.

Professor Hudson-Williams also from Bangor tried to address the meeting and said it was the first time he'd ever known a fellow Welshman not get a fair hearing in Wales – and suggested that the hecklers were using the methods adopted by the Suffragettes.

The jostling and shaking of the reporter's table made their position untenable and they had to jump onto the stage, followed by the crowd. Miss Gawthorpe disappeared from view, but the young men who'd been most prominent in the heckling formed a protective cordon around her.

However, Miss Gawthorpe didn't want protection. She told the youth she considered to be the ring-leader of the heckling and the cordon, that what she did want was for him to get a hearing for her. He denied being the ring-leader, but explained to her that the reason for the uproar was the Suffragettes' interruption of the Eisteddfod. She asked for peace so she could explain fully, but it was futile and a vote of confidence in Mr Lloyd George was passed.

John Hughes, a librarian with a genial and persuasive manner, drew Miss Gawthorpe's attention to a by-law relating to the letting of the hall, but she took no notice whatsoever.

Her voice still piped higher than the rest, but it wasn't possible to hear what she was saying. Stern police looked on helpless as frivolous youths played games on the stage.

Miss Gawthorpe tried all her artifices to get converts to 'The Cause' and everyone admired her persistence, if not discretion. Soon afterwards she announced that it had been a successful meeting and left with the words: 'God bless you all'.

She was considered lucky to have made it to Conwy Station unscathed, guarded by police and militia. She told the *North Wales Weekly News* reporter that she did not think what had happened at the meeting was a true reflection of the feelings of the people of Conwy. The ring-leader and his supporters regretted very much the storm they had raised and she had been told by two or three of these young men – and she believed they were sincere in what they said, that they would arrange at the earliest possible convenience for her to speak at a Welsh Liberals Meeting. Miss Gawthorpe said that were she to be so invited the only condition she would impose would be that she should have a fair hearing and after explaining the Suffragettes' tactics, she would answer any questions which might be put.

Further, she would challenge Mr Lloyd George to meet her along with local Liberals.

£4 worth of damage was done to the hall – a large number of the best armchairs were seriously damaged, the seats of some of the cane chairs were broken and the front of the stage was damaged.

August
Early in the month Miss Gawthorpe held her first meeting on Llandudno shore, inviting those seated on the sands and passing promenaders, to gather round and hear why women should have the vote. The crowd was large and attentive but at the end of her talk Miss Gawthorpe faced some fairly hostile questions, particularly about the WSPU's militant activities.

Further meetings were held both at Llandudno and Colwyn Bay. At her first meeting on Colwyn Bay sands, Miss Gawthorpe was approached by a Promenade Inspector, who asked if she had permission to hold such an assembly. To which she cheerfully replied 'No'. It was reported that the Inspector immediately realised that although he had the might of the District Council behind him, he was a mere male and somewhat lamely asked for her address. Miss Gawthorpe provided both her Manchester and Llandudno addresses and explained that she hadn't sought permission, because having previously made a request to the Town Clerk at Llandudno and having been told he didn't think there'd be any objection, she'd subsequently been told by the Llandudno Promenade Inspector that she needed written permission. She had obediently, immediately gone to the Council, which was sitting, to request written permission, but had been refused leave to speak to the council members. She did not know if she would be thrown into Caernarfon Gaol in the near future, but the Suffragettes' motto was 'Always carry on until you're stopped' and that was precisely what she intended to do! And precisely what she did for the rest of the summer.

Little did Miss Gawthorpe know that whilst she was proselytizing, the Arcadia Pierrots were performing a screamingly funny (and doubtless derogatory) Suffragette sketch just a few yards away.

But the last word must go to a rather matronly lady who commented: 'I'd like to see the man who could stand up to her.'

On one occasion at Colwyn Bay, Miss Gawthorpe was accompanied by a Miss Barry who addressed her audience from the top of two boxes arranged precariously one on top of the other. It was reported that Miss Barry was admired as much for her ability to balance as for her oratory, proving that Suffragettes had the same contempt for the Law of Gravity as they had for men, maybe because women had no part in forming that law either! Miss Barry's delivery was quiet and sedate and her speech was not interrupted, but her final point – that it ought to be possible for Mrs Lloyd

George to have a place in the cabinet, was heartily cheered.

Catching sight of a *Weekly News* reporter, Miss Gawthorpe thanked him for his coverage of her own speeches but pointed out that she wasn't a Suffragist but a Suffragette, not a non-militant but a militant. And added as an afterthought, 'but we aren't so very much worse than the other sort!'

From 1909 the north Wales coast became a magnet for the Liverpool branch of the WFL. The women lodged in Llanfairfechan for the month of August and held meetings there and at Penmaenmawr, Conwy, Llandudno, Colwyn Bay and Abergele – not primarily for locals, but for the crowds of holidaymakers who flocked to our shores. Abergele was the furthest they went because Rhyl had banned WFL meetings – not wanting visitors to be put off their high-class resort!

The WFL applied to the Surveyor at Penmaenmawr Council for permission to use the shore, but as no council meeting was due until September, the Surveyor, together with the Chairman, decided they couldn't authorise it. The ladies went ahead and commenced operations on the shore on Monday regardless, but within a few moments the Promenade Inspector arrived on the scene followed by the Surveyor who politely requested the ladies, around whom a large crowd had already gathered, to move on.

The ladies hurried into the village and found a benefactor in Mr H. R. Williams, a butcher, who gave them the use of his field close to the square. Miss Manning addressed a large crowd but was subjected to continual interruptions and questions.

The ladies attempted to hold a further meeting at the Gladstone Memorial on Saturday evening, but were moved on by the police who claimed they were obstructing the main road by allowing a large crowd to congregate.

The first report on the WFL's activities further afield concerned Miss Millicent Browne and two other (unnamed) ladies visiting Colwyn Bay early in August and holding a meeting on the sands, which were thronged with thousands of visitors, the majority of whom paid no attention whatsoever to the speakers. There was plenty of good-natured badinage from those who did gather round to listen and Miss Browne took it in excellent spirit, but as she was about to leave, a local gentleman launched into a tirade of derogatory comments.

Several visitors surrounded him and tried to hustle him away, but Miss Browne and her companions became caught up in the melee and the crowd feared for their safety.

But suddenly, to the relief of spectators Miss Browne ducked out of the circle and ran towards the high wall of the Promenade with the evident intention of scaling it. This would have been impossible unaided, but some people standing on the edge of the wall reached down and hauled her up, whereupon she started to speak again – just as if nothing had happened. By this time a much bigger crowd had gathered and suddenly out of the blue, someone gave Miss Browne an almighty push and had it not been for the swift action of Mr Owen of Grove Park in reaching out and seizing her arm, she and several other ladies nearby would undoubtedly have fallen onto the throng below. Undaunted Miss Browne continued her speech, continually heckled by the gentleman on the shore, whom she dismissed with sarcastic wit.

She and her friends eventually left for the station, but they had gone only a few yards when there were shrieks of : 'A fight, a fight!' The ladies present withdrew and in the clearing could be seen the obnoxious local gentleman and a visitor engaged in fisticuffs. A couple of blows were exchanged before they were separated by their friends, but they continued to glare at each-other and utter threats.

The ladies who had been present were scandalised and the rowdyism on the Promenade was the subject of much conversation in the town, the general opinion being that the council had a duty to ensure that there could be no repetition of such a regrettable incident.

Miss Gawthorpe and Miss Hayes (from Manchester) then gave Colwyn Bay the benefit of their opinions. There were few interruptions on this occasion and it was said there would have been even fewer had the ladies not indulged in sarcasm at the expense of those who already possessed the vote – namely men!

In mid-August Miss Hayes visited Conwy, accompanied by Miss John (from London) and Miss Manning. Unusually they addressed their audience from inside the cab in which they had arrived on the Quay. Miss John said that if a man's wife ended up in the workhouse – and most women did everything in their power to avoid that fate – then her husband was made to pay for her maintenance not for the sake of his wife, but for the sake of ratepayers. It was ratepayers who were protected – not women.

Miss Hayes spoke next, but although she was continually heckled particularly by the special reserve soldiers from Camp Morfa, she had an answer for every comment.

Miss Manning waxed indignant over the fact that in free England and Wales women didn't have the vote, but in Russia they did! But, she added, she thought there were three stages in their campaign – ridicule, opposition and success and they were well on their way to success. This was news to their audience!

Miss Gawthorpe and Miss Browne also visited Rhyl, where Miss Gawthorpe was constantly interrupted, to the extent that she eventually lost patience and told the man concerned to desist or leave. She proceeded to criticise the Liberals in a very severe manner, which resulted in wild cheers from the audience every time Mr Lloyd George's name was mentioned. Miss Gawthorpe then told one man that he should have 'paid his 6d like a man' to get into her meeting instead of sneaking in, another that if he was a specimen of north Wales Liberals; she didn't think they'd do very well at the next election and addressing a third man she said: 'Why don't you just say what you mean – that you men think you have the right to rule the earth and we women should just leave you to it?'

Some time later Miss Gawthorpe and Miss Browne held another meeting at Rhyl, this time at the Town Hall and there was a good attendance. Miss Browne took the chair and Miss Gawthorpe explained that after the rowdy meeting in Conwy she had been inundated with invitations to return to the district and had decided to hold a meeting at Llandudno. Miss Bowes had made arrangements with the Grand Theatre for the meeting to be held there and all the printing of advertising had gone ahead, when the theatre manager, concerned for the fabric of the building, suddenly cancelled. However, said Miss Gawthorpe, Miss Bowes had shown great pluck and organised this meeting at Rhyl at very short notice.

Miss Gawthorpe then opened her speech by saying that 'criminals, paupers, lunatics and women' were not qualified to vote. She was sorry for those in asylums and some people thought Suffragettes should be there [laughter], but her main point was that female doctors, teachers and women in all other occupations earned less than men and the reason they were in this situation was because they hadn't got the vote. But they didn't want just the vote – they wanted equal wages for equal work.

Miss Clarkson, a Suffragette from Manchester who had recently been released from prison, suddenly appeared on the sands near Rhyl Pier and predictably began to speak about women's suffrage. She was in the company of a few local Suffragettes including Miss Francis and some of her own supporters from Manchester. A crowd quickly gathered. At first Miss Clarkson had a fair hearing, but once she started trying to explain about the interruptions at the Albert Hall Eisteddfod, the heckling and abuse threatened to drown her completely. This, combined with the intense heat, which Miss Clarkson was obviously finding it difficult to contend with, would have silenced a less determined person but she doggedly carried on, until she was surrounded by a mob of protestors who lifted her bodily off the box on which she was standing and transported her across the sands until she fell into another part of the crowd.

It was clear that despite the protestors, Miss Clarkson actually had many sympathisers and even though she looked ill and exhausted, she called for her box to be retrieved and started addressing the crowd again from her new vantage point. The protestors once again surrounded her. The situation looked as if it was turning ugly and parents started to take their children away from the immediate vicinity, but at this point Police Inspector Hayes intervened, asking Miss Clarkson to desist – claiming she was causing an obstruction.

Miss Clarkson ignored him and would certainly have ignored his instruction not to take a collection, save for the fact that someone had stolen the collection bag!

Miss Clarkson then invited questions but they were so

childish (e.g. 'would she like a donkey ride on the sands?') that she refused to answer them and declared the meeting closed.

At the end of August a group of Suffragettes including a Miss Hewitt visited Rhyl again and chalked the time and place of their meeting on various footpaths around the town. (This was a popular method of letting people know about meetings). This time they didn't meet at their customary spot near the pier, but on the extreme west end of the foreshore. At first they had an extremely attentive and sympathetic audience and were able to speak without interruption.

But soon the crowd which had gathered between the minstrel plot and the pier learned where the Suffragettes were and hot-footed it down to the west end, after which Miss Hewitt was heckled, poked and showered with bags of sand and other missiles. Finally there was a rush for the tub which was serving as a platform; Miss Hewitt was knocked off it and it rolled away into the sea. Many thought the Suffragettes would be following it for a ducking, given the demeanour of the latecomers, but at this point the Promenade Inspector intervened, removed the most rowdy protestors and ensured a safe exit for Miss Hewitt and her companions.

The WFL also held one meeting in the Market Square at Llanrwst, addressed by the Misses Elliott, Hayes and Manning. A crowd of several hundred had gathered, but as soon as Miss Elliott commenced the introductions the ladies were greeted with motor-hooters, mouth organs and trumpets.

Miss Hayes started to speak, only to be almost immediately interrupted, at which point a woman took hold of the coat collar of the man who was heckling and unceremoniously landed him on the edge of the throng, much to the delight of both the audience and the speaker. Miss Hayes continued for almost an hour, but only those near the front could really hear what she said.

Once the crowd started singing choruses the local police officer requested a fair hearing for the speakers, but although the racket continued Miss Manning was much more successful at making herself heard.

Finally Isgoed Jones addressed those still remaining and said that whilst he was in favour of women's suffrage, he disagreed with the Suffragettes' methods of trying to secure that end. He then called for cheers for Mr Asquith, Mr Churchill and Mr Lloyd George, to which the throng readily responded.

Miss Manning asked for a vote in favour of women's suffrage and six or seven women bravely raised their hands, but the overwhelming majority just melted away.

Dr Helena Jones took to the Llandudno shore on behalf of the WSPU saying they didn't want petticoat government and they didn't want trouser government either – they wanted to see petticoats and trousers side-by-side in the cause of progress. The crowd was almost equally divided between those who were genuinely interested in what Dr Jones had to say and those just out for a lark – singing and cheering Mr Lloyd George. Despite this, Dr Jones made a very favourable impression both by her sincerity and witty repartee.

Another group of WFL members concentrated their efforts in the Bangor, Anglesey and Caernarfon area. Bessie Jones of Bod Iorwerth, Newborough, arranged the first meeting which was described as having 'put courage in the hearts of local supporters'. The Chairman, Mr R. P. Jones of Bron Menai, was quite overcome with emotion and in his vote of thanks addressed the WFL thus: 'You have taken all by storm and converted everyone'.

Having stayed with Bessie Jones overnight, the WFL members crossed the Menai Strait by ferry the following morning and made their way to Caernarfon, where about 500 people had gathered in Castle Square. Despite the singing of election songs and '*Hen Wlad fy Nhadau*' and questions about the interruptions to the Eisteddfod at the Albert Hall, the meeting passed off fairly peacefully under the watchful eyes of the police.

Holyhead was the women's next port of call, followed by a gathering of over 600 people at The Reformer's Tree in Bangor. Here it was nearly impossible to hear what the women had to say due to rowdy youths and when after 1½ hours the youths got bored with merely heckling and surged forward surrounding the speakers, the police had great difficulty in extricating the WFL. members and escorting them safely to the station and onto a train.

The WFL continued to hold weekly meetings at Bangor and Caernarfon for the remainder of the summer. At one meeting in mid-August at Caernarfon's Castle Square 3,000 people turned up. But it was a disastrous meeting from the point of view of the speakers, since a London schoolmaster, a native of Caernarfon, persisted in asking 'awkward questions'. Exasperated, one of the women invited him onto the platform, where he held forth for over an hour in support of Mr Lloyd George and the reforms already put in place by the Liberal Government. Needless to say, this delighted the crowd and discomfited the WFL members.

November

Lady Frances Balfour visited Llandudno. In her address she pointed out that in Saxon times women in possession of appropriate qualifications were consulted along with their menfolk, when decisions needed to be made. From then on the situation had deteriorated until in 1832 the Reform Bill finally defined the electorate as 'male'. Had men been treated the same way as women and lost their vote, would they not have resented it?

Lady Balfour said some people felt women should stay at home, but if they did, what would happen to the 2 million homes at that very moment being held together by women's wages? She said that years ago women had made jams, pickles and clothes at home, but men had taken these commodities and many others and transferred them into factories, so men couldn't complain if women took back their traditional work by joining them in the factories.

Women had been campaigning for the vote for the past forty years, but it was only since the Suffragettes had taken militant action that anyone had taken any notice of 'The Cause'. There shouldn't be any need for militancy said Lady Balfour, the reasonableness and justice of the women's request should be sufficient to get it through parliament.

This meeting was described as having given a stimulus to the Suffragists' cause locally, with a considerable increase in the number of members.

Lady Balfour also visited Rhyl, where the platform party at the Town Hall included the Bishop of St Asaph and Mrs Edwards, Mrs Walton-Evans, Mr J. Frimston, Dr Edward Gooddy, Rev. Verrier-Jones, Colonel and Mrs Howard, Mr and Mrs Lloyd of St Asaph, Miss Perks, Secretary of the Rhyl Society, Mrs de Rance, Mr and Mrs Harold Roberts and Rev. T. Vaughan – vicar of Rhuddlan. Lady Balfour was warmly welcomed by the Chairman, who said that had the meeting had any connection with the militant Suffragettes he would not have agreed to chair it.

Lady Balfour opened by saying that she was willing to answer any questions put to her and continued that in the early years the main objection to women getting the vote was that women didn't want the vote anyway, but that argument was rarely heard now.

Another argument had been that they couldn't fight and therefore weren't fit to make decisions about war. There were many men who weren't fit to fight for their country but they still had the vote.

Yet another argument was that women were on a pedestal and should remain there, but, said Lady Balfour, it didn't stop men kicking the pedestal from under women when it suited them. How many men did the listeners know who did the housework? Lady Balfour said that amongst other things, women were almost exclusively responsible for the upbringing of children, which was hard work.

She continued that women weren't men and had no wish to be, but the desire for the vote wasn't confined to Britain; women throughout Europe were also campaigning to be given the vote. Indeed, twenty-one countries had been represented at a recent conference in London and in every one of those countries women's suffrage was high on the agenda, to the extent that if women didn't get the vote soon, the injustice could break up the whole of society.

There was no going back, the Suffrage Movement must fight on and Lady Balfour moved a resolution pledging the meeting to do its utmost to support 'The Movement'. [loud applause]

Dr Edward Goody seconded this and said if he didn't have the vote he would be a rebel and although he didn't approve of the militant's tactics, he could understand them.

He wanted a Royal Commission comprised of intelligent and fair-minded men appointed to deal with women's suffrage – and he was certain they would get the vote.

The resolution was carried with just one (male) dissenter.

Colonel Howard said that although he had been convinced of the rightness of women's suffrage, after hearing Lady Balfour he was even more convinced. [laughter and applause] How could it be right that a lady who employed staff couldn't vote, yet those who were dependent on her for their livelihoods – butler, chauffeur, gardener and other male servants, could vote? Colonel Howard did not, however, approve of the militants – they were neither fair nor honorable and they certainly weren't 'playing the game'. Lady Balfour's NUWSS colleagues did play the game in an honorable and straightforward way and he would always be glad to help them in any way he could. [cheers and applause]

The Bishop of St Asaph expressed his personal thanks to Lady Balfour for her temperate explanation, but he still did not think that intellectually women were equal to men! There was no female equivalent of Shakespeare. But he did admit that in the realm of morality women were superior and he did not think there was any good reason not to give the vote to women. Further, there was not the slightest doubt that in the industries where so many women worked, their conditions would be considerably improved if they had the franchise.

Once the General Election was called the Liverpool WFL, eager to stir up as much opposition to Mr Lloyd George in his constituency as possible, held a meeting at Caernarfon Guild Hall which became extremely rowdy; even the Mayor, Alderman J. T. Roberts failed to get a hearing and the women had to be escorted to their hotel by ten policemen.

Miss Rosa Hovey,
Principal, Penrhos College,
Colwyn Bay

Miss Ethel Hovey,
Matron/Bursar, Penrhos College.
Colwyn Bay Mayor 1945-46

December

On Wednesday 16 December the Colwyn Bay branch of the NUWSS held its first meeting. They met at the Café Royal, Station Road. Miss Hovey was in the chair and expressed herself as being earnestly in favour of votes for women – women had the same responsibilities as men and were therefore entitled to the same rights.

(When I read this newspaper account I assumed that the Miss Hovey referred to was Rosa, Principal of Penrhos College, but her sister Ethel was matron/bursar at Penrhos, so it could have been either of them – certainly both were active in the Colwyn Bay Society.)

There was an excellent address by Miss Rathbone, who expressed gratification that Wales was at last awakening to women's suffrage!

Miss Elizabeth Kenyon was the Colwyn Bay Society's first Secretary and by the end of the afternoon she had enrolled thirty members.

The *North Wales Weekly News* reported that with reference to the action brought by the Corporation against Miss Mabel Pollard, who had hired Conwy Town Hall on behalf of Dr Helena Jones for Miss Gawthorpe's visit, the Borough Accountant had stated that at the last County Court Sitting the Summons had still been outstanding, but since then a cheque had been received fully settling the claim.

Miss Rathbone was the speaker when Bangor's branch of the NUWSS held its first public meeting at the Queen's Head Café. The first Secretary was Miss Hartley, which was almost certainly Mary Gertrude, who was a daily governess; or possibly her sister, Ruth Olwen. Mrs Charlotte Price White became Secretary the following year and remained in post until at least 1913.

It is interesting to note that as early as 1906 a meeting had been called in Bangor to try to establish a branch of the Independent Labour Party (ILP) and the speaker was Philip Snowden, Party Chairman and newly elected ILP MP for Blackburn. After he had spoken, his wife Ethel addressed the meeting, pointing out that the ILP supported women's suffrage and urging the people of Bangor to support both the party and 'The Cause'.

On the penultimate day of the old year the WFL opened Committee Rooms at No. 21 High Street, Caernarfon to co-ordinate their month-long, vigorous campaign to urge locals to 'Vote against your pet, the Chancellor of the Exchequer'. A *Caernarfon and Denbigh Herald* reporter interviewed the 'advance guard' Miss Violet Tillard, who had been sent to make preliminary arrangements prior to the arrival of her friend, Muriel Matters. Miss Tillard told the reporter that their policy was to oppose Cabinet Ministers responsible for

Women's Freedom League Office, Caernarfon

refusing to do justice to women and to oppose known Anti-Suffragists – mostly, but not exclusively, Conservatives.

Miss Muriel Matters

Miss Tillard continued: 'Two years ago people thought it was a new and horrible thing for women to have the vote, but now although they say 'the way you behave is disgusting', they agree that everyone who pays taxes should get the vote'.

She mentioned that they planned to hold outdoor meetings and possibly one indoor meeting.

The interviewer commented that Mr Lloyd George supported women's suffrage and wanted to know why they were opposing him. Miss Tillard replied that the

Cabinet and Mr Lloyd George in the Cabinet, could have done something for women but they had not. The WFL was asking all candidates to include their views on women's suffrage in their election addresses.

Miss Matters, having had the vote in Australia, had come to Britain to help with the women's suffrage campaign here and had spoken every second night for the past seven years.

Chapter 4

1910

Welsh Women Liberals give up political work to support the NUWSS

January

There was an extremely nasty incident on 18 January when a group of Suffragettes wearing the 'purple, white and green' drove into Pwllheli in a car adorned with 'Votes for Women' placards and started to hold a meeting opposing Mr Lloyd George. A large crowd gathered and the women were soon drowned out, then the placards were ripped from the vehicle and flags wrenched from the women's hands. Concluding that 'discretion was the better part of valour' they prepared to beat a hasty retreat, only to find, to their horror, that one of their tyres had been punctured. As they hurried away on foot they were attacked by a large group of irate women and were extremely fortunate to find refuge in the Conservative Club. Even so, they were besieged by '1000's of people' singing pro Lloyd George election songs. When they tried to leave they were again harassed by the crowd and having reached the Whitehall Hotel were forced to remain there for several hours, until the crowd dispersed.

Mrs Walton-Evans, President; Mrs Mary Gooddy, Secretary and Mr Alfred Pugh, Treasurer, of the Llandudno Cell wrote to the *Llandudno Advertiser* explaining that at the forthcoming election, NUWSS members all over the British Isles, intended canvassing gentlemen leaving polling booths, to sign a petition in favour of women's suffrage. The aim being to prevent any future government claiming that it had no mandate from the country to consider giving women the franchise.

In north Wales, NUWSS members stood outside polling stations for hours on end (it was unlawful for them to stand inside), enduring the winter weather and being jeered at by the ignorant. Men leaving polling stations were politely and sometimes coquettishly asked to add their names to the petition.

On leaving Colwyn Bay Council Offices an elderly monoglot Welshman wearing a velvet coat, velvet vest and moleskin trousers, was approached by two very attractive English women. A young man passing by offered to translate. The old man declined to sign, telling the young man to tell the ladies they were 'naughty enough as it was and would be even worse if they got the vote' and went off chuckling.

In Llandudno a less charming man, entreated to sign, declared: 'No – if I had my way I would drown you all!'

There was a snowstorm in Colwyn Bay but the ladies stuck it out until their fur and feathers became so bedraggled a retreat was essential – even Suffragists liked to look their best.

700 signatures were obtained from 1417 voters.

February

The Llandudno Cell held a very well attended reception in the dining room of the Craig y Don Boarding Establishment. The President, Mrs Walton-Evans and committee were hostesses and the speaker was Mrs Fawcett, National NUWSS President, who said their greatest task was to convince the government that women were human-beings. She also complimented the local members on their efforts to obtain voter's signatures on the petition and the success achieved. The evening concluded with refreshments provided by Miss Middleton, proprietor of the hotel.

Mrs Fawcett also addressed a meeting at Colwyn Bay's Pier Pavilion and said that women weren't asking for a revolution, simply for their electoral disabilities to be removed. She continued that although the objectives of the NUWSS and WSPU were the same, she regretted and condemned militant tactics. A small choir was formed for this event and the ladies sang 'Our Appeal' conducted by Mr J. O. Davies (probably J. Owen Davies, boot-maker of The Dingle) and Miss Winifred Ramsey, a mistress at Penrhos College, sang 'Queen of the Earth'.

March

The *North Wales Weekly News* reported on Miss Hovey's illuminating address: 'Women and the State' given to Colwyn Bay Women Liberals. The reporter said:

In our fairly long and by no means passive experience of the agitation for women's rights, we have rarely if ever, known the case to be stated with greater clarity or force. The whole address in fact, by the wide knowledge of the subject which it revealed and the moderation of its tone, was a striking example of the manner in which this and every other cause should be submitted by its advocates to the judgment of the country. We are almost tempted to say that if the women's cause was always put forward in this manner it would meet with greater sympathy and success. And we can say without fear of contradiction that Miss Hovey's method is the method best suited to the time and to the district. Of course with the time at her disposal it was impossible for Miss Hovey to cover the whole ground, but sufficient was said to enable those who have not studied the question for themselves, to lay hold of the right principles as a sound basis for personal investigation and we hope and believe that the subject will henceforward receive more adequate and less prejudiced public attention, as a result of Miss Hovey's capable and scholarly exposition and temperate advocacy.

June

The Colwyn Bay Society held a drawing-room meeting at the home of Dr Lilian Blake in Victoria Park addressed by Lady Barlow and Dr Gordon Clark (described as female) (neither of whom I've been able to identify). Lady Barlow spoke about the situation of married women and the far-reaching effects of mothers. She said present conditions gave the wrong impression to children – particularly boys, on the position of women and there shouldn't be different morals for men and women. She also commented on the growing sisterhood amongst women. And finally she said that although women wanted the vote, not many wanted to enter the House of Commons – they had more important things to do!

Dr Gordon Clark discussed what NUWSS members wanted and what those present thought they could do to help, urging anyone who wasn't already a member to join the NUWSS, or at the very least read a suffrage newspaper.

Dr Blake said that women paid tax, so why couldn't they vote? Women had no more rights than African slaves – lumped together with paupers, criminals and lunatics. Having the vote had helped men in their struggles in the labour market and it would help women too.

The Bangor Society held a public meeting addressed by a Mrs Philipps from London, almost certainly Leonora

Philipps, Lady St David's, wife of Wynford Philipps, MP for Pembrokeshire. Nora Philipps (as she was known in Wales) had developed a deep and abiding love for the principality and its people. She devoted much of her time to developing Welsh institutions and culture. She was a governor of Aberystwyth University College and a keen supporter of the National Eisteddfod. Her speech wasn't reported.

By the invitation of Miss E. M. Hall, members and friends of the Colwyn Bay Society gathered at The Swedish Gymnasium on Prince's Drive in support of the bill to 'Extend the Parliamentary Franchise to Women Occupiers'. Dr Guest of Llandudno moved a resolution praying the government to grant facilities for the passage of the bill, seconded by Miss Spencer and carried unanimously. A copy of the resolution was forwarded to Sir Herbert Roberts MP.

July
At the second reading of the Conciliation Bill on 11 July it was carried with a majority of 110, only for the government to refuse to find time for the committee stage.

In Llandudno, at the height of the holiday season there was a three-week campaign to support the Conciliation Bill, with meetings in private houses and on the streets and Promenade. A small library of books on women's suffrage and social problems was opened in the town.

August
Dr Guest applied to Llandudno Council for permission to sell women's suffrage literature and to deliver speeches on the Promenade and foreshore. The council declared that it was unable to grant permission, but the sales and speeches went ahead anyway.

A further request from Dr Guest to the Library Committee to allow rental of a notice-board in the Public Library on which NUWSS notices could be posted was also declined.

Mrs Pankhurst paid her first visit to Caernarfonshire and spoke to a capacity audience of 700 at Penrhyn Hall, Bangor, chaired by Dr Helena Jones.

Mrs Emmeline Pankhurst, founder WSPU

Mrs Pankhurst also spoke at Caernarfon, but bearing in mind the mixed receptions the WFL had experienced in the town, this meeting was 'women only'. Meanwhile, Dr Helena Jones spoke at Porthmadog, Cricieth and Pwllheli.

Around this time Mr Lloyd George was invited to address Caernarfonshire Women Liberals and outlined his reasons for not supporting the Conciliation Bill, including his opinion that: 'There is no convincing evidence that the majority of women are in favour of the bill'.

Mrs Pankhurst spoke to Mr Lloyd George's most devoted supporters – Caernarfon Women's Liberal Association comprising the majority of the audience when she visited the town. The meeting was chaired by Dr Helena Jones and Mrs Pankhurst had a fair hearing, but there were interruptions when she referred to Mr Lloyd George's attitude to the Conciliation Bill.

When questions were invited Mrs N. Davies commented

that Women Liberals in Caernarfon were Liberals first and Suffragists second and she believed the same applied to the Conservatives. They were more interested in the peer's veto than suffrage at the present time. (The Liberal Government had sought to remove the House of Lords Right of Veto after it had refused to approve Chancellor Lloyd George's 1909 Budget.)

Dr Jones interjected that this did not come under the category of questions and she was not surprised that the President of the Women Liberals had absolute faith in Mr Lloyd George [cheers] but if they wanted to pass a vote of confidence in him would they kindly hold another meeting to do it!

Mrs Pankhurst appealed to the Liberals saying that when candidates opposing women's suffrage realised their seats were in real danger, suffrage would be accomplished very quickly! If they looked carefully at Mr Lloyd George's speeches they would find he'd revolted against any party which didn't give him what he wanted and she commended his excellent example to his women friends!

Afterwards she was entertained by Sir Henry and Lady Lewis at Belmont, Bangor and. Sir Henry was reported to have 'much enjoyed her company'.

September

Following Mr Lloyd George's address to Caernarfonshire Women Liberals, a deputation of five Bangor Society members, together with three representatives from the neighbourhood, visited Mr Lloyd George at his home in Cricieth. Mrs Price White expressed their dissatisfaction with his attitude to the Conciliation Bill and after listening to his justification for his opinion, she concluded that 'Mr Lloyd George cared more for the advantage of the Liberal Party than for principles'. This encounter was reported in

Café Royal – regular meeting place of Colwyn Bay NUWSS

every daily and weekly newspaper in the country. It must have taken real guts for a mere woman – even Mrs Price White – to challenge the powerful and charismatic Mr Lloyd George face to face.

October

The Colwyn Bay Society opened its winter session with a social at their new venue – Cartmell's Restaurant. Short addresses were given by Dr Blake, Miss Hovey, Miss Spencer and Mrs Clara St Leger, followed by recitations, pianoforte solos and songs by Miss Dorothy Coulter, Miss Winnie Jones and Miss Kenyon.

The Bangor Society was responsible for the organisation and financing of a public meeting at Penrhyn Hall at which Mr Henry Brailsford, Secretary of the Conciliation Committee explained the Conciliation Bill.

November

At Colwyn Bay Society's meeting Miss Marie-Louise Eakin

of Llandudno gave an inspiring address on 'The Suffragists' Cause' and referred in scathing terms to Lord Cromer's recent speech (Lord Cromer being a prominent Anti-Suffragist). Miss Spencer informed the meeting that it had been proposed that women members of the Liberal Party in Wales should give up their political work and support the NUWSS instead.

Mrs Price White from Bangor wrote a typically informative and readable article for the *North Wales Chronicle and Advertiser* as follows:

> A series of meetings in support of women's suffrage has recently been held, culminating in a joint demonstration at the Albert Hall on 12th November. This was attended by representatives of the NUWSS and 200 affiliated societies campaigning for women's suffrage, as well as many other political and independent organisations with the same aim.
>
> In view of these important proceedings, we ask to be allowed to offer your readers on behalf of Bangor NUWSS some information with regard to the Bill:
>
> Why is it described as a Conciliation Bill? Who does it conciliate? Certainly not the Anti-Suffragists for it embodies the principle of the removal of the disability of (the female) sex to which they are unalterably opposed. Neither is it designed to banish differences of aim between the various Women's Suffrage Societies, because these do not exist. But amongst MP's who are more or less favourable towards women's suffrage there are differences as to the kind of measure they are willing to support with the vigour and determination needed to carry the bill through.
>
> Some Conservatives look upon change as dangerous

and are not prepared to go so far as giving the vote to women on the same terms as men.

Some Liberals fear Plural* and particularly Faggot** voting would allow a large number of propertied women to vote and this would be an obstacle to the type of reform they are interested in.

(*Businessmen had two votes – one at their residential address and one at their business address. **If a property owner sub-divided a large property and transferred the title-deeds of each sub-division to a separate person or 'faggot', the faggots could be instructed by the property owner which way to vote and have no alternative but to comply).

The all-party Conciliation Committee has endeavoured in proposing the bill to meet these diverse views.

It gives the vote to those women only who are on the Municipal Register and this commends itself to Conservatives as a moderate measure, adding only about a million women to the present male electorate of nearly 8 million and the new element would consist of persons who have already had some experience as municipal voters.

It meets the fears of the Liberals as regards Plural and Faggot voting by excluding the ownership qualification except where the owner actually occupies her property.

The Bill has the support of influential members of all parties in the House of Commons. At its second reading on 12 July it was passed by a majority of 110, a larger majority than the government has been able to secure for other recent bills.

We appeal to all who are convinced of the justice of the claim and who desire to see the measure passed by the common consent of reasonable men of all parties, to use their utmost efforts at this critical moment in support of the bill.

I am etc. Charlotte Price White, Hon. Sec.

Surprisingly both the Suffragettes and Suffragists supported the bill on the grounds that 'a few crumbs' were better than no bread at all.

The Bangor Society was also successful in getting Bangor City Council to pass a resolution in favour of the Conciliation Bill, urging the government to give facilities for its passage into law. Copies of the resolution were forwarded to Mr Asquith, Mr Lloyd George and Mr Brailsford, Secretary of the Conciliation Committee.

A meeting at Rhyl Town Hall at the end of November was to have been addressed by Lady Constance Lytton, but she was unable to be present due to having suffered a serious heart attack. Miss Ada Flatman, the Liverpool WSPU Organiser had been asked to chair the meeting and so she spoke instead of Lady Lytton.

Lady Constance Lytton

Miss Flatman said she was pleased to see so many people present because it showed that they were willing to consider the militant's point of view. They had been fighting for the vote for fifty years and were determined to get it before much longer, they wanted to be able to return men to parliament who would put forward women's points of view.

Miss Flatman proposed a resolution in favour of the Women's Franchise Bill currently before parliament and called upon Mr Frederick Pethick-Lawrence editor of *Votes for Women* to second it.

Mr Pethick-Lawrence replied that step by step the women of Britain – including Wales, were coming together and saying that they would not undertake any further political canvassing for men unless they got the vote. The evils in their midst, he said, would never be solved until the half of the population most able to deal with them got the vote. Being polite and law-abiding had got the NUWSS nowhere and the WSPU intended to remedy that by any means available to them – and if that meant taking militant action then so be it.

The resolution was carried unanimously.

Miss Selina Martin then addressed the meeting. Interestingly Selina Martin and another working-class woman, Leslie Hall, had been arrested in Liverpool in 1909 for throwing a ginger-beer bottle at the Prime Minister's car – after he'd stepped out of it. No damage was done – but for this misdemeanor the two women were arrested, refused bail and taken to Walton Gaol, where, against prison rules, they were denied access to visitors.

Miss Martin barricaded herself into her cell and refused food, at which point wardresses broke into her cell, handcuffed her, dragged her to a punishment room, flung her onto the stone floor and threatened her with forcible feeding.

Lady Lytton – who should have addressed the meeting that night – outraged by Miss Martin's treatment, had travelled to Liverpool, assumed the name of 'Jane Wharton', disguised herself as a seamstress and joined a protest outside Walton Gaol. She had then led the protestors to the Prison Governor's house, demanded the release of Suffragettes and thrown a stone wrapped in brown paper at the window.

'Jane Wharton' was sentenced to fourteen day's imprisonment with hard labour and when she went on hunger strike was forcibly fed on eight separate occasions, without first being tested for signs of heart disease, again against prison rules. This proved Lady Lytton's contention that working-class women were treated far more harshly than 'ladies'; she had spent previous incarcerations in prison hospital wings, due to her title and known heart condition.

The Rhyl Society held their AGM at the Grosvenor Hotel, chaired by Mr Joseph Lloyd. Mrs A. Sarson, Secretary, thanked Mrs de Rance for putting her home at the disposal of the committee for all their meetings and made special mention of Mr Boyd Robertson and Mr Jonathan Jones who had travelled from St Asaph to every one of these meetings. Miss Rosa Hovey from Colwyn Bay then spoke about the current Conciliation Bill drafted by all parties in the House of Commons and awaiting further progress.

December

The Colwyn Bay Society met for their final meeting of 1910 when Dr Blake and Miss Kenyon took part in an interesting debate: 'Shall women have the vote?' Discussion followed, questions were answered and the resolution that: 'women should indeed have the vote' was carried unanimously.

The Bangor Society held their AGM at the Queen's Head Café to review their first year's work. Mrs Price White, Secretary, reported that since its inception in November 1909 the society had more than justified its existence – they had started out with ten members and now, just one year later, had well over 100 and this number was continually increasing. She continued that 'The Cause' of women's suffrage had made huge strides and Bangor had made an effective contribution in north Wales. They had held public meetings and smaller drawing room meetings to which they had attracted high profile speakers.

Members had canvassed women who had the municipal vote about their attitude towards the parliamentary franchise for women. The society had financed a leaflet explaining the Conciliation Bill being translated into Welsh; this leaflet had been distributed, again at Bangor's expense, to societies all over Wales, including south Wales.

Bangor had also appointed a Press Secretary to try to extend coverage of their activities in local newspapers.

Bangor Men's Society for Women's Suffrage sent a telegram to Mr Lloyd George: 'We, your undersigned constituents pray you will use your influence to pledge the government to give full facilities next session for a reasonable and moderate women's suffrage measure on lines certain to secure a majority in the House' and was informed that Mr Lloyd George had nothing to add to his previous exposition on the Conciliation Bill.

This is the only reference I have found to Bangor Men's Society supporting women's suffrage. It was said to be well supported by university staff, but not by male students – loyal to Mr Lloyd George. No mention of Suffragettes or Suffragists appeared in college newspapers or magazines.

Further support came from habitations of the Primrose League (Women Conservatives) in Llandudno, Bangor and Caernarfon; eight leading trades unions in the Bangor area and members of the Caernarfon Labour Council were asked to support women's suffrage.

Chapter 5

1911

Penmaenmawr Society formed

January
Early in 1911 Llandudno Urban District Council passed a resolution in favour of the Conciliation Bill.

February
The Colwyn Bay Society presented *How the Vote was Won* at the Craig y Don Boarding Establishment, Llandudno. The premise of the play was that on a given date, all single women should descend on their nearest male relative and announce that they were taking up residence with him, until such time as the government enfranchised them. This, they thought would concentrate the minds of every male involved, on the urgent necessity of getting women the vote! The play was 'capitally staged, splendidly acted and rapturously received'.

> Cast: Miss Daisy Allen, Miss Alice Andress, Dr Lilian Blake, Mr Charles Elcock, Miss M. Johnstone, Mr Cyril Keeble, Miss Elizabeth Kenyon, Miss Mildred Spencer and Mrs Clara St Leger
> Stage Manager: Mrs Margaret Fleet
> Wigs and Make-up: Mr John Barker (Hairdresser, Station Road)
> Furniture: Daniel Allen, Station Road.

The Colwyn Bay Society also held their AGM, presided over by Miss Ethel Hovey and it was reported that they had sixty members. Miss Eskrigge of Liverpool, the north Wales Organiser, spoke about the Second Conciliation Bill, the second reading of which was due in May.

The Rhyl Society held a Whist Drive followed by a Dance at the Town Hall – the biggest event they had organised to date and there were upwards of 200 people present.

Mrs Sarson had made all the arrangements – the hall was splendidly decorated with the red, white and green NUWSS colours loaned by Mr Fell of the Bon Marche and the tables had been set out by Mr Fred Bell, Mr Hubbard and Mr Sykes. Mr James of the Mostyn Hotel was responsible for the catering and Mrs de Rance for the prizes. The MC was Mr Hubbard and dance music was provided by Mr de Quincey's Orchestra.

Mr E. Bevington introduced a Miss Brown of Liverpool and it was commented that there was a lengthy talk before the entertainment got under way!

March
At the Colwyn Bay Society's meeting Miss Rosa Hovey spoke on some facts relating to women. A very fine address concluded that in the past children and home were women's provinces, but those duties had been largely taken away. And whereas in medieval times it was very important that there should be a large number of children – mortality being very high due to war, disease, famine and ignorance – what was important now was that children should be well born, well cared for and have every opportunity to be well educated. No one should lament the falling birth rate, but rather rejoice in the decreasing death rate of children in Britain.

Miss Hovey continued that the left-wing Fabian Society had passed a resolution that: 'the economic independence of the wife was a fundamental factor in social progress'.

A woman's work ought by no means to be limited to her home. Marriage would become even more popular if women were trained to be equal to men, because it would remove from men's shoulders the worry of what would happen to their wives should they be widowed and left un-provided for.

It was universally acknowledged that children should have the best possible education to encourage the development of their fullest potential and the same must apply to women. Indeed there were no circumstances in which education would lessen a woman's value as a wife and mother.

Miss Hovey said their role model should be Mary Somerville, mathematician, scientist, supporter of women's education and suffrage, described as 'having her head among the stars but her feet firmly on earth'.

This meeting was attended by Miss Gibbs, Secretary of the Scarborough NUWSS.

The *North Wales Weekly News* published:

Chancellor and Suffragettes – Own Constituency Chosen to Disprove his Assertion

and stated that in order to test the exact social position of women municipal voters (i.e. householders – whom Mr Lloyd George had described as 'wealthy') a careful investigation had been undertaken in Bangor and Caernarfon – his constituency, to disprove his assertion that women householders were rich, propertied women. These were the results:

	Bangor	C'fon
Business women keeping 1 or more servants	61	29
Farmers keeping no servants	163	174
Working class housewives	144	79
Women of means engaged in no paying occupation & keeping 1 or more servants	36	63
Total:	**404**	**345**

It was the editor's opinion that if Mr Lloyd George and Mr Churchill were to oppose the Second Conciliation Bill it would have to be on some other plea than not wanting to enfranchise only wealthy propertied women.

At Rhyl Society's meeting it was reported that they now had 100 members. Two members had attended the recent Federation Meeting in Liverpool and returned with many fresh and interesting ideas about how their society could attract even more women. It was hoped it would be possible to put these ideas into practice in the coming months.

At a meeting held in Colwyn Bay Church Rooms, Francis Nunn, a Colwyn Bay solicitor, presided and said he knew about the Second Conciliation Bill only what had been reported in the local paper and he hoped to be educated. He added that it was always a small, intelligent and determined body which brought about legislative reform. He had an open mind about the bill – he wasn't interested in how it would benefit any party – only that it was fair and just.

Miss Eskrigge explained that every woman possessed of a household qualified and a woman would not be disqualified by marriage provided husband and wife were not both registered as voters in the same parliamentary borough – which, presumably, would have excluded most married women. Miss Eskrigge said the bill didn't by any means satisfy the suffrage societies' demands, but they were willing to take what they could get as a first step.

Miss Eskrigge proposed a resolution in favour of the Second Conciliation Bill, urging Sir Herbert Roberts MP to do all he could to secure its passage into law, which was seconded and carried unanimously.

Miss Eskrigge was asked if a couple divorced, but both continued to live in the same parliamentary borough, would the wife still be barred from voting? She didn't know – but said she'd jolly well find out! [laughter]

Towards the end of March the Bangor Society held a meeting at the Oxford Hall, Penmaenmawr, presided over by Colonel Darbishire, quarry owner; the speaker was Miss Rathbone. Colonel Darbishire introduced her by saying that her late father was often in Penmaenmawr when he was MP for Arfon and was much respected and admired. He was absolutely unselfish, with the highest ideals and desired only to right wrongs and leave the world a better place than he found it.

Miss Rathbone then delivered a very effective speech, stating that she was there to explain what she considered to be wrong with regard to the treatment of women and to suggest how it should be put right.

The Rev. Dewi Williams moved a resolution that: 'this meeting of inhabitants of Penmaenmawr believe the Second Conciliation Bill now before the House of Commons to be the most practicable measure for securing votes for women and urges Mr William Jones MP to do all in his power to secure its passage into law'.

Mrs Phillips (a member of the Women's Liberal Association) seconded the resolution and the vote was carried unanimously.

Miss Eskrigge said everywhere in north Wales she had

found men and women agreeing that women householders ought to have the vote, but there seemed to be the impression abroad that it was coming without the need for active effort on their part. If people realised what a mass of both indifference and hard opposition the NUWSS faced, many would rise up and join the ranks of active workers.

A considerable number came forward to give their names and it was hoped there would soon be a society at Penmaenmawr.

As well as this meeting, the Bangor Society arranged meetings at Llanfairfechan, Bethesda, Bangor and Holyhead during March and an 'At Home' in Menai Bridge. As a result, Llanfairfechan became an offshoot of the Bangor Society.

Bangor had also produced *Fourteen Reasons*, a leaflet in both English and Welsh concerning the Second Conciliation Bill and this had been distributed throughout Wales.

April

Many Suffragettes returned their Census Forms endorsed: 'No Vote – No Census'. The Suffragists did not follow their example, however – fortunately for historians. Had they done so, much of the information contained in Appendices B-G would not have been available.

May

On 3 May Mrs Price White, together with representatives from Bethesda, Llanfairfechan and Penmaenmawr attended an NUWSS Convention at the Portman Rooms, Baker Street, London. Every one of over 200 societies was represented with a tall shield bearing its name and grouped together in Federations. It was felt to be delightful and exhilarating to meet with fellow workers. The platform, walls and tables were draped with the Suffragists' red, white and green and the colours were repeated in the ladies sashes and badges and the multitude of banners on display – beautiful in colour and workmanship and stirring with mottoes and battle-cries.

There were eloquent speeches by Mrs Fawcett, President and Miss Ashton from Manchester, both characterised by quiet determination, restrained passion and hope – speeches which no one present was ever likely to forget.

Delegates signed a petition asking for the Second Conciliation Bill to be carried to effective issue during the present session of parliament.

The women felt that there was plenty of evidence that their non-militant tactics were paying off and also that within the NUWSS all classes felt bound together in a strong fellowship, unheard of prior to the past five years.

A lady who was interviewed by the *North Wales Weekly News* mentioned the things she personally remembered:

The Suffrage Clock with 'Votes for Women' on the dial outside the Women's Press.

The Suffrage Shop with pamphlets, newspapers, books, photos and song sheets.

The lady selling *Votes for Women* at Oxford Circus.

Visiting the offices of the Actresses' Franchise League in Adelphi Terrace to find plays to perform.

Smiling at a lady driving up Whitehall in purple, white and green – the Suffragettes' colours.

Marching, holding a 'Carry the Bill' banner along Downing Street and quite enjoying being shadowed by policemen.

Visiting the Little Theatre to see a new suffrage play by

George Bernard Shaw – a feast of wit and merriment, but at the same time conveying profound truths of social philosophy, with his inimitable light touch.

There was another suffrage play on in London, Jerome's *The Master of Mrs Chilvers*, but it lacked the scintillating wit of Shaw and his rapier thrusts at people and prejudices. This play was described as ponderous and sentimental although very funny in parts and the acting was excellent.

But many Suffragists thought it obscured and confused the issues and might be cited by Suffragettes and Antis alike to support their different convictions.

However, this may have been intentional on the part of the management, who were naturally and cheerfully prepared to extract shillings impartially from the pockets of believers and unbelievers alike.

On 4 May the Suffragists' magazine, *The Common Cause* contained an article by Miss Eskrigge:

One of the most satisfactory results of the campaign during March in Caernarvonshire and Anglesea has been that in each place visited the Urban District Council has since passed a suffrage resolution viz: Holyhead, Penmaenmawr, Llanfairfechan and Bethesda. Holyhead, Penmaenmawr and Bethesda have also started suffrage societies and the Llanfairfechan people have become a branch of the Bangor Society. Bethesda will be the first society in north Wales that is composed entirely of Welsh women and it is hoped that this progressive little quarry town will prove a centre from which 'The Movement' will spread to other quarry villages, hidden away among the hills.

Dolgelly [*sic*], where I spent the week 6-13th, is an

entirely different character and I had only ventured to take a small hall for a public meeting. However, it was crowded to the doors and the audience gave a most attentive hearing to speeches both in English and in Welsh. Here, as in other places the success of the meeting was very largely due to the co-operation of well-known local men. It is most encouraging to find in these small Welsh towns keen Suffragists, who have in many cases been in touch with either the Bangor or Cardiff Society. I was very glad while in Dolgelly to have the help of Miss Jones (from Bethesda) who spoke in Welsh at the meeting and visited some of the women ratepayers in the town to explain the Conciliation Bill.

After an interval I am now (27 April) again in Wales, this time in Eirion (south Caernarvonshire) making Portmadoc my headquarters. The difficulty in this country is not that of opposition but that of converting the passive aquiescence, which is the usual attitude, into an active enthusiasm. Still, I have received so much real help and such invariable courtesy everywhere that the work has been pleasant and helpful. I should not be giving any idea of the situation as I found it, without saying that nine out of ten people who have expressed agreement with our aims would not have even listened to me for a minute, had I not first explained that I was 'non-militant'.

Edith Eskrigge

(A society was formed at Dolgellau and by 1913 there was also one at Aberdyfi).

Mrs Pankhurst addressed a very well attended meeting at Rhyl Town Hall, chaired by Miss Rachel Barrett, South Wales WSPU Organiser, who said that the question before them was the most important of modern times. The Women's Suffrage Movement had existed for fifty years and the only thing preventing women from getting the vote was their sex – not their intellect.

The forthcoming Second Conciliation Bill offered an acceptable compromise – for the time being [applause] and accordingly she proposed a resolution approving of the bill and called upon Mrs Pankhurst to second it.

Mrs Pankhurst said that Rhyl to a large extent was disenfranchised because such a large number of ratepayers (i.e. women) had no say in who represented them. Women took no small part in running such a town as Rhyl, making it attractive to visitors and maintaining it and if women had the vote, the town could become even more important as a holiday resort than it already was.

Further, Mrs Pankhurst contended that most of the current evils besetting Britain – particularly poverty – were caused by men failing to protect women and women being powerless to protect themselves. In the economic conditions in which women presently worked, it was adding insult to injury to say that men could protect women.

The Rhyl Society held a very successful social evening at The Queen's Hotel, despite supporters arriving in a snowstorm.

The evening opened with a talk by Miss Eskrigge about the different methods employed by the law-abiding NUWSS and the militant WSPU, but stressed the unity of their purpose. She said that whilst the Suffragists pledged themselves to be law-abiding there was no reason whatsoever why they could not be as dedicated, self-sacrificing and courageous as the Suffragettes.

Miss Eskrigge added that when Mrs Lloyd George had opened a bazaar in Huddersfield the previous week she had said: 'Women throughout the country were looking to the time when they would be able to help in sending representatives to parliament'.

Musical entertainment was provided by Miss Alice Edwards, Miss Louie Hubbard, Miss Hughes, Mr Vickery and Mr Boyd Robertson, accompanied by Mrs Bromley.

The Bangor Society, together with staff from the Caernarfonshire and Anglesey Infirmary, put on a very successful production of Ibsen's *The Doll's House* at the Penrhyn Hall, Bangor.

> The lead character, Nora Helmer, was played very successfully by Mona Smith
> Torvald Helmer by Dr Emyr Price
> Mrs Linden by Mrs Annie Orton
> the villain, Nils Krogstad, by Mr Ffoulkes Price White
> Dr Rank by Mr A. E. Chapman
> the Helmers' three children by Walter Milner-Barry, Will Orton and Margery White
> Annie, their nurse, by Miss D. Chapman
> the housemaid by Miss Edith Orton
>   The porter and Stage Manager was Mr H. A. S. Wortley, assisted by Mr E. Baker; the Business Manager was Prof. E. L. Milner-Barry and the Musical Director was Mr J. R. Whitehead.
>   This production raised £18 13 6d for society funds.

In late May and early June local newspapers reported that recent weeks had been an anxious, busy and memorable time for local Suffragists, who had travelled to London awaiting the fate of the Second Conciliation Bill. Feeble knees were confirmed, wobblers steadied, the lukewarm rekindled with fresh enthusiasm and MP's were not allowed to forget that there was a vast mass of political activity they could no longer afford to ignore. London was full of Suffragettes and Suffragists from all over Britain and the Men's League for Women's Suffrage was much in evidence too.

When the bill was passed with a majority of 167 none of them could have imagined that the government would employ the same delaying tactics as before and refuse to find time for the committee stage. There were demonstrations, meetings and dinners to attend and two suffrage plays to see at the theatre.

June

On 23 June the *North Wales Weekly News* published a 'Special' entitled 'National Demonstration in London – A Colwyn Bay Lady's Impressions'. It opened as follows:

The day of women is at hand. What was considered a few months ago to be an utter impossibility, is about to become an accomplished fact. At all events, that is the impression that assails the steady thinking man and woman of today when he or she reads the glowing account of the tremendous success which crowned the national demonstration in London last Saturday, in connection with those societies which advocate women's suffrage.

It was indeed a great national demonstration. Each branch of the kindred societies took their members by the hundred to the great city which has been the scene of the many stirring events which the women (Suffragettes and Suffragists) have propagated, in order to more prominently put before the public the justice of their cause. The huge procession was marshalled between Westminster Bridge and The Embankment and about 5

Supporters in Welsh costume in London

a.m. the task commenced. So great was the number of women present that day, that they overflowed from the main line of the procession into the side streets, but the marshalling had been so carefully arranged that there was not the slightest hitch in the proceedings. One outstanding feature of the gathering was the hundreds of banners displayed by the different branches of the societies with the names of the branches on them. There were representatives from England, Ireland, Scotland and Wales, each branch headed by a contingent in emblematic costume. America and Finland also sent quotas to swell the ranks. The pageant was cosmopolitan in character, there being women from universities and workers from Lancashire factories walking side by side for the good of one common cause. Never had a political procession inspired such interest as on this occasion, the streets being thronged for a distance of seven miles. So great was the length of the army of women that long before the arrival of the tail end of the procession, the speaking had begun in the Albert Hall, where so many political meetings have taken place. This meeting was only one of three, however, each of the buildings being packed from floor to ceiling. Undoubtedly one of the most pleasing sections of the pageant was composed of Welsh ladies in their national costume, led by Mrs Ellis Griffith, Mrs Roch and Mrs Llewelyn Williams who earned much admiration by their beautiful singing of the Marching Song, which was played by all the bands taking part.

It was not until 7 p.m. that the procession completed its circuit of London's principle thoroughfares, but long before that crowds had assembled in the vicinity of the Albert Hall, to watch the end of the remarkable demonstration.
There was a conspicuous difference between the reception given to a similar event twelve months previously and the hearty greeting given by Londoners on this occasion.

Being well aware of the great interest taken in this movement in Colwyn Bay and neighbourhood, one of our representatives had the great pleasure of interviewing a prominent member of the Colwyn Bay NUWSS (almost certainly Miss Spencer) who, together with four other local ladies, made the journey to London to take part in the demonstration.

She said they joined the procession at 5.30 in the morning and were processing until 9.30 in the evening. In Trafalgar Square the police were standing shoulder to shoulder in order to keep the way clear because a great number of people were watching.

The interviewer asked if they were in Welsh costume?
The interviewee replied that they weren't, but they were under the Colwyn Bay banner which had been painted by

local ladies. Each banner was clearly inscribed with the name of the branch it represented.

The interviewer asked if they'd seen the contingent in Welsh costume or any distinctive tableaux?
The interviewee said they'd seen only one lady in Welsh costume. They'd driven along the embankment in a carriage as the guests of Lady Barlow and had seen the whole procession except the section in national costume. The procession lined up on the Embankment and extended all the way from Westminster Bridge to Blackfriar's Bridge, it was indeed an impressive sight. She added that the Car of Empire with girls walking beside it carrying festoons of roses was especially memorable.

The interviewer asked if they'd attended the meeting in the Albert Hall?
The interviewee replied that two of them had.

The interviewer asked what was her overall impression of the event?
She said that she felt the mood was very much changed in London and the opinion was expressed that women would most certainly get the vote in 1912 and that the government would be obliged as a matter of honour, to grant enfranchisement as quickly as possible.

The interviewer referred to a comment made a few days earlier by the Prime Minister.
The interviewee agreed that the comment did encourage them, but what encouraged them even more was the friendliness of the crowd towards them, they'd lined the whole seven miles of the route and cheered enthusiastically, in fact she hadn't heard one single jeering remark.

The interviewer concluded 'You had a very pleasant experience altogether then?

The interviewee warmly agreed, but said that the people at the end of the procession who had to stand for two hours before they started to march must have felt very tired. It was a great physical strain for them. The weather was all in favour of the event, it rained lightly in the morning but that settled the dust and made the walk more pleasant. Everyone seemed interested and some of the spectators actually paid for 10/- seats on the Coronation Stand.

The interviewer asked if she was satisfied with the experience?

And she replied that it was most inspiring to see so many people – 40-50,000 taking part.

The interviewer asked if they had any plans for the coming months?

The interviewee said that the Colwyn Bay Society didn't meet in the summer but would be campaigning again in the autumn and winter.

She added that she earnestly wished that Colwyn Bay District Council had seen fit to pass a resolution of sympathy with 'The Movement', as other town councils had done. One of the features of the banners was that they were inscribed with the names of all the councils which had expressed sympathy with 'The Movement'. This showed that some of the municipal bodies composed entirely of men, had felt the justice of their petition.

Going on to speak on the subject in general, this enthusiastic Suffragist said that the giving of the vote was a matter of justice. The Insurance Bill affected women and was not quite fair in some of the clauses. In matters of taxation women ought to be allowed to speak.

In conclusion she said the whole country felt that

women's enfranchisement was a serious matter, which ought to be given urgent attention.

Bangor was well represented with ladies carrying not only their own society's banner but also a banner representing Bangor Council which had already passed a resolution in favour of women's suffrage. They had been joined by an ex-Bangorite, now living in London. The Bangor representatives said that they walked five abreast, all wearing sashes in the NUWSS colours – red, white and green and those on the outside columns carried pennons in the colours.

There were many other colours in the procession:

> The Actresses Franchise League's pink and green were carried out in arches of roses and leaves
> Artists carried blue and silver arches
> The Suffrage Atelier's colours were blue, black and yellow (the Suffrage Atelier was an Arts and Crafts Movement supporting Women's Suffrage)
> The WFL's colours were green, white and gold and
> The WSPU's purple, white and green.
> Pageants included Queens, the Empire, Famous Women and Prisoners.

At St James's Mrs Elizabeth Wolstenholme-Elmy, then aged seventy-nine and one of the oldest Suffragettes, sat on a balcony to view the procession and all banners and pennons were lowered in respect as they passed.

Also in attendance were:

Mrs Andrew Fisher, wife of the Australian PM
Mrs George Bernard Shaw

Mrs Millicent Fawcett, NUWSS President

Mrs Emmeline Pankhurst, WSPU founder

Miss Annie Besant, Match Girls representative and Trades Unionist

Mrs Charlotte Despard – who had broken away from the WSPU to form the WFL

and actresses Princess Bariatinsky, Lena Ashwell, Lilian McCarthy and Eva Moore.

July

Caernarfonshire County Council passed without discussion and without one dissenting vote, a resolution urging the government to facilitate the passing of the Second Conciliation Bill, moved by Mr C. E. Breese of Porthmadog and seconded by James Marks of Llandudno. (Pwllheli, where the meeting was held, was one of the Caernarfonshire boroughs represented by Mr Lloyd George).

Other public bodies soon added their support – Pwllheli Town Council, Pwllheli Board of Guardians and Pwllheli Free Church Council passed reolutions in favour of the Conciliation Bill, as did Llŷn Rural District Council, Llŷn Temperance Association and Nefyn Parish Council. Even Caernarfonshire Women's Liberal Association bravely raised their voice in favour.

The great Mrs Pankhurst addressed a very well-attended meeting at Colwyn Bay. The audience was almost entirely women, with not more than six men present. 'Harmony' was the keynote and there was not a single hint of discord – even the little crowd which had gathered outside the venue was welcoming.

Miss Barrett presided and explained that this was one of a series of meetings being held in Wales not only for Welsh women, but also for summer visitors to Welsh resorts. She asserted that the tide had turned – after many years of strong antipathy towards 'The Movement', who could now be so imprudent as to suggest the militant Suffragettes had failed? Votes for women had taken on a very hopeful aspect and after fifty years of wandering in the wilderness she was beginning to think they could now be sure of the promised land. It wasn't logical that women should be debarred from citizenship. Men qualified for the vote by paying rent, rates and taxes and why shouldn't women qualify in the same way?

Miss Barrett said she'd like to know how many other societies could have gathered such an audience on a hot, summer's day? 'The Movement' had more interest and sympathy than any other political organisation. Suffrage was very much alive, but Miss Barrett hoped it wouldn't live much longer – she wanted to see the end of the fight. If they couldn't have the whole loaf they wouldn't starve, they'd have half. She hoped the next meeting would be to discuss what they'd do with the vote after they'd got it.

Gwladys Meredith sang 'The Suffragettes' Marching Song' and the audience joined in the last verse:

Life, strife, – those two are one,
Naught can ye win but by faith and daring.
On, on, that ye have done,
But for the work of today preparing,
Firm in reliance, laugh a defiance,
Laugh in hope, for sure is the end,
March, march – many as one,
Shoulder to shoulder and friend to friend.

(For full text see pages 263-264)

Mrs Pankhurst was greeted with warm applause as she

rose to speak. She said unfortunately the House of Commons had not agreed on what sort of bill would be best. The Second Conciliation Bill had tried to please all parties and hardly a man or woman in the country didn't think it should go through, but the Prime Minister had refused to give time for its second reading. The Suffragettes were determined to keep the Prime Minister to his promise, that the bill would be given time to become law.

No-one who was able to contrast these present day meetings with those of five years earlier could fail to realise the necessity at that time for action and the outspoken expression of what was in every intelligent woman's heart. Very few women attended meetings in the early days, Mrs Pankhurst said and that had made some people say that women were indifferent to the vote – not so, women hadn't known then what immense benefits they could derive from the vote, but now that they did know, things were very much altered. Many men didn't know the value of the vote, they'd said to her, 'You can have my vote if you want it – I don't want it.' But women knew what a valuable weapon the vote was – they would be able to refuse to support candidates who didn't agree with them on matters relating to women and children.

Mrs Pankhurst said she was glad Miss Barrett had explained the situation with regard to the Second Conciliation Bill. Although a great many people didn't agree with the Suffragettes' methods, they still thought that given certain circumstances, women should be given the vote.

But there were threats, women's suffrage had its enemies, some open; some more dangerous, who pretended to be friends. The real danger was not from the relatively few Anti-Suffragists, but from people who tried to split up supporters of the Suffrage Movement, so that when a third reading came it would be defeated by making the scope of the bill too wide. If both man and wife were allowed to vote there would be 7 million new voters at a single stroke of the pen and the country wasn't ready for that. One of the greatest objections Mrs Pankhurst had to face was the fact that there would be more female voters than male. But if the bill was passed without amendments it would only entitle 1 million women, already trained in the use of the municipal vote, to exercise parliamentary franchise and that surely wasn't dangerous?

Mrs Pankhurst said Mr Lloyd George was not sincere in his supposed support of women's suffrage [indignant interjections!] and he ought to be asked whether he was prepared to force through the measures he advocated and compel colleagues to make it a success, as he had with the Insurance and Old Age Pension Bills. Mr Lloyd George was worse than an avowed enemy like Mr Asquith – at least Mr. Asquith was honest about his opposition to the women's cause.

Suffragettes were willing to accept the Second Conciliation Bill as an installment of what they really wanted. Mrs Pankhurst urged them to tell their MP's how they felt. To those attending a suffrage meeting for the first time, she said women were no longer inferior or subordinate to men. Women might with good training, be able to grapple with some of those grave imperial questions now of such importance, which even men didn't very much understand. And it was high time they did consider imperial matters, when they read of millions of women suffering in India through no fault of their own – their plight could only be fully understood by other women. Mrs Pankhurst said she knew what women suffered in prison [warm applause] and she was prepared to give up the rest of her life and indeed her very life if need be, to this cause.

A lady in the audience asked if the WPSU would be

disbanded if they got the vote? Mrs Pankhurst replied that it wouldn't be disbanded until women's rights were set on a firm footing.

It was reported that the following evening Mrs Pankhurst spoke at a well-attended meeting at Llandudno Town Hall. Admission cost 6d–2/6d, the implication being that Colwyn Bay's meeting had been free. There was also a collection for the WSPU's 'missionary work'.

As at Colwyn Bay, Rachel Barrett was in the chair.

Mrs Pankhurst said she was spending her whole holiday travelling to seaside resorts by motor-car (donated by a WSPU supporter and driven by a female chauffeur), to advocate the women's cause and hoped to speak at all the principal resorts in north Wales and along the west coast of England and Scotland.

Whilst they were awaiting the final reading of the Second Conciliation Bill, the Suffrage Movement must not stand still. They knew they had opponents like Mr Asquith, Lord Cromer and Mrs Humphrey Ward, but it was the opponents who were not so outspoken who were more dangerous – wolves in sheep's clothing. Mr Lloyd George had been against the extension of the scope of other bills, so why had he not adopted the same stance on the Second Conciliation Bill? It was because he was trying to divide and rule. If people in Wales weren't so accepting of everything Mr Lloyd George said and showed a businesslike intelligence about measures in his custody, then, Mrs Pankhurst thought, he might have more respect for his constituent's wishes.

Liberal doctrine was that successful government was dependent on the consent of the governed. So unless women were to be regarded as slaves, they had a right to be consulted about the laws by which they were affected and therefore the right to vote for MP's was important to them.

A large crowd gathered outside to see Mrs Pankhurst driven away – almost certainly by Miss Vera Holme – and Mrs Pankhurst departed from Llandudno to boos and cheers in equal measure.

August

Suffragettes made their annual visit to Penmaenmawr to further their cause. A morning meeting commenced on the Promenade but the Promenade Inspector insisted it should be broken up and it had to be held elsewhere.

An evening meeting attended by a large number of visitors went ahead, as did a further evening meeting near the Gladstone Memorial when a fairly large crowd was addressed by Miss Vida Goldstein, who had been instrumental in obtaining the vote for women in the state of Victoria, Australia. In 1903 she became the first woman to stand for parliament in the British Empire when she tried, unsuccessfully to gain a seat in the Australian Federal Elections.

The WSPU held a meeting at Rhyl Town Hall at which the Chairman, Miss E. Evans, stated that she would be supporting the bill due to come before the next session of parliament. This would give 8 million women the vote, eighty-two per cent of them, she claimed, working class. Whilst nature decreed that both a father and a mother were necessary for a family, legislators in the past had considered that there was only one head of the family and that was the father. Women were sick and tired of men telling them what was 'womanly' and what was 'unwomanly' and they wanted the power of the franchise to enable them to solve the problems which particularly concerned women and children. The main speaker, Miss Goldstein, said she had been amazed during her time in England and Wales to hear the same tired old argument that women didn't want the vote.

Women in Australia had used the vote excellently. In her home country, just as in Britain, machinery had taken over what had been home industries and women were forced to go out of their homes to work and earn their living. In fact, 6 million Australian women had to go out to work; lace-makers currently earned less than a ha'penny an hour, but now that women had the vote they were striving to remedy this situation. Also their marriage and divorce laws still favoured men – and Australian women had been promised settlements comparable with those already won by women in New Zealand.

Miss Goldstein closed by saying that since they had won the vote, Australian women were taking a far greater interest in politics than men ever had. Eighty-two per cent of women had voted at the last election compared with only sixty-four per cent of men and she recounted her own experience of standing as a parliamentary candidate. In conclusion she wished the women well with their struggle.

October
A drawing-room meeting was held at Bryn Eithin, Upper Colwyn Bay, home of Mrs and Miss Crosfield, (who were members of the wealthy Warrington Soap Manufacturing family), to hear an address by Miss Evelyn Deakin of Liverpool, who explained that the Second Conciliation Bill presently under consideration would enfranchise women *householders* only. Mostly widows would get the vote, but it was right that they should be first as they were acting as both fathers and mothers to their families.

November

Llandudno held an 'American Sixpenny Sale' at York House, home of Miss Caroline Raw and Miss Mabel Bennett, joint principals of Lansdowne House School, Abbey Road. Ladies brought an item worth a specified amount to sell and bought an item someone else had brought, so that nothing was left at the end. There were prizes for the best value and most original sixpenny-worths and Mrs Dearden did a roaring trade in sixpenny palm readings!

The speaker was Mrs Jessie Keeble, wife of the newly arrived Rev. Samuel Keeble, Minister of St John's Wesleyan Methodist Church, who effectively demolished all the arguments of the Anti-Suffragists.

Bangor held their AGM and reported that their society was by now recognised as the most enterprising in north Wales. In 1910 there had been three suffrage societies in Caernarfonshire and now there were nine. They had raised £53 17 3d during the year. They had a nominal 1/- per year subscription, thirty-five per cent of which went to NUWSS affiliation fees.

Mrs Vaughan-Davies addressed the meeting alternately in English and Welsh.

Mrs Price White spoke first about the Anti-Suffragists, whose opinion was that women had done very well without the vote. Mrs Price White continued that the Suffrage Movement had started fifty years ago, not five; women who paid rates and taxes had the right to citizenship and the right to be equal to men. A woman's place was no longer just in the home, millions of women had to earn their own livings and they had a right to expect reasonable working conditions. Much more time was spent in parliament on social questions than intellectual ones and social questions

Queen's Head Cafe – regular meeting place of Bangor NUWSS

were within a woman's sphere of experience. Why was it a better idea to give the vote to male youths of twenty-one than women with far more experience? Married women weren't considered to be equal to their child's father in parenting, but unmarried mothers were their child's only parent.

At the Colwyn Bay Society meeting Miss McPherson, Treasurer of the West Lancashire, West Cheshire and North Wales Federation spoke and the banner which Colwyn Bay had carried in London was on display.

Mr Asquith announced that the government intended to

introduce a Franchise and Registration Bill in the next session of parliament, to include some concession to campaigners for women's suffrage. Mrs Fawcett of the NUWSS thought this was their best ever chance of winning the vote and urged Suffragists to campaign for the success of the bill. Mrs Pankhurst, on the other hand, expressed her utter contempt for the government and in particular Mr Lloyd George, writing in *Votes for Women*: 'the government's latest attempt to cheat women of the vote is, of course, inspired by Mr Lloyd George. The whole crooked and discreditable scheme is characteristic of the man and of the methods he has from the first employed against the suffrage cause'.

December

At the Colwyn Bay Society meeting, Miss Crosfield presiding, spoke first about the year's successes:

> The Second Conciliation Bill had been passed in House of Commons with a majority of 169.
>
> 2-3 million had watched the Suffrage Procession in London in July and had been very sympathetic.
>
> Sir Edward Grey had promised on behalf of Mr Asquith to give facilities for the final reading of the bill that session.
>
> 110 town and city councils had passed resolutions for the bill.
>
> The long press boycott of suffrage news had ended and *The Standard* now included a whole page dealing with women's suffrage issues every week and it was one of the brightest pages in the paper. Maybe, she suggested, the publishers had an eye on increasing their circulation.

And then Mr Asquith's bolt from the blue in the shape of the

Manhood Suffrage Bill which would give the vote to every male aged twenty-one and over. Despite vague references to the fact that Mr Asquith may consider an amendment to include some women, this bill was designed to split the majority who had been in favour of women's suffrage. Eighty Irish Unionist MP's had made up nearly half of the 169 majority who had voted in favour of the Second Conciliation Bill, but they weren't really interested in it – only in keeping 'well in' with the Liberals so that the Irish Home Rule Bill would go through.

Miss Crosfield said she didn't care whether they got the vote from a Liberal Government or a Conservative Government, but they would get it! She then proposed a resolution that: 'This meeting calls upon the member for this division to do all in his power to ensure the enfranchisement of women in 1912'. This was seconded by Miss Andress of Penrhos College, who said that when she heard of the Reform Bill she was filled with amazement and indignation – a monstrous thing to treat as nought the hundreds of meetings held by suffrage societies, processions greater than any organised by men at any time, deputations to MP's and petitions – all presented in a constitutional manner; to pass over women and enfranchise youths of twenty-one and men who had never organised themselves to ask for the vote, was a direct insult to women. Needless to say, the resolution was carried unanimously.

Bangor Society held their AGM and put out a press release reminding the public that 'in view of recent disturbances and the threat of future disturbances, the NUWSS wishes to state that such incidents are organised by one society alone (WSPU) and injure women's suffrage supporters far more than anyone else'.

Chapter 6
1912

Welsh-speaking women join the campaign

By the beginning of 1912 a lot had happened – as well as the original suffragists' cell in Llandudno there were active societies in Rhyl, Colwyn Bay, Bangor and Penmaenmawr, where there were both English and middle-class influences.

The Bangor Society had almost 200 members and had assumed leadership of all the societies throughout Caernarfonshire. Under its influence new societies had sprung up in Llanfairfechan, Menai Bridge, Caernarfon, Porthmadog, Criccieth and Pwllheli and also in the predominantly Welsh-speaking slate quarrying villages of Bethesda, Tal-y-sarn and Pen-y-groes, Bethesda being particularly active. Miss Agnes Huws, daughter of Rev. J. Rhys Huws was their Secretary. A report of one of their early meetings from the *North Wales Chronicle and Advertiser* has been translated for me:

> Under the presidency of her father, there was an excellent paper by Miss Agnes Huws on 'Votes for Women'. A good paper was given by Mr Jacob Parry against. There was an overwhelming majority for Votes for Women.

Bangor was probably so influential due to its high profile supporters giving it an air of 'respectability'. Academics:

Professors Milner-Barry, Witton Davies, James Gibson, Lewis Jones, Previte Orton and Hudson Williams were supporters; as were the Bishop of Bangor, the Mayor of Bangor, doctors, solicitors, headmasters, several Nonconformist ministers, Sir Henry Lewis – a corn merchant and prominent Calvinistic Methodist in the town – and his daughter Nora. Eleanor Rathbone was a frequent visitor to Bangor, her father, together with Henry Lewis, had played a vital part in establishing the university. Indeed William Rathbone had been President 1892–1900. Eleanor's uncle and cousin, Richard and Mary Rathbone, lived at Glan Menai, Llandegfan and she stayed with them whenever she was speaking in Caernarfonshire and took a real interest in Bangor's NUWSS activities.

But perhaps the single most significant contribution to the Bangor Society was made by Charlotte, wife of Price Foulkes White, who in 1901 had been appointed Manager of Bangor's newly-built electricity station. Mrs Price White was Secretary of the society from soon after its inception and insisted that if 'The Cause' was to have any measure of success beyond Bangor and the coastal towns, its literature must be translated into Welsh. To this end she tirelessly organised French Auctions with sealed bids, Garden Fetes, Cake Sales, Garment Sales, Rummage Sales and Whist Drives to finance translation to and publication in Welsh.

All this activity triggered a new organisation in Bangor – the National League Opposing Women's Suffrage (NLOWS).

On 12 January delegates from several local suffrage societies met at the Queen's Head Café. Representatives from Bangor. Llanfairfechan, Bethesda and Menai Bridge reported on progress with having their literature translated into Welsh and the Llandudno spokeswoman gave an account of their meetings and said they hoped to arrange a mass meeting with political parties in the near future.

February

Members and friends of the Colwyn Bay Society performed two one-act Suffrage Plays at St Paul's Church Rooms, one of the plays having been adapted from Mrs Gaskell's Cranford. There was a good attendance and the acting was greatly appreciated.

Colwyn Bay also organised an 'At Home' in the Church Rooms with Miss Crosfield and Mrs Heenan acting as hostesses. Mrs Brock should also have been a hostess, but wrote that 'an unavoidable absence from home meant she couldn't attend; she'd have enjoyed hearing the speaker and had hoped to have her ideas enlarged and one or two small

prejudices dispelled. She disagreed with those whose zeal outran their wisdom, but was sorry on this occasion not to be able to assist those who believed women should take a greater part in the work of the world'.

The speaker, Miss Maude Royden said that if anyone's sympathies had been alienated by the militants, they must remember that there were militants in every organisation – even the Christian Church. She went on to point out that in fact men had invited women into politics, men didn't want

Miss Maude Royden

94

to canvass without getting paid, so they'd got women to do it for them! Suffragists agreed that women could find their duty, work and happiness within the home but it didn't mean they had to be imprisoned there. It was because women cared about their husbands and children that they wanted the vote. Acts of Parliament affected women's lives from cradle to grave, but they had no part in making the laws.

Mr John Porter said that three or four of the largest establishments in Colwyn Bay were managed by women; many members of staff's livelihoods depended on these women and he believed women had the right to vote.

At the end of the month Colwyn Bay held their AGM at the Café Royal. Dr Blake presided and gave a brief resume of the Chairman's duties – 'Stand up, speak up and shut up' – which was, she said, exactly what she intended to do. The Treasurer announced a balance of £3 10 3d.

The meeting was addressed by Miss Evelyn Lamport, Bangor Society's President, who spoke on 'The Legal Disabilities of Women' and said she didn't think one woman in a thousand knew how unjust the law was towards women, men didn't know either and neither did some lawyers. A Liverpool barrister had recently stated that although the old marriage law was unjust to women, recent amendments had put women in a more privileged position than men. She explained that statute law was made by parliament with the King's assent, whereas common law gradually evolved from judge's decisions; but what was right 200 years ago may not be fair and just today, given changing conditions. Magistrates simply did what they had always done – didn't use their imagination and didn't try to see things from a woman's point of view.

Marriage was unequal, said Miss Lamport, because husbands didn't promise to obey their wives! Divorce was unequal because husbands could leave their wives and wives could not compel their husbands to maintain them and their children; often the workhouse was their only option. Further, fathers had sole responsibility for children – they could appoint anyone they chose to be their children's guardian and this person took precedence over the children's own mother. Work was unequal because a woman working in business with her husband had no claim to a share of the income.

Miss Lamport closed with a rallying cry to fight indifference.

Dr Blake urged everyone to vote in the local elections. She then announced that their committee had taken a room at Fron Heulog, next door to the Public Hall on Abergele Road, Colwyn Bay, which it would be running as a Suffrage Shop from 14 to 20 March and she hoped as many people as possible would volunteer to help.

The Llandudno Cell held a meeting at the Town Hall addressed by Mrs Snowden. It seems incongruous that at this women's suffrage meeting, presided over by Mr E. Bone (a Llandudno solicitor), the platform party consisted of a row of clergy and ministers, behind them a row of men holding public office and businessmen and a back row of prominent women supporters!

Mrs Snowden proposed the following resolution, drafted by the local Secretary and handed to her only five minutes earlier that: 'this meeting approves of the principle of admitting women to vote in parliamentary elections on the same terms as men and pledges itself to do all in its power to secure their enfranchisement during the present session of parliament'. Mrs Snowden said she thought this would commend itself to all present and she was convinced women would get the vote in this session.

In the United States, where women could vote, they had acquired a dignity, self-respect and self-reliance which was remarkable, but had lost none of their love of home and of those duties regarded as a woman's sphere. Democracy could never be complete until women could vote; the state needed the nurturing hand of the mother as well as the strength of the father.

The objection that women should not vote because they did not fight for their country was particularly childish when only one per cent of the male population was trained for war and whilst she did not advocate war, she'd like to point out that it was brain force not physical force which won military campaigns. The Rev. Samuel Keeble seconded the resolution, saying he'd supported women's suffrage for forty years and sat on many platforms during that time, but this was the first where there'd been more men than women!

Only one hand lifted in opposition to the resolution.

The Bangor Society held a meeting at the Penrhyn Hall in February, the entrance fee cost 6d–2/- but the hall was still almost full.

Pentir Williams presided and was joined on the platform by Mrs Snowden, well-known writer Flora Annie Steel, Miss Lamport, Mrs Hudson-Williams and the Mayor of Bangor, who said in plain language that he had agreed to attend because the meeting had been organised by the NUWSS; although he was in favour of giving women the franchise, if the meeting had been organised by the WSPU he would have had nothing to do with it.

Mrs Snowden moved a resolution in favour of women's suffrage and went on to say that the NUWSS was one of twenty-two suffrage organisations. Tens of thousands of women were already prepared to make huge sacrifices for 'The Cause' and there were tens of thousands more who felt that they would like to support the Suffrage Movement but didn't really know how to go about it.

Women's discontent was becoming a serious factor in national life. All the enthusiasm and devotion going into fighting for the vote could so easily be channelled into other worthwhile projects once the vote was won. It was an insult to give the vote to men who had never asked for it, whilst passing over women who had striven so hard to gain it. And she could guarantee that forty-two Labour members would vote against the latest bill unless it was amended to contain some degree of women's suffrage.

Bangor held a drawing-room meeting at Craig Menai by invitation of Miss Pughe-Jones. Despite stormy weather, several Bangor members and a gratifying number of non-members attended to hear an address by Miss Eskrigge, who explained how the NUWSS differed from other suffrage organisations.

Miss Pughe-Jones spoke about the current McCann National Court Case where, due to existing laws, the children's mother was obliged to fight through the courts to have charge of her own children and how this situation must be remedied.

As a result of this meeting seventeen new members were added to the Bangor Society.

March

The WSPU had managed to engineer a Third Conciliation Bill, but before it could be debated, they committed political suicide by unleashing a frenzy of window-smashing. As well as the established targets of government and Liberal Party offices, they attacked the Guards Club, two hotels, the *Daily Mail* and *Daily Star*, Dunn's Hat Shop, Lyons, Swan and Edgar's Department Store and numerous other small businesses and private properties in the West End,

Kensington and Knightsbridge. It was even rumoured that there had been a plot to assassinate Mr Lloyd George, but that this had been foiled.

The following letter appeared in the *North Wales Chronicle and Advertiser* dated 8 March 1912 under the headline: 'Suffragettes in Bond Street – Mr Wartski's Experience':

> Mr Isidore Wartski writes to us from London stating that his Bond Street shop was one of the few which escaped serious damage at the hands of the Suffragettes on Friday. His Manager, Mr Armstrong and Mr Snowman (a member of the Wartski family) got out of the shop just in time to prevent a woman getting out of a taxi from attacking their premises. She was armed with a stone ready to dash against the windows. With assistance they managed to secure the ammunition and hustle her away. Mr Wartski continued: When anyone laid hands on the Suffragettes and attempted to take away hammers and stones from their possession, they invariably screamed 'Don't touch me – if you insult me I will have you punished'. The feeling against them is very bitter and were it not that amongst most men there is a repugnance to deal violently with women, they would be very seriously dealt with in spite of police protection. Regent Street and parts of Oxford Street had a worse experience than ourselves and in Kilburn High Road the windows of very small shops owned by people likely to be uninsured were all smashed. There is a tremendous sensation in London tonight and the very fact that rumours of burning the General Post Office, kidnapping the Prime Minister's children and placing inflammable matter in every letter-box are seriously discussed, shows a horrible spirit of unrest abroad.

(Wartski's was actually founded in Bangor but when they opened their jeweller's shop in London's prestigious Bond Street, it had a sign over the door proclaiming 'Wartski's of Llandudno').

Unsurprisingly, when the Third Conciliation Bill came up for its second reading it was overwhelmingly defeated. As a result of the defeat, even the moderate Suffragists realised that gaining support from the Liberals was a lost cause. They therefore set about getting backing from Labour by opening a Fighting Fund, to back Labour in constituencies where the Liberal candidate was known to be anti women's suffrage. But the Labour Party wasn't too keen to be seen as pro-suffrage – fearing it may lose votes. And committed Liberals in the NUWSS (e.g. Eleanor Rathbone) weren't too keen to be aligned with Labour. As a result, Miss Rathbone resigned from the National Executive of the NUWSS.

However, this campaign had two significant results – at two by-elections where Suffragists supported Labour candidates, the Conservative candidates won and at another two by-elections, where the Suffragists supported Labour candidates, the Liberal majority was drastically reduced.

Even more importantly, for the first time the Suffragists were actively trying to gain the support of working-class women who traditionally supported Labour and the Trades Unions. The injustices suffered by working women were added to the litany of woes in NUWSS propaganda.

Llandudno Young Liberals organised a debate at the Liberal Club. Miss Crosfield from Colwyn Bay stated that women were earning only one third of what men earned and indirectly the government employed 160,000 women sewing uniforms etc. Rev. J. Raymond opposed women's suffrage. A Miss Chad then referred to the government filching 6,000 barmaid's jobs in Scotland and giving them to men, at which point the Reverend Gentleman said that the government didn't want women to be working in uncongenial surroundings, nor in jobs which didn't raise their moral character. (A Mr Driffield interjected that if women tried half as hard to help their poorer sisters as they did to get the vote, things wouldn't be in such a deplorable state.) Miss Crosfield indignantly replied that women may have to be employed in considerably more deplorable positions if they lost their jobs as barmaids!

A string of bunting across Abergele Road greeted visitors to Colwyn Bay's Suffrage Shop at Fron Heulog, next door to the Public Hall, which opened at 11 am on 22 March. The room was liberally decorated with flags, banners, mottoes and flowers. Along one side were daintily-set tables where refreshments could be enjoyed – the *Advertiser* reporter waxed lyrical about the freshly cooked potato cakes! On the other side of the room a tempting array of hand-made articles created by the Suffrage Sewing Group over the previous three months were for sale. These items included embroidered footstools, pictures, items of clothing and aprons. There was also a china stall. All proceeds from both the café and the stalls went to the society's funds.

The walls were covered with posters giving information about societies supporting the Women's Movement and there was a literature stall with a whole range of reading matter from short pamphlets to quite substantial books.

Those responsible for running the shop were Miss Ayles, Dr Blake, Miss Crosfield, Mrs Elcock, Miss Guest, Miss Kenyon, Miss Spencer and Miss Wood. Well over 100 people came on the first morning. There wasn't a formal opening, but in the afternoon Miss Eskrigge addressed a large crowd. She said that for the past few weeks the

Suffragists had been existing under a cloud of depression since the defeat of the Third Conciliation Bill and the attack on shop windows in London by the Suffragettes and she heartily congratulated Colwyn Bay for continuing to work so hard. Miss Eskrigge said many people were under the impression that the Suffragists agreed with militancy but were too scared to do the deeds themselves, but they couldn't be more wrong. However, she didn't think militants should be treated too harshly because they truly believed they were fighting a holy war and severe punishment would only lead to greater violence. She appealed to everyone present not to let 'The Cause' suffer due to the actions of a small group of misguided women.

On Saturday evening there was a classical concert at the shop with recitations, songs and violin solos. Refreshments were served during the interval.

On Monday evening a public meeting was held at the shop, presided over by Mr Charles Elcock, a local Architect who said how disappointed he was with the Suffragettes and that the Suffragists must continue their work. Miss Eskrigge said how difficult it was to get political parties to pass resolutions in favour of women's suffrage. Unjust laws were passed concerning women's health, children and homes, without women having any voice in making them. At the close of the meeting Dr Blake presented the retiring Secretary, Miss Kenyon, who had served for three years, with a handsome writing desk and a woollen shawl.

On Wednesday evening there was an amateur dramatic entertainment at the shop – 'Scenes from Cranford'.

The special week closed with a meeting on Friday evening at the Victoria Pier addressed by Mrs Snowden. Mr James Marks of Llandudno presided and the platform party included Dr Duff, Mr Elcock and the Rev. and Mrs Thomas Lloyd.

Mrs Snowden said that there were 370 NUWSS

branches throughout Britain. She said all organisations (even the Christian Church) had members whose way of tackling things the majority of members disagreed with, which was a somewhat confusing comment since the Suffragettes didn't belong to the NUWSS but the WSPU. Already 200 women had withdrawn their support from the NUWSS due to Suffragettes' actions and men in parliament were saying that this simply proved what they'd always said – that most women didn't want the vote.

Mrs Snowden continued that it was enough to make the Suffragists despair, but they must not despair, they must believe that in the end they would triumph. They were not asking for more or less than men, but for equality.

That year, 1912, 6-7 million people, through resolutions passed at the AGMs of various organisations, had asked parliament to enfranchise women. It was a definite plank of Labour's programme; the Labour Party had 2 million members and whatever constitutional reform was proposed they would oppose, unless there was some measure of enfranchisement for women. The British Women's Temperance Association (155,000 members), the Co-operative Guild (50,000 members), the Women's Conservative and Unionist Association and the Women's Liberal Association had all demanded the vote. 4 million women were working long hours in factories and shops for between 2/6d and 7/6d per week and it just wasn't good enough. They weren't encouraged to join trades unions and even if they did join they couldn't vote.

A resolution supporting women's suffrage was carried with two dissenters.

The Bangor Society held an afternoon Cake and Apron Sale at the Bryn Rooms, Upper Bangor. Tea cost 6d and their Dramatic Society performed a play.

Delegates from north Wales attended a Federation Meeting in Liverpool chaired by Miss Rathbone, where the best methods of bringing pressure to bear on neutral MP's and ensuring press coverage of NUWSS events, were discussed. Reports were read from Bangor, Llandudno, Colwyn Bay, Rhyl and Llangollen.

Then on the last day of the month there was a good attendance at Bangor's Queen's Head Café for a meeting addressed by Miss Rathbone, who spoke about the proposed new bill relating to women's suffrage.

Mr Pentir Williams was in the chair and referred warmly to the philanthropy of Miss Rathbone's father particularly with reference to Bangor University and said it was an anachronism that at the beginning of the twentieth-century British women were excluded from the vote.

Bangor then drafted a memorial from constituents and supporters and collected 155 signatures in Bangor, sixty in Caernarfon and thirty-five in Pwllheli within two days and telegraphed it to Mr Lloyd George.

April
The sinking of the *Titanic* on 15 April and the inadequacy of the lifeboats, meaning that many men were lost because there was simply no room for them in the craft; added to the shop window-breaking campaign of the previous month, elicited a tidal wave of ill-feeling against both the militant Suffragettes and law-abiding Suffragists – the general public not being sufficiently interested to tell the difference!

It was pointed out that it had been 'women and children first' when Titanic's lifeboats were launched; 'Votes for Women' was parodied as 'Votes for Boats', but the Suffragettes took this up with 'Votes for Women – Boats for Men' in other words, equality for both sexes.

On the day following the *Titanic* disaster another historic event took place, but it involved a woman and received very little coverage in the newspapers of the day, with the possible exception of the *Daily Mirror* which sponsored her. On that day American, Harriet Quimby, in her trademark purple silk flying-suit, became the first woman to fly solo across the English Channel from Dover to Calais. The *Daily Mirror* had sent a tug ahead carrying photographers, but unfortunately they weren't able to record the event due to fog. Sadly, Harriet Quimby was killed in a flying accident only a few months later.

Miss Spencer, Colwyn Bay's Secretary, sent a letter from Mrs Fawcett, NUWSS President, to the *North Wales Weekly News* for publication. Miss Spencer wrote:

Colwyn Bay Suffrage Society thinks it is very important that the real facts relating to the defeat of the Conciliation Bill should be clearly understood and Mrs Fawcett's letter with its careful analysis of the causes, its diagnosis of the present situation and the future prospects of suffrage, is opportune and cogent:

Mrs Fawcett's letter stated:

Sir,

The Executive Committee of the NUWSS wishes to make it quite clear that the defeat of the Conciliation Bill by the narrow majority of fourteen, must not be interpreted as a sign that the House of Commons is hostile to the principle of women's suffrage.

The Irish Nationalists, led by Mr J. Redmond, believed discussion on the Conciliation Bill would weaken and perhaps break up the government and this they desired beyond all things to prevent for the sake of the success of Home Rule. They therefore entirely withdrew their support from the Conciliation Bill. Last year the thirty-one Irish Nationalists voted for women's suffrage, this year thirty-four voted against it, only three voting for it. This serious defection more than covers the small majority against the bill.

Thirteen members of the Labour Party who represent mining areas were compelled to visit their constituencies due to the coal strike. If they had been in the house they would certainly have voted for the bill.

The disastrous effect of militancy (of the Suffragettes) on public opinion, rendered it easy for those members who desired to break their pledge, to do so.

The cordial thanks of all Suffragists are heartily given to those friends of 'The Movement' in the House of Commons, who supported the bill by voice and vote.

There is no cause for faint heartedness or discouragement. Our object must be to work unceasingly, vigorously and discreetly for the Women's Suffrage Amendment to the government's Reform Bill.

Mr Asquith gave a positive promise on 17 November 1911 that the government intended to proceed with this bill during this session and this pledge was repeated with the strongest possible emphasis by Mr Lloyd George on 23 February 1912 at the Albert Hall.

Yours etc. Millicent Fawcett.

May

The Colwyn Bay Society held a very well attended meeting at the Café Royal at which the speaker was Miss Royden, her eloquent speech a few months earlier having attracted a considerable number of new members to 'The Cause'.

Miss Kenyon presided and suggested that all members of the society should write to Sir Herbert Roberts MP expressing their gratitude and encourage as many voters as possible to write to him, adding that the definition of gratitude was 'a lively sense of thankfulness for favours to come'!

Miss Royden said it was not philanthropy that would lift women workers earning less than 5/- per week, but political power. That was why women of her class were sacrificing a comfortable life to support the Suffrage Movement.

Miss McPherson, Secretary of the Federation, offered practical advice to those about to become involved in propaganda work in the Denbighshire hills.

Mr Vincent, Mayor of Bangor, presided when Miss Royden spoke at the Queen's Head Café, Bangor, about the Anti-Suffragists in general and their handbook in particular, selecting some choice quotes:

1. women's wages won't be affected by legislation so votes are un-necessary
2. we (the Antis) are obliged to conclude that since infant mortality has considerably reduced in Australia and New Zealand since they got the vote, women's suffrage changes natural conditions
   In fact there were four paragraphs on infant mortality and only one on education -
3. the only difficulty is a religious one – women are religious and that increases the difficulty of educating them.

Miss Royden continued that academic supporters of women's suffrage should realise was that no reform came about without hard work. The general opinion was that men didn't need to get involved, but they did – women couldn't win the vote without men's support. Many people thought the Women's Suffrage Movement was dying or even dead, but it would only die when women got the vote. Miss Royden said she had no interest in politics, her interest was in the welfare of women and children.

Miss Royden also spoke at Rhyl. The very well-attended meeting was chaired by Councillor Cheetham. On this occasion Miss Royden spoke about the progress of women's suffrage in other countries and refuted the view that it was disastrous to give women the vote, by pointing out that originally only one state in America had given women the vote but now six neighbouring states had enfranchised women. Australia had started the same way and now all women had the vote. Miss Royden said they weren't just struggling for the vote, but for reform and freedom for those who could not fight for themselves.

Miss Royden then proposed the resolution that: 'This meeting calls upon parliament to pass some measure of women's suffrage this session', which was seconded and passed unanimously.

Miss Royden added that she was strongly against law breakers – if they broke the law themselves, how could they expect other people to keep it?

Councillor Llew Evans mentioned that in his native New Zealand every woman over twenty-one had the vote and this appeared to be perfectly satisfactory.

Penmaenmawr Suffragists met at Hewan Hall and Mrs Phillips, Paradise Crescent, presided.

Miss Royden proposed that: 'this meeting cordially thanks Mr William Jones MP for his consistent support of women's suffrage measures in the House of Commons and expresses the hope that he will advocate women's suffrage on his next visit to the constituency'.

Miss Royden then dealt with the claims women had to the vote and pointed out that there was a big difference between administering the law and making it. Women's share of law-making would never be as prominent as men's, because the nature of women's work made it impossible for many of them to take part in politics, but they had great work to do in the sphere of local government. She pointed out that women had the vote before 1835, so they were simply asking to be given something back which had been taken away from them. Now parliament voted on subjects in which only women were experts – it had been made a criminal offence to sell food not fit to eat, but it wasn't criminal for landlords to let houses not fit to live in. When women had the vote they'd use it to protect their homes and their children. The Empire wasn't built on square miles, but on homes and human beings. Miss Royden continued that in countries where women already had the vote there had been a marked decrease in infant mortality.

She mentioned that after the Suffrage Bill was thrown out, the next item to go was the Criminal Law Amendment Bill drafted to deal with White Slave Traffic and someone – some man – rose and said 'I object', so it wasn't proceeded with. That was a bill which would have dealt with a subject which could only be described as an infinite disgrace to a country calling itself Christian, which presently neither inflicted penalties on the perpetrators, nor protected the virtuous, the innocent, the vulnerable and the young.

Mrs Phillips then appealed for more members and Miss Annie Harker, Secretary, said she would be pleased to provide information.

But the most momentous meeting that month must have

been at The Pavilion, Caernarfon, which held 5,000 and was packed and overflowing with people wanting to hear Mr Lloyd George speak about the campaign for the Disestablishment of the Church in Wales. This venue was at the heart of his constituency and it was here that he had delivered some of his most electrifying speeches to the Liberal Party faithful. Long before proceedings began, the capacity crowd was singing – as only the Welsh can – election songs, patriotic songs and hymns.

As Mr Lloyd George rose to speak there was absolute silence, but after only a few sentences a young lady in the 5/- reserved seats jumped up and shouted 'Votes for Women!' She was bundled out, but six further interruptions (two by men) ensued in rapid succession. Even a man who just wanted to ask a perfectly reasonable question was pounced on and dragged out. The women were very roughly treated – their clothes were torn, clumps of their hair were ripped out and they were beaten with fists and umbrellas.

Afterwards Mr Lloyd George was able to continue. Sir Henry Lewis observed that the interruptions would have been far more effective had they been spaced out, rather than occurring within such a short time.

It transpired that the Suffragettes and male supporters had left London on the 10 p.m. train on Friday night. Not wishing to draw attention to themselves, they had got off the train at Bangor at 4.30 a.m. on Saturday morning, then spent some time with friends before walking to Caernarfon!

The Welsh press, whilst deploring the Suffragettes' actions, did admonish the youths who had set upon the women, saying that, had members of the audience retaliated in the heat of the moment that would have been understandable, but as these youths had not been present at the meeting, they could not have known why the women had been ejected.

A few weeks later Mr Lloyd George was scheduled to preside over an afternoon event at the National Eisteddfod which was being held at Wrexham. He spoke with 'a vibrancy and thrill only heard from Mr Lloyd George when he is with his own people at home' but was soon interrupted by about ten men and women who were 'violently thrust forth from our midst, expelled from this fierce frying pan only to fall into the fiercer fire which burned among the mob outside'. One woman reported even her undergarments being ripped to shreds.

Thanks to an article in New Zealand's *Poverty Bay Herald*, I learned that small strips of women's clothing were sent to prominent men who had been present at the Eisteddfod that afternoon and one Caernarfonshire magistrate was particularly proud of his 'Wrexham trophy'!

July

The government's Franchise Bill received its second reading; attention focused on which of three amendments (by Dickinson, Grey or Henderson) would stand the greatest chance of success. Any one of them would give over 6 million women the vote, which was a huge increase on the 1 million covered by the failed Conciliation Bills. Fears were voiced that if any one of the amendments was passed it would so fundamentally change the bill that the government would withdraw it.

Bangor, Llandudno and Colwyn Bay were represented at the West Lancashire, West Cheshire and North Wales Federation Committee Meeting in Liverpool, where discussion took place on the latest bill.

A local sub-committee met at the home of Mrs Elsie Marks in Llandudno to discuss arrangements for the forthcoming autumn campaign. Bangor was printing 1,000 Welsh-language leaflets to be distributed in both north and south Wales. This meeting was attended by Mr Thomas and Mrs Anna Maria Haslam, by then both well into their eighties, dedicated Suffragists from Ireland.

August

The *North Wales Weekly News* reported that a letter from Miss Mildred Spencer had been submitted to the District Council General Purposes Committee sitting in private on 2 August and as a result the following resolution had been passed that: 'This Council calls upon the Government to grant the Parliamentary Franchise 1912 to Women' and that a copy of the Resolution be sent to Sir Herbert Roberts MP, the Prime Minister and the Chancellor.

September

Suffragettes attempted to heckle Mr Lloyd George as he opened Llanystumdwy Village Hall, despite local Suffragists having appealed for him to be allowed to undertake this engagement, in his home village, in peace. At the first cry of 'Votes for Women', the offending Suffragette was surrounded by men chanting '*I'r afon a hi*' – it being their intention to duck her and anyone else who interrupted Mr Lloyd George, in the river! But other interruptions followed and the Suffragettes came under merciless attack – having their clothes ripped from them and clumps of their hair torn out; one woman reported that she was left naked to the waist. They were beaten and kicked and the police had a real struggle to protect them. Thwarted in their attempt to reach the river one Suffragettes' captors would definitely have ducked her under the village pump had they been able to get anywhere near it, but the crowd was too dense for them to be able to drag her through. But although the police

Suffragette at Llanystumdwy

couldn't find anyone willing to offer the Suffragettes sanctuary, they did manage to commandeer a pony and trap, bundle the women in and transport them to Cricieth Station, where they were told they must travel in the guard's van on the train, for fear of recriminations if they were seated with other passengers.

The press had been out in force at this event and it was extensively covered, even making the pages of the *Illustrated London News*. The Welsh press was divided between pouring scorn on the English women for daring to come to Wales to interrupt the great Welsh hero and admonishing the ruffian element for tarnishing the image of God-fearing, chapel-going Welshmen. The Conservative element of the English press relished the opportunity to vilify its arch-enemy, Mr Lloyd George and his uncivilised followers and *The Times* emphasised how unfit women were to vote.

The previously mentioned *Poverty Bay Herald* took a different angle. In an item headed 'Like Porcupines', it explained that women who had been roughly treated at the Wrexham Eisteddfod a few months earlier, had come to Llanystumdwy prepared. They wore padded garments into which an ingenious arrangement of sharp needles had been inserted with their points outward. The needles were of course, invisible and their presence was only felt when anyone attempted to manhandle the women!

But once again, strips of women's clothing were sent to prominent men who had been present in Llanystumdwy that afternoon, ripped from those women who had come unprepared.

After Mr Lloyd George's death, amongst his correspondence, a letter was found from Evan William Evans, a Calvinistic Methodist, local historian, journalist, editor, publisher and owner of a Dolgellau printing office where many local newspapers and journals were produced.

Mr Evans wrote:

I find in today's paper that questions are to be asked in the House of Commons on Monday about the treatment of the Suffragists (as explained above, they were actually Suffragettes – the Suffragists having begged the Suffragettes not to disrupt this event) at Llanystumdwy. I was present at the meeting and quite close to two of the women who disturbed the proceedings and who were ejected.

The reports published in many of the newspapers were greatly exaggerated. It has been repeatedly asserted that the hair of one of the disturbers was actually pulled off in handfuls by the crowd. I was close by at the time and saw what did take place. The hat of the woman was taken off and handfuls of hair did come off with it. A friend of mine picked up the hat and I have it now in my possession as well as a considerable quantity of the 'hair' said to have been plucked off. But will you allow me to assure you that this woman did not on that occasion suffer the loss of any of her own hair! It was false hair that was artfully inserted inside the hat in such a way that it looked like natural hair and of course 'it came off in handfuls'. I have been endeavouring to find out the name and address of the owner of the hat and false hair, but so far I have failed. It was I think a very clever bit of stage acting and it came off well!

Evan William Evans

(The letter is preserved in the National Library of Wales).

October

The Colwyn Bay Society's first meeting of the 1912-1913 session was held at the Café Royal and it was noted that the group was increasing both numerically and in enthusiasm.

Mr Charles Elcock presided and Miss Ashton from Manchester was the speaker. She said they were at a critical moment in history. They wanted the vote to affect legislation and improve social conditions. She said women were at the bottom of every walk of life and profession, but women were now going to university and worked harder for less money than men. The Insurance Act covered 9 million men but only 3 million women, because women didn't earn enough to qualify. The health of mothers was important because future generations depended on it.

Miss Ashton said women should to write to their MP's urging them to support women's suffrage, or at the very least to abstain from voting against it.

Miss Hovey gave the vote of thanks and said that even though Sir Herbert Roberts MP had supported them previously, they should each try to get one man to write to him urging him to continue to support women's suffrage.

Miss Kenyon said how sorry they all were that the Elcocks were moving to Manchester; Colwyn Bay Suffragists really didn't know how they'd manage without them. Mr Elcock passed on a message from his wife, who was ill, saying it had been a great privilege to be associated with the Colwyn Bay NUWSS.

November
Bangor Society met at 'Wellfield' by kind permission of Mrs Edith Milner-Barry.

Miss Deakin, who had that day returned from speaking in Dublin, said it was impossible to over-estimate the gravity of the current position – they were facing the very real possibility that the government was about to enfranchise every male over twenty-one, no matter how ignorant, but no women no matter how intelligent.

She went on to warn that an invasion of Bangor by the Anti-Suffragists was imminent.

But Miss Deakin needn't have worried about the Anti-Suffragists – next day Mrs Gladstone Solomon spoke at the Queen's Head Café on 'No Votes for Women' but her audience was comprised largely of NUWSS members!

Mrs Solomon pointed out that since there were more women in Britain than men, they could have to assume responsibility for military and naval forces, the rule of Empire and questions of war and peace, all subjects she contended about which women were profoundly ignorant.

The Colwyn Bay Society met at the Café Royal and Miss Deakin spoke on 'The Reform Bill and Women's Suffrage'. A resolution was passed calling on Sir Herbert Roberts MP 'to do his utmost to secure some measure of women's suffrage in the Reform Bill'.

Miss Deakin said twenty-three MP's were said to have

voted against the Conciliation Bill as a protest against the violence of the militant's window-smashing campaign; but in Wales women were lynched merely for interrupting Mr Lloyd George's meetings and there were no arrests – the male perpetrators were allowed to go free.

If law-abiding Suffragists could have equalled the enthusiasm and self-sacrifice of the Suffragettes, 'The Cause' would already have been won.

Women needed the protection of the vote to enable them to solve grave social problems.

Colwyn Bay's members were also invited to a somewhat luridly entitled talk: 'Horrors of the White Slave Trade' – under the auspices of the British Women's Temperance Association, chaired by Miss Rosa Hovey and addressed by Miss Hessell, who said that her subject was the saddest in the world. The subsequent newspaper report was headlined:

AWFUL REVELATIONS AT COLWYN BAY – GIRLS BOUGHT AND SOLD, DRUGGED, DISHONOURED AND EXILED

Miss Hessell said in every city in the country there was a great army of outcast or fallen women, estimated at 60,000 in London alone and 1,200,000 fallen men, but unlike women, they were received into society.

Only five per cent of women went into this life willingly and the other causes were starvation wages: women paid 7/6d, for hours, maybe days, spent hand-stitching a fur coat which would be sold for 21 guineas; shop girls earning less than 7/- per week; widows and deserted wives suffering the same plight.

They had only three options: the workhouse, with no prospect of ever getting their home and family back together; struggling on but having to let their children starve; or supplementing their earnings by working on the streets.

But, said Miss Hessell, girls coming to London and other big cities to take up respectable posts were at high risk from procurers who met them at railway stations (pretending to have been sent by their prospective employers to transport them for interview) and then bundled them into cabs with well-dressed women who proceeded to drug them and take them to houses of ill repute. The girls would then wake up to find their clothes had been taken away and if they didn't do as they were told they would be beaten and starved. Many were taken abroad to countries where they couldn't speak the language and had almost no chance of escape. Procurers also advertised perfectly respectable jobs, offered interviews and then simply abducted applicants.

Miss Hessell said there were estimated to be nearly 1½ million white slaves in America and a staggering £60 million per year was spent on vice. In London, Miss Hessel said, in the past twelve weeks fifty-four girls under the age of twenty-one were known to have gone missing and the total so far for the year was 1,118 girls and 2,696 women who were unaccounted for in London alone.

The maximum penalty for injuring a horse was fourteen years; for injuring a child – two years!

Anything the NUWSS could do, through gaining enfranchisement, which would help to alleviate the suffering of these poor women, would be supported by the British Women's Temperance Association.

The Bangor Society intended to hold a debate between the Anti's and Pro's but the Anti-Suffrage speaker, Cordelia

Moir failed to turn up, so Mrs Corbett Ashby (NUWSS Secretary and Editor of *The Common Cause*) put her personal view to the audience. She said many women were now better educated and had greater responsibilities in family, local and indeed national life than in the past and consequently more need of the vote. She agreed that it was for men to be in charge of the armed forces, but they must not forget that it was women who must see that their husbands and sons were well fed and fit to fight. She mentioned that for the Boer War the height restriction had to be lowered as there simply weren't enough males reaching the requirement.

At the end of November Suffragettes poured acid, ink, lampblack (the soot from oil-lamps) and tar into pillar-boxes in the City of London, the West End and numerous provincial cities. Thousands of pieces of mail were destroyed and in Newcastle on Tyne alone 2,000 letters were damaged. The Suffragettes achieved this without a single arrest. One of the Suffragettes interviewed by historian Sir Brian Harrison explained that she, as a live-in maid, felt able to take part in this campaign because the damage could be done discreetly, whereas she wouldn't have dared take part in any protest where there was a chance of being arrested and then dismissed by her employer. This is the reason that this particular campaign was so crucial – it gave ordinary working-class women the chance to demonstrate their support for what their wealthier and more leisured sisters were trying to achieve for them.

December
'The Exclusion of Women from the Parliamentary Franchise Blocks the Way for Social Reform' was the subject for debate at Colwyn Bay Society's meeting at the Café

Royal. Colonel Sarson presided and 150 women and four men were present.

Miss Crosfield said women wanted votes as protection – 5 million women were earning their own livings and ninety per cent of them were engaged in sweated labour. Lord Haldane was convinced they were better off without the vote, if they got it there'd be no chivalry. Miss Crosfield asked where was the chivalry now, when women had the worst paid jobs? There should be no taxation without representation and those who obeyed laws should take part in making them – the introduction of the White Slave Traffic Bill had been successful due to women's agitation.

Miss Crosfield said the Salvation Army was a wonderful organisation and Mrs Booth was no less valuable than General Booth. She also said that a popular excuse for women not having the vote was that they couldn't fight, but few people knew that the soldiers who actually did the fighting didn't have the vote.

Miss Crosfield ended triumphantly that cooking was extremely important and beyond the capabilities of the majority of men.

Against Miss Crosfield, R. Thompson argued that there was social reform: the Poor Law, the Illegitimate Children's Act, the Married Women's Act, Health, Insurance, Old Age Pensions, Education and Criminal Law had all been improved.

Miss Clayton supported Miss Crosfield and an invitation was given to the audience to support Mr Thompson, but no support was forthcoming for him.

Miss Spencer said that a Royal Commission had recently shown the futility of the Poor Law Acts and deemed it necessary to appoint women to the Commission to deal with the shortcomings. She continued that Mr Thompson had paid a glowing tribute to his mother and said that he wouldn't be half the man he was without her, so didn't he think his mother deserved the vote?

When the vote on the debate was taken only four people were in favour of Mr Thompson.

The Colwyn Bay Society also held a Sale of Work (sale of needlework produced by members in their 'spare' time!) in the Lecture Hall (possibly at Penrhos College). Mrs Edith Mould was ill, so the sale was opened by Dr Mary Deacon.

Mrs Thomas Lloyd presided and said that women should press forward and break through barriers that were preventing them from taking their rightful place as citizens. They could not be happy with only men making laws which both men and women had to obey. But Mrs Lloyd had no sympathy with those who behaved in a way the Suffragists couldn't possibly imitate and she was very sorry for what had been done by the misguided women who had adopted such methods.

Miss Kenyon addressed her listeners as 'My fellow ought-to-be citizens'. [laughter] She deplored the excesses which had taken place recently, especially the pillar-box outrage, but said they must encourage people to write to Sir Herbert Roberts MP to tell him public opinion in his constituency was still in favour of women's suffrage.

Miss Kenyon added that they had started out with fifty members, now had 150 and were hoping for 200 by Christmas.

Dr Deacon, declaring the sale open, said that women's suffrage was at a crisis point and it was therefore important to raise funds for whatever lay ahead. Miss Ethel Hovey gave the vote of thanks to Mrs Lloyd and Dr Deacon and said women doctors were equal to men and were very kind to be fighting the suffrage battle for women far less fortunate than themselves, who hadn't had their opportunities. Finally she warned that Suffragists were rapidly losing support due to the actions of the Suffragettes.

The Sale of Work was followed in the evening by a musical concert performed by Penrhos College staff.

Mrs Jennie Cornwallis-West of Ruthin Castle, President of the North Wales Anti-Suffrage League, (widow of Randolph Churchill and mother of Winston), addressing St Asaph Intermediate School's prize-giving, said:

> I could always manage boys, but never girls. My advice to you is hit out and hit straight. When you live your life, live straight – never drink and above all, if you can possibly help it, never swear – except at a Suffragette!

Chapter 7

1913

The year of 'The Pilgrimage'

At the beginning of 1913 the government's latest Franchise Bill was withdrawn and it was obvious no progress could be made before the next election, which had to be held by the end of 1915. By this time the Labour Party was rapidly losing patience and resolved to oppose any bill which did not include women's suffrage on the same terms as men's.

Suffragists spent 1913 and the early months of 1914 on educational and propaganda campaigns to promote women's suffrage as a popular cause, which prospective parliamentary candidates could no longer afford to ignore.

Mrs Pankhurst, meanwhile, announced that Suffragettes were warranted in employing all methods of war. Human life would be held sacred, but if it was necessary in order to win the vote, maximum damage would be done to property.

January
Bangor Society started off the new year with a Rummage Sale which raised £12 19 6d.

February
The Colwyn Bay Society held their AGM.

Income for the year had been £158 9 7d and expenditure £121 18 8d, leaving a balance of £36 10 11d.

The speaker, Miss Royden, said that so far suffrage campaigners had not been defeated in the House of

Commons, but defrauded. They must never give up. It had taken twenty-seven years to get the White Slave Traffic Bill passed and that only finally happened because William Stead, who had dedicated his whole life to that cause, was lost on the *Titanic* and it was thought that the bill would be a suitable memorial to him.

At the Bangor Committee Meeting Mrs Price White reported that she had been invited by Liverpool NUWSS to stand for election to the National Executive, but felt unable to allow her name to go forward due to the time and incidental expenses involved if elected. (By 1913 Mrs Price White had a six-year old son and five year old daughter and only one general servant to help her.) Knowing how hard Mrs Price White was working for equality, particularly for Welsh-speaking women in the quarrying villages here – and indeed, in the mining villages of south Wales, through the translation of women's suffrage literature into Welsh, I felt very sad when I read that she had declined to let her name go forward for the usual reasons – lack of time and lack of money. I'm sure she could have made a tremendous contribution to the National Executive, had she stood and been elected.

Miss Wortham reported that all women municipal voters in Bangor West Ward had been canvassed by letter and accompanying NUWSS literature, sent through the post. She, Miss Edwards and Mrs Huw Rowland would be following this up by house-to-house canvassing. Mrs Gaunt, Miss Lamport, Miss Matthews and Miss Pinkerton then volunteered to help.

It was decided to adopt the suggestion of Miss Raw of Llandudno that education as well as propaganda should be included in meetings. Miss Raw had included a list of speakers and subjects and these would be used to draw up a programme for the coming year.

Lady Lewis was to be asked for the use of Belmont grounds for the Garden Fete in June and Lady Aberconwy, Mrs Steel or Miss Royden were suggested as possible 'openers'.

Miss Wortham requested the names of regular subscribers to *Suffrage News* in order to manage the insertion of *Suffrage Notes* (which may have been published by the Bangor Society). It was suggested she should make a list of members likely to take the paper, get their consent and place the list with the newsagent.

At the next Bangor Committee Meeting members agreed to canvass for Mrs Ffoulkes-Jones to be appointed to the Board of Guardians (South Ward).

It was decided that attendance of delegates at the NUWSS Council Meetings should be in rotation, to stimulate interest amongst committee members.

It was agreed that they should send 2/- towards the collection for Mrs Fawcett, NUWSS President, a message from Bangor to be drawn up by Mrs Hudson-Williams and Miss Wortham and Mrs Price White to represent them at the presentation.

A letter had been received from Miss Hughes, Bangor Normal College, requesting a date for a public debate on women's suffrage; it was decided they would invite Miss Matters to speak.

Mrs Huw Rowland said only a very small start had been made on house-to-house canvassing in West Ward.

Leonora Cohen (nee Throp), entered the Tower of London with an iron bar concealed beneath her coat and smashed a case containing the insignia of the Order of Merit. Wrapped around the iron bar was a sheet of paper inscribed: 'This is my protest against the government's treachery to the working women of Great Britain'.

Mrs Leonora Cohen

She was charged with 'causing unlawful and malicious damage to an amount exceeding £5'. By the time she returned home to Leeds her action had already made headline news. At her trial Mrs Cohen who defended herself, spoke with such conviction and clarity that she impressed everyone present and when an Expert Witness testified that she had inflicted only £4 10/- worth of damage, the jury was able to acquit her!

March

Miss Spencer addressed a meeting in the English Presbyterian Schoolroom on 'The Law as it affects Women'. She said that everywhere the law was blocking the way to freedom and self-realisation for women. They were still not free from the idea that a wife was one of a man's possessions, but all over the world women were recognising their right to determine their own destinies. Although the Married Women's Property Act and the new Divorce Laws had improved things for women, even as she spoke, the law still regarded the father as the only parent able to make decisions about children. Men got light fines and short sentences for offences against women and children, whereas offences against property by the Suffragettes were severely punished. No wonder women were driven to rebellion and destruction of property, feeling it to be the only way to draw the attention of the apathetic masses to the terrible wrongs in society.

A debate was held in The Penrhyn Hall, Bangor between representatives of the Suffrage and Anti-Suffrage Societies. Despite all the effort expended by the Suffragists, the motion that women should be given the vote was defeated. Mrs Gladstone Solomon went on very successfully to sign up new members to the National League Opposing Women's Suffrage in Penmaenmawr, Llanfairfechan, Bangor, Caernarfon, Holyhead and Valley.

But still the Suffragists didn't give up, they simply carried on quietly with their campaign of education in the hope that if a Liberal Party with a tiny majority won the imminent election, they would be forced to negotiate with Labour and some compromise on women's issues could be reached. (There was no hope of Labour actually winning outright).

Bangor Society organised another Suffrage versus Anti-Suffrage debate on 'Granting the Parliamentary Vote to Women' at The Penrhyn Hall. The Mayor of Bangor presided and the case for the Antis was put by Miss Moir, Organising Secretary of the Manchester Branch of the National League Opposing Women's Suffrage, who started by complaining that she was at a disadvantage due to putting her case first, for others to reply to. Miss Moir contended that getting the vote would be just the first step of many and would strike at the root of social and domestic life. Most women didn't grasp what was involved. Anti-Suffragists agreed there was a need for some reform, but didn't think having the vote was the best way to achieve it. In the past women hadn't felt any indignity regarding not having the vote. The Anti-Suffragists thought it was right that men should make the laws – men carried on the business of the country and the country couldn't manage without them, they were the police, the firemen, the miners, the farmers and the fishermen.

Women were judged by different standards. Women who had to work – and she was one of them, mattered nothing at all to the welfare of the nation – they mattered only as wives and mothers. [loud cheers]

Miss Matters for the NUWSS replied that for laws to be made for women who had no voice, condemned women to slavery. She said the Anti-Suffragists tried to make people believe women didn't want the vote, but both intellectual and industrial bodies were demanding it.

Miss Moir said the Suffragists were trying to make men and women equal, instead of recognising the precious qualities men possessed which women didn't have.

Miss Matters commented that all great reforms, e.g. the ending of slavery in America, were achieved by the burning enthusiasm of a few, whilst the vast majority didn't bother their heads.

April

A public debate was held at Colwyn Bay YMCA between the NUWSS and YMCA members and the room was packed to capacity. Mr T. Arthur Hughes, Solicitor, moved the resolution that: 'Enfranchisement for women was neither necessary nor desirable, as women had not been educated or raised in a manner that equipped them for the use of the ballot. It was like asking for a diploma before learning the ABC'. He continued that they should vote in municipal elections which they were allowed to do – but didn't – before asking for the parliamentary vote.

Miss Spencer opposed the motion but no result was recorded.

At the Bangor Committee Meeting it was noted that forty-two women had been eligible to vote for the South Ward Guardian and thirty-two had done so. It was not recorded whether Mrs Ffoulkes-Jones (whom Bangor NUWSS had supported) was successful.

Miss Edwards reported a deficit of £2 5 9d and that £5 was still owing to Miss Rathbone.

Miss Edwards was asked to approach Miss Hughes, Secretary, National League Opposing Women's Suffrage to try to arrange another debate on their respective views.

It was decided to invite Miss Eskrigge to speak to other local societies during April and May to try to boost NUWSS membership.

Miss Edwards was asked to make a list of members with outstanding subscriptions and another list of people thought to be interested in joining the Bangor Society, to be followed up by the committee.

It was decided to move the bank account from the National Provincial and to see whether London City and Midland or Lloyds would be more suitable to receive future deposits.

With regard to the Fete, Mrs. G. O. Price was to liase with Lady Lewis and Mrs Corbett-Ashby and also with Miss Pinkerton concerning the choice of a play to be performed. There would be a Cake Stall and Mrs Hudson-Williams was to liase with Mrs Grierson regarding Side Shows.

At the next Bangor Committee Meeting it was decided that Mrs Corbett-Ashby or Mrs Steel would be invited to speak at the Fete and if neither was available Miss Beavan was to be consulted about another possible speaker.

Entertainment was to be arranged by Miss Pinkerton, Mrs Price and Miss Sedgwick.

Cakes were to be arranged by Mrs Milner-Barry, Miss Edwards and Mrs Hudson-Williams and Teas by Mrs H. O.

Hughes, Mrs Price and Mrs Price White. Miss Matthews was to seek contributions towards the teas and also arrange the competitions.

Mrs Hudson-Williams was to approach Mrs Gadsby about fancy dancing. (This turned out to be Maypole dancing.)

It was reported that the bank account had been successfully moved to Lloyds.

May

Non-committee members were invited to attend the Bangor Committee Meeting.

Miss Matthews was asked to appoint a delegate to attend the Federation Meeting in Colwyn Bay on 5 May and Miss Lamport indicated that she was willing to attend the Provincial Council at Exeter, representing Bangor.

Over a period of a fortnight during this month, Miss Eskrigge and the Bangor Suffragists spoke in Bangor, Bethesda, Llanfairfechan and Holyhead – stressing that the NUWSS was law-abiding and non-militant a number of full members and friends were enlisted.

An application was made to the Vicar of Penmaenmawr for the use of Church House for the purpose of a women's suffrage meeting.

In the parish magazine the vicar wrote:

It may be well to state one's convictions when the doings of some women of splendid courage but extraordinary antics, which for public safety should be stopped with a firm hand, are alienating many and filling them with disgust. Of the righteousness of 'The Cause' there can be no doubt and of the unselfish and equally sincere desire of its advocates, who willingly sacrifice much for it, there can be no doubt either. The hysterical doings of some misguided women do not therefore make 'The Cause' less righteous, although they do damage it considerably. I therefore place the parlour at the disposal of the friends of women's suffrage and heartily wish them success.

The local newspapers reported that a round-the-clock watch was being kept on Gwyrch Castle, home of the Earl and Countess Dundonald, while it was being extensively renovated and the same applied to Bryngwenallt, home of Sir Herbert and Lady Roberts, as a precaution against attack by Suffragettes.

A railwayman cycling to work on the Rhiwlas to Glanadda road found that a tree had been felled near Perfeddgoed obstructing the road and nailed to it was a sheet of paper printed 'Votes for Women'. Similar sheets were scattered around.

June

On 4 June Suffragette Emily Wilding Davison tried, it's now thought, to attach a 'Votes for Women' scarf to the King's horse at the Epsom Derby in the hope that the message would stream out as the jockey in the King's colours raced the horse to victory.

She and the horse came into contact and she died four days later of her injuries.

Miss Emily Davison at the Epsom Derby

Miss Emily Davison's funeral

(For full details of this incident see 'Appendix A – Visiting Dignitaries – Who was Who'.)

Early June provided several dramatic headlines for local newspapers too. Suffragettes visited Llanrwst, handing out leaflets and pasting them up on buildings. Subsequently a package was found on the windowsill of the Town Hall. PC Jones, 'with great boldness', disassembled the 'bomb' of glue and copper wire.

A sudden fire in a heap of cut timber above Gwydyr Castle was also attributed to Suffragettes and golfers who had left their hats and coats on the course due to the heat, returned to find 'Votes for Women' pennants flying above them.

A few days later, as two ladies were paying for admission to Conwy Castle, an eagle-eyed keeper noticed their Suffragettes' badges and immediately summoned a corporation employee to act as detective. On arrival he searched various nooks and crannies before coming upon the ladies sitting talking in the Banqueting Hall. Keeping them under observation, he was startled to see them reach beneath their cloaks, but breathed again when they took out sketch books and started drawing. After they had left, a thorough search was carried out but nothing untoward was found.

The Bangor Committee met primarily to discuss the forthcoming Fete.

Sixpenny tickets would include admission and a plain tea.

Mrs Bayne was to be invited to adjudicate the competitions.

On a notion of Mrs Huw Rowland, seconded by Mrs Hudson-Williams, it was agreed to insure the Fete for £25 (presumably approximately the amount they were hoping to raise) against rain. Mr Roberts, Insurance Agent, had been consulted and had promised to deal with the matter – the premium he thought would not exceed £1.

And a sure sign of the times they were living in – several ladies were to be asked to loan their maids to assist.

Mrs Gadsby had agreed to organise the Maypole Dances.

Mrs Huw Rowland was to be responsible for the Flower Stall,

Miss Edwards for the Gramophone Concert and

Miss Wortham was to arrange to have advertisements placed in the *North Wales Chronicle and Advertiser* and possibly *The Observer*.

Tea would be at 3.30 p.m. and Fru Ankers (from Norway) would speak at 5.30 p.m.

It was reported that ten delegates would be going to the NUWSS Women Worker's Conference at Hull. The forthcoming Pilgrimage was also discussed.

The Colwyn Bay Society sought permission from Abergele and Pensarn District Council to hold a meeting on the Promenade to plead for support and denounce militancy. Permission was refused because the council didn't want to open the door to 'the other variety' (WSPU) who were described as 'a regular nuisance to everyone'. One Councillor, Percy Davies, appealed for the Suffragists to be allowed to hold their meeting since they were against militancy. The clerk then very rudely commented that perhaps Percy was hoping to pick himself up a suitable wife from amongst 'the dear little things'.

In mid-June Dr Blake opened the Colwyn Bay Society's meeting by expressing her admiration and respect for the heroism and self-sacrifice of Emily Wilding Davison, followed by a minute's silence to honour Miss Davison's demise.

Miss Eskrigge agreed that whilst they all admired the courage and devotion shown by the militants, they were doing great harm to 'The Cause', both in parliament and in the country at large. Some thought the Suffragists should lie dormant for a few months, but they shouldn't, because if they did they would lose ground.

The forthcoming Pilgrimage was to be a huge advertising campaign and each of the 400 societies in the nineteen NUWSS Federations had been asked to help in organising it. The women would be walking to London, joining other suffrage societies along the way, holding meetings, distributing literature and collecting subscriptions and promises, the final goal being to meet in London on Saturday 26 July.

The NUWSS had attracted 12,000 new members in the past year alone despite all the setbacks caused by militant's actions and it was hoped that the Pilgrimage would enlist even more support.

M90/6/7/3/1

NATIONAL UNION OF WOMEN'S SUFFRAGE SOCIETIES

LAW-ABIDING   NON-PARTY

WOMEN'S SUFFRAGE PILGRIMAGE

TO TELL ALL ENGLAND WHY WOMEN WANT THE VOTE

THE WATLING STREET ROUTE

FROM

CARLISLE, JUNE 18TH, TO LONDON, JULY 26TH

MEETINGS WILL BE HELD ALL ALONG THE ROUTE AT

CARLISLE	JUNE 18th	ORMSKIRK	JULY 2nd	WOLVERHAMP'N	JULY 11th
WIGTON	" 18th	COLWYN BAY	" 3rd	BIRMINGHAM	" 12th
ASPATRIA	" 19th	PRESCOT	" 3rd	KNOWLE	" 14th
KESWICK	" 21st	RHYL	" 4th	LEAMINGTON	" 15th
GRASMERE	" 23rd	LIVERPOOL	" 4th	STRATFORD	" 16th
WINDERMERE	" 24th	CHESTER	" 5th	KINETON	" 17th
KENDAL	" 25th	MANCHESTER	" 5th	BANBURY	" 18th
ARNSIDE	" 26th	STOCKPORT	" 5th	OXFORD	" 19th
LANCASTER	" 27th	TARPORLEY	" 7th	THAME	" 21st
GARSTANG	" 28th	MACCLESFIELD	" 7th	HIGH WYCOMBE	" 22nd
PRESTON	" 30th	NANTWICH	" 8th	BEACONSFIELD	" 23rd
SOUTHPORT	JULY 1st	CONGLETON	" 8th	UXBRIDGE	" 24th
BANGOR	" 2nd	STOKE	" 9th	EALING	" 25th
PENMAENMAWR	" 2nd	STAFFORD	" 10th		

AND LONDON   -   JULY 26th

MID-DAY MEETINGS WILL BE HELD AT INTERMEDIATE PLACES ALONG THE ROUTE

ALL LAW-ABIDING SUFFRAGISTS ARE INVITED TO JOIN THE PILGRIMAGE

Full particulars may be obtained from the National Union of Women's Suffrage Societies, 14 Gt. Smith St., Westminster, and the Watling St. Route Secretary, Manchester and District Federation of Women's Suffrage Societies, 16 Deansgate, Manchester.

NUWSS 1913 Pilgrimage Poster

Federations along the route were being asked to offer hospitality – accommodation was promised on at least alternate nights and traps and motor cars would carry luggage and provide lifts when ladies were tired.

Miss Hovey announced that she had already received several promises, namely two £5's, two double bedrooms and the use of a bicycle with luggage carrier for the whole distance and return fare for same. She added that Colwyn Bay would be well represented on the Pilgrimage and two ladies intended walking all the way to London. Miss Hovey had also received another donation of £100 and I think this huge amount may well have come from Mrs Crosfield (of the soap manufacturing family). Meanwhile, in Llandudno, Mrs Walton-Evans had donated 1 guinea to the fund.

Miss Eskrigge said they would try to arrange accommodation for each pilgrim, but there may be hitches and they would have to be prepared to take their chances! She also demonstrated the little bright red, waterproof haversack with white and green straps (the NUWSS colours) in which it was hoped, each pilgrim would carry her personal belongings.

Mrs Ankers spoke at Colwyn Bay, one week after Norwegian women had been given the vote (having campaigned for it since 1814). She said that although there were more women than men in Norway, the men were not afraid of them! They believed that everyone who worked for their living was entitled to vote. As well as the vote, women who worked outside the home had been given two weeks off work before their babies were born and eight weeks afterwards, with sixty per cent of earnings throughout this time, which was revolutionary in 1913. They believed that women who were not tied exclusively to the kitchen and nursery were better able to educate their children and give them a broader outlook on life. She added that now Denmark was proposing to introduce Universal Suffrage too.

At the end of June Mrs Ankers went on to give the same address at a drawing-room meeting at the Plas Gwilym Hotel courtesy of Mrs Helby, organised by the Penmaenmawr Society and finally at Llandudno Town Hall. On the latter occasion, the Chairman was Dr Blake, who recounted how, several years earlier, she and a number of other Colwyn Bay ladies had attended a meeting in the same hall to hear Lady Balfour and been so inspired by her address that they had set up the Colwyn Bay NUWSS.

The Bangor Committee met to make final preparations for the Fete. In addition to the activities already planned, there was to be a Sale of Work.

Mrs Price White and Miss Edwards reported on arrangements for the open-air meeting on 2 July to launch the Pilgrimage. It was decided to order posters (a sample was on display) and also to engage the services of a sandwich(board)-man on the day. Mrs Price White was asked to order twelve hat badges for intending pilgrims. Mr Milner-Barry was to be asked to chair the open-air meeting and names were suggested of people who may be willing to take a collection in support of Pilgrimage expenses.

A letter was read out offering five £1 scholarships for the Summer School at Tal-y-cafn from 25 August to 6 September, dependent upon those taking up the scholarships being willing to provide secretarial help to the Bangor Society. If no applicants were forthcoming then Miss Edwards or Mrs Price White would be the Bangor representative.

The Bangor Society held their Fete in the well kept

grounds of Sir Henry and Lady Lewis's mansion 'Belmont'. It must have been a lovely afternoon with a Cake Stall, a Flower Stall, a 'Sale of Work', Side-shows, Maypole Dancing to gramophone records followed by a Gramophone Concert, Competitions, Tennis and Teas. And for good measure there was a stirring address from Mrs Ankers and two inspiring Suffrage Plays – *A Chat with Mrs Chicky*, in which a blunt Suffragist charwoman played by Miss Sedgewick silenced an aristocratic 'Anti' played by Miss Matthews and *A Change of Tenant*. Typically, the society having insured against the event being rained off, the sun shone all day!

July

This was the high point of the year, when the NUWSS organised the pilgrimage to London involving 70,000 women from all over England and Wales. Pilgrims could join for any distance, at any point on the route convenient to themselves. There were four routes – from Newcastle on Tyne; from Land's End; through Kent and from Carlisle – 'The Watling Street Route' which was the one the north Wales pilgrims eventually joined. Passing through villages, towns and cities, the columns of walkers gave huge publicity to the NUWSS cause.

On **Wednesday 2nd July** supporters from Caernarfon, Pen-y-groes, Pwllheli and Cricieth met at the Reformer's Tree, Bangor. After brief speeches they travelled to Penmaenmawr where they were joined by local Suffragists and nearly forty women walked through the town wearing their 'uniform' of a white, grey, navy-blue or black coat and matching dress or skirt – if skirt, then their blouse was either to match in colour or be white. They were to wear matching coloured hats, simple in style, to which must be pinned a

*The Reformer's Tree, Bishops's Park, Bangor – starting point
for north Wales contingent*

raffia badge in the shape of a cockle-shell (the traditional symbol of pilgrimage) available from NUWSS HQ at 3d each. They also wore their red, white and green shoulder sashes and red haversacks and could carry umbrellas if desired – so long as were encased in red white or green covers. They carried their 'Law-abiding Suffragists' banner aloft.

They were entertained to tea by Mrs Margaret Jenkins, President of the local NUWSS, at her home, Tan-y-Berllan and in the evening held a meeting in Mr H. R. Willliams' field at Pant-yr-Afon, where Dr Herbert Jenkins presided. He said that these were law-abiding ladies who hadn't broken any windows or set fire to any letter-boxes. Mrs Price White explained the aims of the NUWSS and the purpose of the Pilgrimage, with a few heckles from rowdy youths thrown in for good measure.

Dr Jenkins then proposed a resolution in favour of women's suffrage, which was declared carried.

A London Suffragist who was on holiday in

Penmaenmawr at the time of the Pilgrimage, wrote to the local papers afterwards 'to thank the men and women of the beautiful town of Pen for the good reception and fair hearing they gave to the Suffragists'.

Next day the women walked to Conwy, where they were joined by Llandudno members and Miss Spencer, Secretary of the Colwyn Bay Society. From then on Mrs Price White and Miss Spencer took it in turns to speak at each place they visited. Mrs Price White admitted to having been terrified when she left Bangor, but felt she was gaining confidence each time she spoke.

At Conwy, a policeman was heard to remark that it was difficult to believe that these women were engaged in a campaign for the franchise – they looked more like a Sunday School Procession. The women were described as ranging in age from 'a maiden of seventeen' to 'a lady with the lines of time deeply implanted on her face'.

Mr and Mrs Thomas Haslam from Ireland, spoke words of encouragement to the pilgrims before they left for Colwyn Bay, where they were greeted by the town band.

There was an evening meeting on the Rhos on Sea side of the pier, attended by thousands – and constantly interrupted by rowdy youths. However, Mrs Price White decided to hold a meeting on the other side of the pier and her delivery was described as clear, forceful and convincing. The faces of her growing audience proved their interest, as Mrs Price White explained that they were law-abiding and did not want the vote for idle purposes. By now the rowdy youths had gathered around her and continued to interrupt, but she dealt with every one of their comments patiently without showing any irritation and well deserved the applause accorded to her. Afterwards she said 'Experience shows that where men and women will listen to reasoned argument we can gain sympathy and support, but it is the attitude of those who turn deaf and contemptuous ears we find upsetting'.

On **Friday 4th**, preceded by a gaily decorated motor-car and the town band, thirty-four women set off from the Imperial Hotel and were joined by further supporters at Old Colwyn. At Llysfaen a crowd of about 200 quarrymen lined the road and cheered them on their way. At Abergele Station the pilgrims stopped to talk to a crowd of poverty-stricken looking women and children who had just arrived by train on a day trip from the Manchester area. These women listened attentively to what the pilgrims had to say and many expressed the opinion that although they had never realised before what having the vote could do for them – how it could raise them out of extreme poverty – they did realise now and would support the Suffrage Movement in future. And they too cheered the pilgrims on their way.

During lunch at the Mountjoy Café hundreds gathered outside, peering in through the windows. When the pilgrims emerged, an irate female Abergele resident told them in no uncertain terms that if she had her way, she'd put Mrs Pankhurst in a big cannon loaded full with powder and shoot her to the moon! Just for good measure, she added that she didn't think they were any better than the Pankhursts and if someone would give her some rotten eggs she'd be delighted to throw them! Miss Spencer then bravely spoke from a motor-car in Bridge Street.

On Friday evening their planned meeting on Rhyl Promenade had to be abandoned when youths and girls got bored with merely heckling and started throwing stones into the assembled crowd of some thousands. Most pilgrims escaped in taxis organised by the police. But Mrs Hutton, whom it's thought was probably carrying the Rhyl Society's flag, was pursued by a large section of the crowd along West Parade and down John Street and despite the protection of every available police officer, was advised for her own safety to hide in a house in River Street until the crowd had dispersed. Mrs Bromley, another member of the Rhyl Society, managed to give her followers the slip by speeding away on her bicycle.

On Saturday morning the women were allowed to walk through Prestatyn, the last town on their itinerary, in peace … but some women travelled on to Chester to meet up with the Cheshire contingent and another two speakers, Miss Ashton of Manchester and Mrs Earp of Rotherham. There was an evening meeting and the Market Square was absolutely packed out, in fact it was said that there had not been such interest in a political meeting in Chester in living memory.

Sunday 6th was a rest day. On Monday they set off for Tarvin, which turned out to be extremely anti-Suffragist, inhabitants refusing to listen to the pilgrims and tearing posters and pennants from their caravans. In contrast, their evening meeting at Tarporley was a great success, they particularly noted how polite and well-behaved the young people were, many buying badges and signing the 'Friends of the Suffragists' cards.

On **Tuesday 8th** their route took the pilgrims through Barbridge, where the women on the narrow-boats tied up in the canal-basin listened attentively. The local Conservative Political Agent turned up and announced that he was an 'Anti'. But having listened to the conversation between the pilgrims and bargees and asked some questions of his own, realised that he did in fact, support a limited franchise for women. He therefore offered to go to Nantwich the following night and ask the same questions.

He kept his promise, but the pilgrims found the adults at Nantwich disinterested and the children extremely ill-mannered. The pilgrims said they intended to commend Nantwich to the care of Crewe NUWSS to see if they could bring any influence to bear on the stolid, apathetic adults and mud-slinging, stone-throwing little boys.

On **Thursday 10th** they moved on to Burslem. Mrs Price White noted that the Suffragists were initially told 'We don't want to listen to you and we don't want to read your rubbishy papers'. She said what made the Suffragists sick at heart was the number of jeering women and girls of the poorer classes who had no notion that it was for their protection and uplifting that she and her companions were campaigning. 'But,' she continued, 'when we could speak to

The Watling Street group – which four north Wales women joined

just small groups of these women and girls, they listened
with surprise, then interest and finally thanked us and even
cheered us on our way'. In fact, before the pilgrims left Burslem
a resolution in favour of women's suffrage was carried
almost without dissent – save for an extremely well-heeled
and haughty woman who stuck her nose in the air and told
the pilgrims they ought to be 'dipped in a barrel of tar'!

It is at this point that Miss Marjory Lees and the women
from Oldham NUWSS joined the 'Watling Street pilgrims'
(the group to which the north Wales ladies belonged). The
Oldham women were accompanied by two horse-drawn
caravans, the horses being Noah and Ham and these were
driven by two of Miss Lees' employees, Messrs Scholes and
Clapham.

Next day the pilgrims entered Hanley led by a band which
appeared to know only two tunes – 'Marching through
Georgia' and 'The Old Folks at Home', played alternately at
a very fast pace. The pilgrim's arrival could certainly not be
described as dignified, with the leaflet distributors and
donation collectors having to dart amongst the crowds at
break-neck speed. Major Cecil Wedgwood came out to
support them and both he and his wife spoke, as well as Miss
Ashton, who addressed a large and sympathetic crowd and
the resolution for women's suffrage was passed. But the
hooligan element made reaching their lodgings very difficult
and not a little frightening, to the extent that some pilgrims
took temporary refuge in the Police Station.

That night the Birkenhead women's caravan was totally
wrecked by hooligans.

On **Saturday 12th** the pilgrims were led into Stafford by a
very poor band, but this was more than compensated for by
the fact that local NUWSS members provided strawberries

and cream for tea. There was a huge meeting in the town square where Miss Cicely Leadley-Brown from Liverpool's Church League for Women's Suffrage (CLWS) had a sympathetic audience. However, at another meeting a small band of rough youths pelted Miss Ashton with eggs, flour and oranges, whilst the rest of the assembled crowd apologised profusely and a band of chivalrous young men offered to travel with the pilgrims to Wolverhampton and act as bodyguards the following evening.

After another rest day on Sunday, the pilgrims made their way to Birmingham. From this point until the pilgrims reached High Wycombe we have only Miss Lees' diary to provide information, because this section wasn't reported on in our local newspapers.

On **Tuesday 15th** July the pilgrims walked to Knowle, which was described as 'a charming little village'. The following day was described as 'lovely' and the women set off through pretty countryside for Warwick. About two miles from Warwick the weather changed, there was a torrential downpour and the Oldham women packed as many pilgrims as possible into the caravans. There were meetings both at Warwick and Leamington. The walk into Leamington was led by a Salvation Army Band playing 'a weird and melancholy tune'.

On **Thursday 17th** the pilgrim's destination was Stratford-on-Avon. After tea they had time for half an hour's sail on the river before visiting Shakespeare's grave and laying a wreath. A large crowd attended the meeting and there was organised opposition by a group of men who jeered and cat-called so loudly that it was impossible for Miss Ashton and Miss Leadley-Brown to be heard. (Miss Eskrigge had more success speaking a little way away from the main meeting). Finally the men linked arms and charged across the platform sweeping the speakers off their feet, but having done that, they dispersed and the pilgrims were able to return to their caravans or lodgings without any further harassment.

Mr Scholes, Miss Lees' groom, reported that, having seen one young male supporter of the Suffragists being badly bullied by other men he had reported it to the police, who told him in no uncertain terms that they didn't intend going any nearer or getting involved!

Friday was another lovely day from the point of view of weather, but the villages of the Compton Valley lived up to their reputation of being rough and the pilgrims encountered a lot of hostility, one man being heard to remark that 'it was lucky for them they hadn't come after dark'. Fortunately several policemen were sent to keep an eye on their progress.

But one thing made Miss Lees' day – a hot lunch of lamb and green peas, followed by raspberries, washed down with stone ginger from the local pub, consumed in one of the caravans. After lunch the pilgrim contingent made its way to Compton Verney, where Lord and Lady Willoughby de Broke had offered to accommodate the caravans and other pilgrims in tents which had been used for a Red Cross demonstration, in their grounds. Tea was followed by an uneventful meeting addressed by Miss Ashton and Miss Matters. Lady Willoughby de Broke provided milk, eggs and bread and butter. As well as the tents, the Red Cross had left their campfire and a large quantity of beef tea.

On leaving Compton Verney on **Saturday 19th**, the pilgrims were advised to avoid Edge Hill, which was terribly steep and after some time unexpectedly found themselves on the road to Banbury.

Two of the women had been fancying cheese on toast ever since they'd left Oldham and this was the day they got it, only for one of them to step out of the caravan and launch her lunch off her plate and onto the grass. She ate it just the same! The meeting that night was described as very noisy with one man constantly blowing a cornet in the direction of the speaker's ear.

On Sunday they woke to find it had been pouring with rain all night, the horses were wet through and feeling sorry for themselves and it was still pouring down. The caravans and all cars accompanying the pilgrims were utilised to transport everyone to Oxford, the cars performing a shuttle service. They were able to relax in the afternoon. You can imagine the amazement of some of the pilgrims when, leaving Balliol College, they came upon an elderly, benevolent-looking gentleman and a young girl getting out of a cab and walking towards the college and suspected that it was none other than their sworn enemy, Mr Asquith. One of the women asked the cab driver if it was in fact the Prime Minister and he confirmed that it was!

The evening meeting was held in the Town Hall and the pilgrims processed the length of the hall and onto the stage, accompanied by organ music, to cheers and jeers in equal measure. A very long-winded Chairman denounced the militants and the Suffragists discovered later that feelings were running high because the Oxford Boathouse had been destroyed by a fire, set – it was presumed – by Suffragettes. To the amazement of the pilgrims the crowd started chanting that they wanted Miss Ashton and Miss Ashton they got – and she was magnificent! A few of the jeerers got bored and left, but others actually became interested in what she was saying and the resolution in favour of women's suffrage was passed, despite the efforts of a group of male Anti-Suffragists.

The pilgrims were asked to remain until the audience had departed and were then ushered out through a door at the back of the building, to the strains of the overture to *Tannhauser*!

Miss Lees said there was a beautiful sunset 'with the spires of Oxford piercing the twilight'.

On **Monday 21st** a crowd of Oxford women came out to bid them godspeed. En route to Wheatley they were asked whether they would like cutlets, or ham and eggs for lunch? Nearly everyone ordered cutlets but most went hungry as the inn had only seven cutlets and the innkeeper seemed completely overwhelmed by the sheer number of pilgrims. In the afternoon they walked on to Thame, where they were allocated the very nice field – often used by circuses. Some of the women were hungry and tired and decided not to go to the evening meeting but to have a meal in the caravans. Much later they were just ready to get undressed and go to bed when there was a huge commotion outside.

A policeman arrived and told them to lock their doors, shut their windows and put out their candles – which they did and huddled together as far back in the vans as possible. The noise of boos, jeers, hooters and whistles and things being thrown at the vans continued for what seemed like ages – Miss Lees thought probably about twenty minutes. Eventually the estimated 150 men lost interest and left, but one policeman remained on duty throughout the night – fortified by drinks of hot milk and Oxo provided by the grateful pilgrims. (At this time Oxo made with milk was advertised as 'making milk more palatable and digestible' and 'an excellent nerve and body food').

Tuesday morning dawned bright and sunny and they set off for Princes Risborough. The afternoon walk was extremely hilly and between that and their largely sleepless night, they were very tired. But much worse was to come – they had been warned there would probably be trouble at High Wycombe and had taken the precaution of sending the caravans to a nearby village. The pilgrims trudging wearily behind the town band were met by a crowd of several thousand extremely hostile people; indeed Miss Lees said she had never seen so many evil faces gathered together. The police seemed unable to control the crowd and they pressed in on the pilgrims from all sides. Some of the Oldham pilgrims were helped by a local woman who explained how to get to their pitch and after climbing what seemed like a mountain they were re-united with their caravans. Meanwhile the attempt to hold a meeting had to be abandoned after rushes had been made at the platform and rotten eggs and tomatoes thrown. Further, the crowd chased the pilgrims, making it necessary for many to escape in taxis and others to plead for refuge in private houses.

Wednesday 23rd was wet and colder. After attending a church service the pilgrims set off for Beaconsfield. An NUWSS member had arranged for them to stay at a delightful pitch, sheltered by pine trees and on the private road up to a farm where they were able to buy milk, butter and eggs and there was a pump for water. The pilgrims were tremendously grateful for this tranquil oasis after their recent experiences. They were just getting into bed when two manly voices outside enquired if they were alright?

It turned out to be a Mr Mottram and a Mr Fairbrother, two more of Miss Lees' employees, despatched by her mother after reading a report of events at High Wycombe in that morning's *Manchester Guardian*!

Thursday brought another lovely morning and Messrs

Mottram and Fairbrother said they would return to Oldham as Mrs Lees would now be on her way – she intended driving down to join the pilgrims. She overtook the pilgrims soon after they'd left Beaconsfield en route for Gerrard's Cross and decided to address the inhabitants of the town herself whilst waiting for the pilgrims to catch up. Mrs Lees then drove on to Uxbridge and arranged dinner for the Oldham women at the Chequers Hotel. Many felt that by this stage they weren't fit to be seen at such a grand establishment, but hunger triumphed.

Members of the Uxbridge Branch of the New Constitutional Society for Women's Suffrage (NCSWS) prepared meals for other Watling Street pilgrims. (The NCSWS supported the campaign to try to prevent candidates who did not support women's suffrage, from standing for election).

On **Friday 25th** it was time for Miss Lees to make arrangements for Noah, Ham and the caravans to be transported back to Oldham. First she and the other women packed up their supplies – by now mainly marmalade and biscuits. Passing Ealing Common, Noah recognised the Watling Street pilgrims who were holding a meeting there and wanted to stop, indeed it proved very difficult to persuade him to move on. After the horses had been given nosebags they set off again for St Pancras. Arrangements for the transport of the caravans were soon made, but the horses proved a different matter. It was the railway's intention for them to travel in an open cattle truck and it was not going to be possible for Mr Scholes and Mr Clapham to travel on the same train. Finally arrangements were made for both horses and men and to travel by passenger train.

Miss Lees then took a taxi to Bayswater where the Watling Street Group was camping.

During the three-week pilgrimage over half a million leaflets had been distributed and £7,800 raised.

On **Saturday 26th** July, with bands playing and banners waving, the four columns of pilgrims, numbering some 70,000 in total, plus multitudes of curious Londoners, converged on Hyde Park, where there were nineteen stands – one for each NUWSS Federation, distributing literature and providing platforms for speakers who explained the Suffragists' aims. The red, white and green colours were everywhere. WSPU members supported the Suffragists, as did the Women's Tax Resistance Group (WTRG) with their 'No Vote – No Tax' banners. At 6 p.m. a bugle sounded and the resolution of 'Votes for Women' was proclaimed from all nineteen platforms and carried with ringing cheers and infinitesimal dissent.

The Pilgrimage ended with a service in St Paul's Cathedral the following morning, where seats had been reserved for pilgrims under the dome. Miss Lees described the service as

Culmination of the Pilgrimage – rally in Hyde Park

'dull' with inaudible prayers and the vicar preaching on 'Elijah and depression'. Afterwards they went on to the Ethical Church, where Miss Royden spoke beautifully about 'The Spirit of Pilgrimage', which she defined as 'repentance, dedication and joy'.

An article written by one of the pilgrims mentioned that she had never seen the hedgerows so covered with wild roses as that summer and that their red-edged white flowers reminded her of the Suffragists' colours – red for enthusiasm, white for purity and green for hope.

And one lady, probably Mrs Price White, returning to Bangor, told a newspaper reporter that 'We all felt it was only the beginning of much greater and better work which the Pilgrim Spirit is going to enable us to do'.

A very thoughtful Editorial appeared in the *North Wales Weekly News* referring to The Pilgrimage:

> There is something to command respect in the spectacle of thousands of women of all classes walking, at the cost of so much self-sacrifice, from the four corners of the kingdom to the great metropolis, in order to prove their sincerity. What is it that has inspired them with the determination and strength to take part in this epoch-making Pilgrimage? It is a feeling shared by them all as one, that the time has arrived to prove to the world that non-militant Suffragists are no less earnest in their desire for citizen's rights because they seek to obtain them by quiet, constitutional methods, instead of the methods of hooliganism and anarchy employed by others.

August

The NUWSS, in association with Oxford and St Andrews

Universities, held a Summer School on 'The Art of Public Speaking' at Walden, Tal-y-bont. The lecturer was Miss Dora Mason MA who had been a lecturer in Classics at Liverpool University 1907-1912 and resigned to become NUWSS Organiser for Oxfordshire, Berkshire and Buckinghamshire.

Miss Mason organised the Conwy Valley School so that she lectured on a different subject each morning, then after lunch students delivered their speeches on the same topic to imaginary audiences, e.g. the Conservative Women's Primrose League, factory girls, Women Liberals, married working women or a Trades Union. In the evenings students addressed anyone willing to listen down at Y Bedol, although one student did wonder aloud what these poor people (the inhabitants of Tal-y-cafn and Tal-y-bont) had done to deserve this?

Students came from Menai Bridge, Bangor, Wrexham, Liverpool, Southport, Warrington and even as far away as Portsmouth. There were also day students from the local area.

On the final evening there was an open-air meeting outside Y Bedol chaired by Miss Mason, at which Mrs Price White, amongst others, spoke and answered difficult questions put by Mr Henry Davies of The School House posing as an 'Anti'.

Mrs Gladstone Solomon held another successful Anti-Suffrage campaign with meetings at Caernarfon, Bangor and Colwyn Bay – where she was forced to give up after two hours when she lost her voice. With the additional support of Lord and Lady Sheffield, further Anti-Suffrage meetings were held at Valley, Holyhead and Caernarfon – after which a number of fires broke out.

At Caernarfon Grammar School the caretaker found

several window frames in the main building and the door to the gymnasium alight; a haystack went up in flames at Cae Gwyn on the Bethel road and after a meeting at Bangor, fires broke out at two houses being built on College Road. In each instance Welsh Suffragette literature was scattered at the scene and inevitably Suffragettes were blamed for retaliation.

Colwyn Bay's 1913-14 winter session was opened by Miss Spencer who said that, this being the first meeting of the session, the number present was highly satisfactory. They had 140 members and aimed to have 200 by Christmas, the minimum subscription being 1/-. Miss Spencer said that what they needed was more of the 'missionary spirit', with volunteers willing to organise small meetings up and down the county. She said that the previous season they'd organised small, informal, public speaking classes which had proved very popular and these would continue.

The meeting was then addressed by Miss Matters, who opened by saying that many people thought women who didn't have husbands wanted the vote instead. [laughter] On this occasion Miss Matters discussed the progress of women from biblical times to the present day. She was noted for the length of her speeches!

Miss Crosfield, who was chairing the meeting, referred to International Feministic Congress where Commissioners were about to urge the introduction of an international law for the protection of women in time of war, to join the law which already existed to ensure the humane treatment of horses in time of war.

In proposing the vote of thanks, Miss Kenyon said that it was interesting that unmarried women formerly called 'old maids' were now known as 'bachelor girls'.

After leaving Colwyn Bay Miss Matters was attending

the Miners' Federation Congress, this being the most powerful of all Trades Unions at that time counting for 600,000 votes. A special Suffragists' Demonstration was planned to take place in Colwyn Bay to coincide with the Congress in Scarborough.

October
At the Bangor Committee Meeting Mrs Price White reported that she had attended the Conwy Valley Summer School and received £1 as arranged.

Miss Matthews proposed that Miss Witton-Davies (Press Secretary) and Mrs Hudson-Williams should attend the next Federation Meeting to have the opportunity of meeting other Press Secretaries.

Miss Spencer of Colwyn Bay and Miss Colquitt of Liverpool were to be asked to carry out a canvass of the Friends of Women's Suffrage to see if they were willing to become more involved and a survey of those who were already members to see if they wished to subscribe to *The Common Cause* magazine.

Bangor opened their winter session with a social at the Queen's Head Café for both members and 'friends' – friends being in sympathy with 'The Cause', but not having sufficient leisure time to take an active role.

Mrs Price White welcomed everyone and said she hoped they could continue in the friendly spirit of the Summer Pilgrimage and that there would be no class barriers. Mr Lloyd George should remember that any setbacks in the campaign for women's suffrage were due entirely to the militant WSPU and not the law-abiding NUWSS.

She referred to the Women Citizen's Association which had been set up in Liverpool and said she hoped they would be able to organise something similar in Bangor. The aim was to encourage self-education on political matters and to enable as many women as possible to work on Boards of Guardians.

Mrs Price White said she agreed with the Anti-Suffragists' stance that a woman's place was in the home – it was, but women ought to be able to contribute to legislation which affected that home. It was women's mothering instinct which made them such good nurses, doctors and social workers.

Entertainment was provided by Miss Baker, piano, Miss Gaynor Phillips, violin and Miss Witton-Davies, who sang. There was a French Auction where items could only be bid for in 1d increments. And finally the Bangor Suffrage Drama Group presented *A Chat with Mrs Chicky*.

Non-committee members Miss Witton-Davies, Miss Gwalyn Edwards, Miss Goodwin, Miss Nora Lewis and Mrs Whitehead were invited to attend the Bangor Committee Meeting. Miss Lewis and Mrs Whitehead were asked if they would consider providing secretarial assistance.

Mrs Hudson-Williams proposed, seconded by Mrs Price White, that Mrs Hugh Rowland-Jones should be invited to be Organising Secretary.

Miss Edwards, Treasurer, would be away for part of the winter and was requested to hand the accounts to Miss Matthews or Miss Pinkerton before she left.

Mrs Price White was asked to look into forming a Women's Citizenship Association and if there was sufficient interest, to seek assistance from Miss Colquitt in canvassing the Bangor population at large.

November

The Llandudno Cell held a meeting at the Town Hall chaired by Charles Montgomery, a master at Tan y Bryn

School, Fferm Bach Road, who said that it had been organised as part of the Llandudno Committee's Educational Campaign.

Miss Fraser gave a hard-hitting lecture on 'The Child and the State' and took the audience back 100 years to a time when children were supposed to be seen and not heard, whose education was not the responsibility of the state and when they were working in factories at the age of eight.

Miss Fraser continued that it was now acknowledged that a child's character was established during the first seven years of its life and during that time most children were almost exclusively in the care of their mothers. Forty per cent of babies who died within the first month of life did so from infections from sexually transmitted diseases suffered by their mothers and a committee was looking into this hidden plague. They couldn't make people good by legislation, but they could stop commercial trafficking in immorality.

She went on to say that the end of the last parliament had been called 'the slaughter of the innocents' because so many bills had been thrown out due to lack of time – including 'The Pure Milk and Dairies Bill' which would have improved the lives of women and children. She said women were demanding a voice in what should go through to become law and what should be discarded. Women didn't want just the vote – they wanted the opportunity.to do good.

Finally Miss Fraser commented that some churches were holding special services in connection with the Women's Movement and she was pleased that women and children were considered to be of importance by Christianity.

Shortly after this, Mrs Fawcett had a letter published in many national and local newspapers – including the *North*

Wales Weekly News, referring to the fact that the Bishop of Winchester had recently made a very powerful and statesmanlike appeal through the press for truth and an amnesty between the militant Suffragettes and the government. Mrs Fawcett said that on behalf of the non-militant NUWSS she wished to express their determination that no effort should be found wanting on their part to promote so far as they possibly could, the well considered effort for peace which the Bishop had inaugurated.

There was a spirited lecture at the Colwyn Bay Society's meeting, chaired by Francis Nunn, a local solicitor. Mr Herbert Taylor, a Mochdre farmer read a paper on 'The Case for Women's Suffrage' and was applauded when he addressed the audience as 'future electors' and said he was in favour of women's suffrage because of the justice of the demand. He referred to Lord Curzon's fifteen reasons why women shouldn't get the vote and said Lord Curzon didn't really want the vote for anyone – he'd prefer to run the country himself. [laughter] Referring to the militants, Mr Taylor said these women had been law-abiding citizens and when women like this turned against the law, didn't it make them think there was something very unjust to make them do such awful things?

The meeting was then opened to the floor. Mrs Margaret Nunn said she was an Anti-Suffragist and Mr Taylor hadn't converted her. She continued that if Anti-Suffragists didn't want the vote, they must fight against being given it as strongly as the Suffragettes and Suffragists fought for it. Many women, Mrs Nunn claimed, shared her opinion, but they were apathetic – she had never seen an 'Anti' book or heard of an 'Anti' meeting. One of her greatest objections to women having the vote was that there were more women than men and the reins of government would be in women's

hands. 'Antis' should be more like militant Suffragettes –
burning innocent peoples' houses and pouring noxious
liquids into letterboxes. That showed what the Suffragettes
would do for money – they were paid to do it. At this point
the audience erupted with cries of 'No, No!' But by now
Mrs Nunn was at full throttle and continued 'When they're
sent to prison they whimper and whine til they're let out,
then they're considered heroines and martyrs. I'd admire
them more if they served their sentences like men!'

At this point Miss Spencer remarked drily that if the
Antis refrained from voting, it would make the number of
votes cast by men and women about equal. [laughter]

Mrs Nunn suddenly proclaimed that she didn't believe in
free education either.

At the close of the meeting Miss Spencer announced that
the Colwyn Bay Society had opened an office for the benefit
of members at Longman's Library, Station Road.

It must have been an interesting meeting – and an
interesting marriage, with Mr and Mrs Nunn holding such
opposing views!

The Bangor Committee met on 17 November. Miss
Matthews was appointed Temporary Treasurer. Mrs
Milner-Barry had resigned from the committee and Mrs
Dingad Davies had left Bangor, so it was decided to
approach Mrs Conan Davies, Mrs Hugh Rowland-Jones,
Mrs J. D. Jones, Mrs Jones-Roberts, Miss Williams, Llys
Tirion and Mrs Williams, Treflan, to join the committee.

A letter from Newcastle-on-Tyne's Suffrage Society was
read out recommending the adoption, as in their
constitution, of a rule making it a condition of enrolling new
members that they should not be supporters of militancy.
However, it was decided on the proposal of Mrs Price
White, seconded by Mrs G. O. Price to adopt a similar rule

to that which was part of the Manchester Society's Constitution, so that in future Bangor's Rule No. 3 would read:

> The methods of the society shall be those of orderly propaganda and public discussion. Approval of the objects and methods of the society and an annual subscription of any amount not less than 1/- shall constitute membership.

The Treasurer's Report was adopted and it was decided that Miss Rathbone's loan must be repaid.

December

Penmaenmawr Committee invited members and friends to a social gathering and a good number mustered together at Hewan Hall, kindly loaned by Colonel Darbishire. The proceedings were presided over by Mrs Jenkins, President. At the outset she emphasised that the society was law-abiding and non-political and condemned in severe terms the destructive tactics of the militants, as being likely to do more harm than good to 'The Cause'.

Following the Presidential address Mrs Price White, in a very able and lucid manner described what work had already been accomplished towards securing the franchise for women.

A very appropriate recitation was well rendered by Miss Hilda Roberts.

Refreshments were handed round and justice having been done to all the good things, the arguments in favour of votes for women were further expanded – this time in the form of a witty dialogue entitled *A Chat with Mrs Chicky*, acted by the President and Mrs Coxon of Llanfairfechan. The acting of both ladies was delightful and the humour, as well as the commonsense side of the question, was so ably presented as to create roars of laughter.

During the evening ten new members were enrolled, so the meeting could be described as a great success from every point of view and reflected great credit on the indefatigable President, Mrs Jenkins and energetic Secretary, Miss Harker.

Colwyn Bay Society held a 'Women Only' meeting in the Church Rooms, chaired by Dr Deacon and addressed by Miss Adaban from London who spoke on 'The Moral Issues of Women's Suffrage'. As well as NUWSS members, women from the British Women's Temperance Association, the Christian Social Union, the Women's Co-Operative Guild and the Women's Liberal Association attended.

Miss Adaban spoke about the four causes of social evil, namely:

1. Terrible poverty, a politician had said 'so long as you have overwhelmingly rich men and overwhelmingly poor women there will be prostitution'. Miss Adaban said that a minimum decent wage for women was a crying need – eighty per cent of the women on the streets were driven there as a last resort by sheer poverty.
2. Failure of the government to protect feeble-minded children, which was in the process of being remedied.
3. Property being regarded as more valuable than the life and the honour of women and children and
4. Double standards – the law failed to protect women and girls, but not the men who took advantage of them.

Miss Adaban concluded that other countries had proved

that when women got the vote the first thing they did was to secure greater protection for themselves and their children.

Chapter 8
1914

The end of an era...

January

By kind permission of Colonel Darbishire, Penmaenmawr Society held a meeting at Hewan Hall, presided over by Mrs Jenkins, President, assisted by Miss Harker and Mrs Phillips-Williams.

Miss Fraser spoke of the work being done by women all over the world and the need for women's insight in all matters affecting the welfare of women. She also referred to the effort being made to reduce infant mortality which was so great in large towns, due largely to the bad housing of the poor and the dirty and unsanitary conditions in which they were forced to live whilst earning miserable pittances, which made it impossible to buy good food or milk essential for the preservation of infant life. Miss Fraser said she'd often been told to 'Go home and mind the baby' and her reply was 'Look at the homes where so many mothers are minding their babies'. That women's place was at home she was ready to admit, but she did not admit that women with comfy homes should remain there, with eyes shut to the misery of their poorer sisters.

Now that women were allowed to take degrees, practice as doctors, form the majority of teachers in schools and have a voice on the Poor Law, why should they be debarred from having a voice in the most important affairs of the nation?

The Bangor Committee met on 13 January. The forthcoming Rummage Sale at Tabernacl Schoolroom on 29 January was discussed and it was decided that adverts for the sale should include details of Miss Fraser's talk, 'The Child and The State', on 6 February. It was stressed that helpers should use their judgment in selling, so that buyers suspected of being dealers might be prevented from buying large numbers of articles.

Miss Edwards, Miss Lewis, Mrs Price White and Mrs Hudson-Williams were delegated to attend the NUWSS Council Meeting in London, a payment of £2 per person was granted towards travelling expenses. Delegates were instructed to vote for Miss Harefield of Oxford for the National Executive.

The Secretary was asked to apply for three seats in a box for the Albert Hall Meeting; tickets cost 5/- but were being offered at 2/6d to those travelling from a distance.

Since the AGM sixteen women had joined Friends of Women's Suffrage and it was felt they should be visited by members of the committee. It was further suggested that a sub-committee should be formed to divide the town into districts to aid canvassing.

The Bangor Sub-Committee was duly formed and met on 19 January. The names of 'Friends' who would possibly become full members if visited were distributed between Miss Lewis, Mrs Price White, Mrs Whitehead and Mrs Hudson-Williams.

Proofs of new leaflets with rules and names of officers were approved.

The full Bangor Committee met on 30 January. A canvass throughout the town was to be undertaken shortly by Mrs Huw Rowland (West Ward), Mrs Price White and Miss Rigby (East Ward), Mrs G. O. Price and Mrs H. O. Hughes

(South Ward) and Miss Witton-Davies and Miss E. Matthews (North Ward).

2,000 pamphlets were to be printed.

£1 was to be provided towards travelling expenses of Trades Union members attending the NUWSS Council in London unless the whole sum needed for rail tickets had been raised by the subscribers approached.

February

The Rhyl Society held a well-attended meeting in the Town Hall and several members of Rhyl Council appeared on the platform in support. The Chairman was Miss Eskrigge of the Liverpool Federation, who said that she had found that in north Wales the chief difficulty was not in winning people to a belief in women's suffrage, but to a belief in the rightness of granting women's suffrage in the face of militancy. [applause] That difficulty was created by very muddle-headed thinking, or perhaps more correctly by people who had stopped thinking altogether because of militant outrages. [more applause] Miss Fraser's resolution demanding 'Votes for Women' was carried and Miss Eskrigge mentioned that with one exception, every north Wales MP had voted for women's suffrage.

The Colwyn Bay Society's February meeting was the first reported in 1914 and was poorly attended, especially as of those who did attend, ten were men. Miss Ayles presided and Miss Fraser submitted the resolution that: 'This meeting demands a government measure for women's suffrage'.

She continued that extraordinary progress had been made in persuading men to support 'The Movement'. It was quite impossible to say how many women in Britain believed in 'The Cause' but the NUWSS had increased its membership in the last two years by 1,000 each month.

Miss Spencer stated that a great many new members were needed, there were lots of people on the verge of joining the society and she wanted them to go over the brink and join. But if there were persons who were sympathetic to 'The Cause' but did not want to join, there was a movement called 'Friends of the Suffragists' in which they could be enrolled. They would then be informed of meetings but there would be no subscription to pay.

Miss Ayles said they sometimes found it necessary to state that they were not militants – they were not Suffragettes, their methods were peaceful and they were law-abiding. The Women's Movement to which they belonged wanted a great deal more than simply getting the vote. The Women's Movement was striving for the expression of personality and for the opportunity of serving the community. It was a strongly moral movement and in no way Anti-Christian.

March

The Colwyn Bay Society's meeting was held in the Pier Pavilion and there was a fair attendance, but numbers were definitely affected by the inclement weather. Mr Hammersley-Heenan presided and Mrs Snowden said it was the intention of the meeting to pass a resolution that: 'This meeting demands a government measure for the enfranchisement of women at the earliest possible moment'.

The Rev. Tutton seconded the motion, saying it was his first speech in support of women's suffrage and if 'The Cause' had nothing more behind it than 'shrieking militancy', he would never have made a speech in it's favour at all. He was opposed to force as a means of redress for political or religious grievances and would suggest that in the act which was going to be passed, there should be a clause preventing any woman convicted of violence from obtaining the right to vote for a period to be determined by Her Majesty's Prison Service. He added that it was the educational work undertaken by Miss Spencer and Colwyn Bay NUWSS which had persuaded him to support 'The Cause' – not just because women desired reform, but because the nation needed it. The resolution was carried unanimously.

Mrs Snowden then spoke on 'What women will do with the vote' but addressed most of her remarks to the men in the audience. She said that the justice of the case for women's suffrage was recognised not merely by the majority of men; but by the majority – and a big majority at that, of the thinking minority and it was the thinking minority which determined the life of the country. Mrs Snowden said she was willing to admit that there were thousands of women who didn't care whether they had the vote or not, but then they had no grievances. For the majority of women who had to work alongside men, it was more self-respecting for them to have a voice in the government of their own affairs.

From the earliest times men had worked in pursuit of property, heedless of more important matters. She had recently read in the press of a case in which a man had been sentenced to three years penal servitude for having stolen a number of coats; whilst in the same paper she had read of another man sentenced to just one month in gaol for a criminal assault on a girl of thirteen. She recognised it was wrong to steal, but if the first man deserved three months for stealing coats, one month's gaol was not enough for the second man who had stolen the innocence and purity of a young girl. Mrs Snowden did not say that women were better than men, but she did say that their particular work in the world had developed special characteristics in them. She gave several examples of what women had done and asked men to consider that they were all the children of women, they had been brought up by women and spent the best days of their youth endeavouring to prevail upon some fair woman to share their life. Women wanted to give their services to the state; there was the housing problem – surely a women's problem, the liquor problem and many more, all of which affected women and yet they had no voice. Finally Mrs Snowden particularly appealed to the males present to support women's suffrage.

Miss Ethel Hovey, Treasurer, appealed for subscriptions – the branch had spent over £90 on education and sent £135 to Head Office.

Colonel A. Sarson proposed the vote of thanks and said that male South African militants had been feted in the House of Commons, given a grand reception and magnificent dinner, but if they had been female militants they'd have been cast into prison and had their dinner forced down their throats. Should that not convince not only women but men, of the injustice of the refusal to grant the vote to women?

During the evening suffrage songs were sung accompanied by Miss Jackson.

The Bangor Committee met on 2 March. Mrs Price White provided a summary of resolutions carried and lost in London, the Liverpool resolution having been lost by five votes. Mrs Hudson-Williams said Bangor delegates had not felt bound to follow instructions concerning voting, as the instructions had been given by the Secretary only, without consultation with the committee. They had therefore abstained from voting for certain resolutions. Mrs Price White explained that the London Council Agenda had not been received in time to bring it to the attention of the last committee and her instructions had been given according to her knowledge of the condition of the society in Bangor and the surrounding area.

It was proposed, seconded and carried that in future a General Meeting of all members would be called prior to each Council Meeting in London and the agenda placed before them. In addition a General Meeting of members would be called before each quarterly Federation Meeting.

The Treasurer reported that the majority of member's subscriptions remained unpaid and they were therefore adopting a system whereby Miss Lewis, Miss Matthews and Mrs Price White would be collecting them!

It was arranged to hold a Cake and Apron Sale at the Queen's Head Café on 26 or 27 March.

Mrs Whitehead tendered her resignation as Assistant Secretary due to moving away from Bangor. Miss Rigby was asked to help Mrs Whitehead for the remainder of her time in the city, with a view to taking on the job when Mrs Whitehead actually left.

An appeal from Miss Crosfield for financial support for the Federation was read out and the Treasurer said that if funds permitted after the Cake Sale, a donation should be made.

A report had been received from the Caretaker of Tabernacl Schoolroom that no payment had been made for cleaning after the Rummage Sale. It was observed that the fee of 10/6d was supposed to include light and cleaning, but resolved that a further 2/- should be paid to the lady Caretaker personally.

The Bangor Committee met again on 30 March and it was proposed that the following be sent to NUWSS for the Agenda for the next Council Meeting:

That as the NUWSS Election Fighting Fund is already committed to work in preparation for the General Election in some twenty-six constituencies and as this will absorb nearly all its resources, the Executive be asked not to sanction work in any fresh constituency, in order that at least some of the fighting strength may be available for the purpose of carrying out the policy to be determined by the Special Council Meeting previous to the General Election.

It was also proposed and seconded that the resolution from Swindon be supported:

That it is important that women's suffrage should be made a prominent issue at the General Election, not only in those constituencies where the NUWSS is working for a Labour candidate, but so far as possible over the whole country. That in order to secure this, the Executive be asked to consider the possibility of organising some large piece of non-party work which would voice the demand for a government measure and induce the electors to take part in that demand.

Delegates for the Federation Meeting were Miss Witton-Davies and Mrs Huw Rowland. Delegates for Council were Mrs Huw Rowland, Mrs Price White and Miss Lamport or Miss Lewis.

It was decided that Bangor should support the Summer School.

The Library Secretary was empowered to make any reasonable rules with regard to the length of time books could be kept and the amount of fines to be charged.

April

The Bangor Committee met on 9 April. It was resolved that the Treasurer be asked to provide a monthly statement and that thanks should be sent to Mr E. T. John MP for including women in his Home Rule Bill for Wales.

With regard to the library, books were to be kept for only two weeks, after which there would be a fine of 3d; if still not returned after notice had been sent there would be a fine of 6d.

It was proposed, seconded and carried that an Amendment should be drawn up to proposal 1A of the Council:

That members of the Executive Committee are not free outside the Executive Committee to take or advocate a course which in the opinion of the Executive expressed in the form of a resolution and carried by a two thirds majority, may prejudice the existing policy of the NUWSS.

Penmaenmawr should be asked to submit this Amendment in Bangor's name, but if they were unwilling to do so then Bangor would submit it.

An Active Service League was discussed and Mrs Price White appointed Group Leader for the district.

On 16 April, Australia's *Hobart Mercury* reported that the previous day, whilst Sir Edward and Lady Carson (Sir Edward being a prominent Irish MP, barrister and judge) were visiting Bangor, north Wales, 'Suffragists' (Suffragettes) had attempted to set fire to the railway station by lighting a candle which had been placed in a wooden box, filled with cotton wool and saturated with paraffin oil.

The Bangor Committee met again on 24 April. It was resolved that delegates to Council should support the resolution submitted either by Penmaenmawr or Bangor, but have freedom to vote on other resolutions, having regard to the feelings expressed at the last meeting of members.

May

On 7 May the following notice appeared in the *North Wales Weekly News*:

> I hope that many more people will endeavour to be present at the meetings likely to be held in the near future. Even those who do not approve of women's suffrage would be showing their sense of fairness and broad outlook on life if they came to hear the other side. Not until we hear the matter explained by women who are well up in the subject and who by practical experience are able to put matters vividly before us, can we realise how great is the work these women are doing and the need for sympathy and co-operation with 'The Cause'.

It is not clear who was responsible for the notice.

The Llandudno Cell organised a meeting in Conwy Town Hall chaired by Mr Leonard and addressed by Miss Fraser. At the advertised time of commencement there was only a meagre attendance but after another half hour a fair number were present. Conwy appears to have been less than enthusiastic about women's suffrage.

Miss Fraser said people thought there was no hope of women ever getting the vote unless the bill to ratify it went through under the present government. There were now 1,500 women on Boards of Guardians, the population at large had got over women being educated and riding bicycles and they were going to have to get over women voting! Women did know about politics because they knew about human suffering. Miss Fraser admitted the WSPU was injuring 'The Cause', but women must have the vote, even if some lost patience and committed violence. The Suffragists must never give up!

The Bangor Committee met on 18 May. A letter was read out from the National Executive asking if any societies in the neighbourhood shared offices with the WSPU or Church League for Women's Suffrage? A negative reply had already been sent.

It was decided to collect subscriptions for a wedding present for their Treasurer, Miss Edwards. If Labour provided a speaker on women's suffrage on a non-party basis, the society would support the meeting financially.

Mrs Huw Rowland and Mrs Hudson-Williams, both Welsh-speakers, indicated that they were willing to speak at Summer School.

They were to seek permission to have a stall for NUWSS literature at the National Eisteddfod, which was to be held in Bangor

The Fete would be held at Belmont on 17 June if possible and jobs were distributed as follows:

Tea: Mrs H. O. Hughes, Mrs G. O. Price and Mrs Price White.

Cakes: Mrs Hughes and Mrs Hudson-Williams.

Flowers and Fruit: Mrs J. D. Jones and Mrs Huw Rowland.

Children at Hirael Infants School would be invited to dance.

The Women's Citizenship Association was discussed

and Mrs Price White's suggestion adopted – that a committee be called at Mrs Gibson's (with her consent) of women in the town representing various societies, with a view to supporting women candidates for the Town and Rural Councils and Boards of Guardians.

June

The Bangor Committee met on 8 June. It was agreed that Secretaries of all women's organisations in Bangor would be contacted with a view to holding a meeting in September.

The fete was to be held on 24 June (not 17) It would open at 3 pm Admission 6d.

Tea – 4d would be served at 4 pm There would be an orchestra and Maypole dancing at 4.30 pm, a play at 5 pm and a Whist Drive 6.30-7 pm.

Lady Verney was to be asked to preside and if she was unavailable, then Mrs Williams, The Palace. They had had an application for an Arts and Crafts stall.

The event was to be advertised in the *North Wales Chronicle and Advertiser* and by posters and handbills and the town was to be divided into districts for selling tickets.

On 11 June the *North Wales Weekly News* reported that at a Llandudno Council Meeting Mr J. R. Pritchard referred to the presence in the county of furious women who damaged tradesmen's windows and behind whom, he thought, there must be some sort of organisation. When that sort of damage was caused, he himself being a tradesman was anxious to know whether the county, as in the case of a riot, was responsible for paying for it? The reply was that the cost had to be borne by the tradesmen themselves.

On 18 June the *North Wales Weekly News* reported that Glan Conwy was an unenlightened village on the question of women's suffrage and villagers were to be educated concerning the justice of the claim of the women. So on Thursday night an open-air meeting was held on the village green outside the Britannia Inn when two ladies and one gentleman from Colwyn Bay delivered addresses.

At first the whole audience was comprised of children and the first lady speaker wisely devoted her speech to the benefits which would accrue to children if their mothers were allowed to vote. By the close of her talk a fairly large crowd had gathered and there were continual interruptions from a group of males. The second lady speaker went into the middle of the trouble-makers to deliver her speech with the result that no one else could hear her. A farmer with half a dozen ducks in a carrier on his bike stopped to listen and the quacking ducks added to the cacophony. He was closely followed by an itinerant musician with a barrel-organ, but he politely declined to play until the meeting had ended.

The gentleman from Colwyn Bay closed by saying that it was clear Glan Conwy needed converting and more meetings would be organised as soon as possible.

Bangor Committee met again on 25 June. A brake (horse-drawn cart or carriage) was to be ordered to bring the children for the Maypole dancing.

Tea would be 6d (not 4d), the Orchestral Concert 3d, the Play 3d, Fortune-telling 3d and the Whist Drive with refreshments 6d, so obviously the Fete had not taken place on 24 June.

July
On 9 July the following Editorial appeared in the *North Wales Weekly News*:

The Women's Suffrage Movement has not created much

enthusiasm in north Wales. At Colwyn Bay, Llandudno, Penmaenmawr and other towns, branches of the NUWSS exist and they have accomplished educational work, but efforts to secure the active support of the general body of women have not been successful and consequently membership of branches is not large. Despite the progressiveness of north Wales, the Women's Cause is not nearly so advanced as it is in England and local opinion concerning the participation of women in public matters may be judged by the fact that there are fewer women representatives on local public bodies than in any other part of Britain.

The same spirit prevails regarding the Suffrage Movement. We are not concerned here with the question of whether or not women should have the vote, what we do wish to emphasise is the sympathy that should be manifested towards 'The Movement' by the public when they realise that the society is working along constitutional lines, as the NUWSS is opposed to militancy and emphasises that fact at every opportunity. Perhaps it is necessary because there are people who have not studied the question closely and make no distinction between the Suffragettes and the Suffragists. When they understand that the methods of the NUWSS are non-militant then the man in the street is willing to listen and often will admit that there is justice in the women's claim for the vote. Inbred in men is the traditional British opinion that representation and taxation should go together, but when he realises that women have to meet the claims of the government Tax Collector on the same basis as men, then, he argues they should be accorded some rights.

The average Welshman has a keen sense of justice, but his ideals receive a rude shock when he sees a section of the womenfolk adopting insane militant methods and he refuses to be intimidated. He is ready to be won over by persuasion, argument and appeals to reason and justice, therefore the NUWSS campaign is likely to succeed when public opinion has been sufficiently advanced by the educative influence of public meetings and the printed page.

Colwyn Bay and Llandudno jointly organised an open-air meeting on the Great Orme; twenty-one people signed support cards and requested further meetings.

As a result, further outdoor meetings were held over a period of about six weeks, at Penrhynside, Old Colwyn, Mochdre, Glan Conwy and Deganwy. The speakers were Miss Spencer and Mrs Keeble. The Penrhynside and

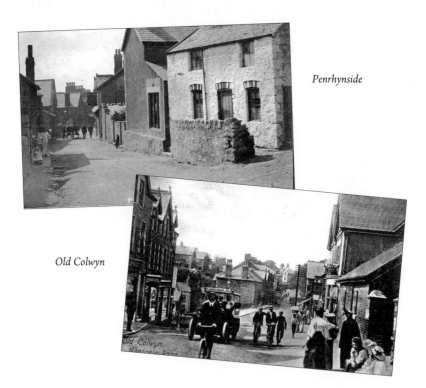

Penrhynside

Old Colwyn

Mochdre

Glan Conwy

Deganwy

Deganwy meetings were held on Saturday afternoons and were not very well-attended, but those who did attend were quiet and attentive and any children present were very well-behaved. The other meetings were held in the evenings and it was decided that would be the best time for any future gatherings.

August

On 6 August the *North Wales Weekly News* led with the headline:

PIER OUTRAGE –
ATTEMPT TO BURN DOWN COLWYN BAY PIER
PAVILION – BUILDING IN FLAMES

The report continued: 'On Saturday last a thrill of surprise and indignation went through Colwyn Bay when it became known that an attempt had been made to set fire to the Pier Pavilion.

Colwyn Bay Pier

It appears that PCs W. Evans and Iorwerth Jones, one of whom was in 'mufti' (plain clothes), were on point duty on the Promenade at 3 a.m. when they saw flames coming from what turned out to be the ladies' lavatory on the pier. Inside the lavatory substantial pieces of cotton wool saturated with cycle lamp oil had been adhered to the wooden walls by means of Seccotine. On the floor just below lay a pile of firelighters and several empty Pryce's Cycle Lamp Oil cans, pointing to a deliberate attempt at arson. Before the Fire Brigade arrived however, PC Evans managed to extinguish the flames.

The indignation in Colwyn Bay was intense – 'the outrage was wanton and dastardly and the consequences to the town if the fine pavilion had been destroyed would have been disastrous'.

The *Welsh Coast Pioneer*'s headline was:

COLWYN BAY PIER PAVILION ON FIRE – ALLEGED OUTRAGE BY SUFFRAGETTES – LYNX-EYED POLICEMEN AVERT A CATASTROPHE!

And contained the additional information that a pair of ladies' gloves, which had been turned inside out as if the wearer had hurriedly snatched them from her hands had been found at the scene and a tattered copy of a Suffragette newspaper nearby.

Elaborate precautions had been taken to ensure the safety of the Pavilion in the future and any suspicious-looking characters would be apprehended as soon as they set foot on the pier.

The following edition of the *North Wales Weekly News* mentioned the police having a lead in that they wished to interview a lady who had been asking strange questions around the town the day before the fire, but so far as I can tell they never traced her.

Chapter 9

The War and afterwards...

With the outbreak of war just a few days after the fire at Colwyn Bay Pier Pavilion both NUWSS and WSPU members were urged to suspend political activity and support the war effort instead. So the 'Votes for Women' campaign in north Wales ended in a puff of smoke rather than a blaze of glory.

On 13 August 1914 the *North Wales Weekly News,* amongst items concerning troop movement, holidaymakers returning home in droves, petrol being scarce and the price of sugar having doubled from tuppence ha'penny to fivepence per pound in a matter of four days, published a paragraph stating that the Chairman of Colwyn Bay NUWSS had informed the Chairman of Colwyn Bay and Colwyn Bay Urban District Councils that her committee was 'prepared to place its services at the disposal of any committee he may call together' and that 'all who are willing to volunteer for personal service of any kind are asked to communicate as soon as possible with the Organising Secretary, Miss Spencer at the Suffrage Office, Station Road, from whom all further information could be obtained'.

On 18 September the *North Wales Chronicle and Advertiser* reported that the women of the Penmaenmawr Suffrage Society were busily preparing clothing for the Belgian refugees who were flooding into north Wales.

By March 1915 Colwyn Bay NUWSS was heavily involved in 'war work'. As at Penmaenmawr, members were busy collecting clothing for Belgian refugees and had raised eight guineas to support a bed at the Welsh Hospital at Netley, near Southampton.

NUWSS members were working on Colwyn Bay's Relief Committee helping those who were in financial difficulty as a result of their menfolk going to war.

And NUWSS members helped in many other ways. Their Committee, chaired by Mrs Gamble Ratonagh, with Miss Spencer as Secretary and Miss Sugden as Treasurer, established a Women's Club and an Enquiry Office to try to deal with any questions women may have – ranging from how could they find out if their husbands and sons were surviving when they hadn't had news of them for several weeks, to how to make tasty meals from leftovers. They set up a workroom where women could make badly-needed medical supplies – bandages and swabs, or knit 'comforts' – socks and scarves for the soldiers. They started the 'Tipperary Club', where the wives and mothers of soldiers and sailors could meet socially for mutual support one night each week and a Girls' Club two nights a week.

But Colwyn Bay NUWSS emphasised that members weren't engaged in war work instead of being Suffragists – there was still a need for equality and enfranchisement for women and they would remain Suffragists until they got the vote!

On 17 July 1915 the WSPU staged a march through Hyde Park entitled: 'Women's Right to Serve' to support the war effort, at the request of their long-time adversary, Mr Lloyd George. The government was having difficulty recruiting sufficient women to staff the munitions factories – which was highly dangerous work – but Mrs Pankhurst agreed to take responsibility for female mobilisation, so long as women received equal pay for equal work. In fact it's not clear if equal pay was achieved but the Mutionettes certainly earned well in excess of the wage of domestic servants.

The march included the traditional floats – Belgium was represented by a girl in rags and France by participants wearing their red caps for liberty. The Union Flag was everywhere – replacing the Suffragettes' customary 'purple, white and green'.

In February 1916 a collection was made to mark the completion of Rosa Hovey's twenty-first year as principal of Penrhos College. Typically, Miss Hovey said she wanted the donations to go towards helping soldiers on the battlefield. £400 provided a fully-equipped ambulance for use in France, with accommodation for the driver, an attendant and eight patients and a further £200 was contributed towards its upkeep.

In June 1918 a Women Citizen's Association was formed in Colwyn Bay. Women engaged in public life and social activities were invited to the inaugural meeting. Mrs Price White from Bangor explained that the Association was working to prepare women for their new role as voters – which she was sure they would achieve when the war ended. When peace came, she said, women who had worked so hard to support the war effort in many and diverse ways, must be able to influence government policy on food, housing, wages, health, welfare, temperance and many other national issues.

Lady Colwyn was elected President of the new Colwyn Bay branch and Miss Spencer was voted onto the Executive Committee.

The First World War probably changed the lives of lower class women beyond recognition. Whilst their well-heeled middle- and upper-class sisters continued much as before – engaged in committee work, but for the War Effort rather than women's suffrage (and largely without customary help from servants in their homes); lower-class women, liberated from low-paid domestic work, needless to say, weren't overly eager to return to domestic drudgery!

Obviously the traditional women's roles as nurses and teachers were as necessary as ever – the former working both at home and in the field hospitals abroad, but for lower-class women a whole new world opened up where there were opportunities for them to work as clerks in businesses and government departments, in active roles in the Police ('Copperettes') and Fire Brigade, Post Office, transport, factories, as surface workers at coal mines and in the shipyards. Other women joined the Land Army, the Women's Auxilary Army and later the Women's Royal Air Force and Women's Royal Naval Service.

Women understood that these jobs were only for the duration of the war and that when the men returned they would re-enter their jobs; but of course many thousands of men never did return, or if they did, were not fit to take up their previous employment.

In 1918, partly in recognition of their magnificent support throughout the war, women householders over thirty years of age were given the vote. (Women between twenty-one and thirty years of age had to wait a further ten years.)

In 1919 Ethel Hovey was the first woman to join the old Colwyn Bay Urban District Council. In 1926 she became the first woman Chairman of an Urban District Council in Wales. When the town received its Charter in 1934 she became the first woman Alderman and was Mayor 1945-46.

In 1921 Miss Selina Williams, Headmistress of Glanadda Infants School, won the Bangor West Ward seat and became the first woman to gain a seat on a Local Council in Caernarfonshire.

In 1926 Mrs Price White became the first woman to be elected to Caernarfonshire County Council and was a diligent and highly respected Councillor until her untimely death in 1932.

Ironically, the first woman to be elected as an MP for a Welsh constituency was Megan, Lloyd George's daughter, who took the seat of Anglesey, predictably for the Liberals in 1929 and held it until 1951. In 1957 she took the seat of Carmarthen for Labour and held it until the time of her death in 1966.

Appendix A

Visiting Dignitaries – Who was Who

Mrs Fru ANKERS was a well-known Norwegian writer on women's matters and was the London Correspondent for several Norwegian newspapers. She had taken an active part in getting Norwegian Divorce Laws reformed and obtaining paid maternity leave for working mothers. Norway was the first European country to enfranchise women.

Mrs Margery CORBETT-ASHBY (neé **Corbett**) was born in 1882, the daughter of Charles Corbett who became a Liberal MP 1906-1910. In 1907 she was appointed NUWSS Secretary and Editor of *The Common Cause* and in 1909 was elected to the Executive Committee. In 1910 she married barrister, Brian Ashby. When the NUWSS launched its Election Fighting Fund to support any candidate who would support women's suffrage if the Liberal candidate refused to do so, she felt compelled to resign from the organisation. She spent the war years working in hospitals and running a canteen for school-children. She was one of the first seventeen women to stand for parliament, but lost her deposit. Together with Eva Hubback, Margery Corbett-Ashby was co-founder of the National Union of Townswomen's Guilds. She continued to be active in politics for the rest of her life and died at the age of ninety-nine in 1981.

Miss Margaret ASHTON was born in 1856. As early as 1900 she was elected to Withington Urban District Council and in 1908 became the first woman to serve on Manchester City Council, where it was said of her that 'As a Councillor she devoted herself to the issues of women's health and education and campaigned to improve the wages and conditions of employment of girls and women'. Her pacifism made her unpopular during the First World War. She was branded 'pro-German' when she refused to 'toe the party line' of supporting the war effort and resigned from the NUWSS to form the Manchester Branch of the Women's International League of Peace and Freedom. Miss Ashton was ousted from the City Council in 1921 and as late as 1936 a portrait commissioned by the Editor of the *Manchester Guardian* to commemorate her seventieth birthday was refused by Manchester City Art Gallery – still disapproving of her pacifism. She died in 1937.

Fortunately 150 years after her birth and eighty years after her portrait was completed, Margaret Ashton was no longer regarded as a traitor and her portrait now hangs in Manchester's Council Chamber.

Lady Frances BALFOUR was born in 1858, daughter of the 8th Duke of Argyll. She married Eustace, an architect, brother of Arthur Balfour, Prime Minister 1902-1905. In 1907 she debated against Christabel Pankhurst that 'Violent Methods (of the WSPU) had put back 'The Cause' and freely admitted that the honours in that debate went to Christabel. When criticised for not being as a conscientious as she might have been, Lady Balfour replied that she had attended sixty suffrage meetings over several years and only three golf matches during the same period! She died in 1931.

Miss Rachel BARRETT was born in 1875. In 1912 she was appointed Editor of the new WSPU paper *The Suffragette* – a prospect which she found terrifying, since she had no experience of journalism. In 1913 she was arrested at the paper's HQ along with the staff, tried for conspiracy, found guilty and sentenced to nine months in Holloway. As a result of going on hunger strike, she was released under 'The Cat and Mouse Act' which the government introduced because they didn't want martyrs. As soon as a woman on hunger strike became ill she was immediately released, then once her condition improved she was re-arrested and re-imprisoned; this could happen countless times, as it did in Rachel Barrett's case. Eventually she escaped to Scotland and published *The Suffragette* from Edinburgh until the outbreak of war in 1914. She died in 1953.

Miss Millicent BROWNE was born in London in 1881, her father, Walter, being a member of the D'Oyly Carte Opera Company. She trained as a teacher and spent her holidays working for the WFL in Wales. She married an artist, Charles Reginald Price, who was a keen supporter of women's suffrage. Both were Quakers and became increasingly disenchanted with the violence of the WSPU's campaign. Reginald was a conscientious objector and spent the war working in a hospital in Belgium. After the war he worked as a librarian at Birmingham College of Art. Millicent Price died at some time after 1952.

Although **Mrs Leonora COHEN OBE** (neé **Throp**) didn't visit north Wales as a speaker, I've included her because she spent the final years of her life at a vegetarian home in Rhos-on-Sea. She was born in Leeds in 1873, the daughter of a stonemason, who died when she was five. Her mother struggled to bring up Leonora and her two younger brothers by working as a seamstress and Leonora always said it was her mother's hard life and lack of empowerment that made her determined to try to change things.

On leaving school Leonora trained to be a milliner and

married Henry Cohen, a watchmaker and jeweller, in 1898. They had a daughter, Rosetta, who died before the age of one and a son, Reginald.

Mrs Cohen joined Leeds WSPU in 1911 and paid her own fare to London to take part in a demonstration, where she was roughly handled by police and subsequently broke a window in a local government office as a protest against her treatment. She was sentenced to seven days in Holloway for her trouble.

As previously mentioned, in 1913 she entered the Tower of London and smashed a case containing the insignia of the Order of Merit. Later that year she spent time in Armley Prison, after throwing stones at a government building when Mr Asquith visited her home town. She went on hunger and thirst strike and was released under the Cat and Mouse Act. At this point she was so ill that her husband wrote to the Home Office stating that if they re-arrested his wife he would refuse to take her back again and they would be forced to accept responsibility for her death.

During the war Mrs Cohen worked in a munitions factory. She served as a magistrate in Leeds for thirty years and was the first woman in Leeds to join a Prison Visiting Committee. Remarkably, given her earlier exploit in the Tower of London, was awarded the OBE in 1928 for her community work. She was also a member of the Theosophical Society, dedicated to the study of comparative religions.

She lived to the age of 105 and delighted in signing her correspondence 'L. Cohen, Centenarian'. In 1974 she was interviewed for radio by Margaret Drabble before the BBC launched a series of television plays – 'Shoulder to Shoulder' about the Suffragettes. Mrs Cohen reminisced about the fact that she was so terrified about what she intended to do, that she missed her stop for the Tower of London and had to complete another circuit of the Circle Line. She recalled the insults they'd had to endure – being spat at, called 'the shrieking sisterhood' and 'the scum of the earth' and the constant worry about whether their families would be targeted Finally she told Margaret Drabble how appalled she was by the shocking indifference of modern women to the vote and entreated her to 'Keep the torch burning'. Leonora Cohen died in 1978.

Again, although **Miss Emily Wilding DAVISON** didn't visit north Wales, I've included her in case any reader isn't aware of the details of her contribution to 'The Cause'. She was born in London in 1872. She joined the WSPU in 1906 and was arrested and imprisoned for the first time in 1909. During her next period of imprisonment she went on hunger strike and during her next hunger strike was forcibly fed. She spent Census Night 1911 in a broom cupboard in the House of Commons, to enable her to use 'The House' as her address on the Census form!

For a century some historians have thought that Miss Davison had either tried to fling herself under the King's horse, Anmer, or tried to catch hold of its bridle at the Epsom Derby on 4 June 1913, because she believed that what the WSPU needed was a martyr. Others have cited the fact that she had a return train ticket and had made arrangements to assist at a WSPU event the following day, as proof that she did not intentionally kill herself. A friend commented that Emily would never have committed suicide without leaving a letter for her mother, to whom she was very close.

However, examination of three separate films in 2013 – 100 years after the event, appears to have revealed that in fact she was trying to throw what turned out to be a scarf over the horse's neck, but had totally misjudged the speed at which it would be travelling. The films show something light-coloured on the ground near her body. It was picked up by Richard Burton, the Epsom Course Clerk and turned out to be a purple, white and green scarf with 'Votes for Women' embroidered on the ends. It is now thought by some that in fact her intention had been that the 'Votes for Women' message would stream out behind the jockey in the King's colours as he raced the horse to victory!

Miss Davison died four days later and was accorded a martyr's funeral. People were asked to attend wearing black and bearing purple irises, or purple and bearing crimson peonies, or white and bearing laurel wreaths. Mr Burton wrapped his small daughter in the scarf and took her to watch the funeral procession. People travelled from all over Britain, Suffragettes and trades unionists marched beside graduates and clergy in their robes and the streets were lined with silent, respectful crowds. After the service at St George's, her coffin was taken to King's Cross and then by train to her family home in Morpeth, Northumberland.

Nevertheless, it was commented that the general public was more concerned about the horse and jockey (both of whom survived) than Miss Davison's demise!

The scarf was neatly folded and put away in a drawer, along with a letter which Mr Burton obtained from a solicitor, explaining how it had come into his possession. And there it lay until the 1990's when Mr Burton's daughter needed to sell something to raise funds for nursing home fees. It was auctioned at Sothebys in 1997, by which time there was so little interest in Miss Davison that there were only two bidders, the Jockey Club and Barbara Gorna, a writer, film-maker and political campaigner. Miss Gorna was the successful bidder and the framed scarf now usually resides in the House of Commons. But it was included in the London 2012 Olympics Opening Ceremony and took pride of place in a Centenary Exhibition in Morpeth marking Miss Davison's death.

However, it has to be said that in 2014 the BBC *Woman's Hour* programme put sixty 'landmark' interviews on-line. One of them was with Mary 'Slasher' Richardson, who in 1914 slashed 'The Rokeby Venus' in the National Gallery, because she didn't approve of women posing nude. Miss Richardson knew Miss Davison and was standing opposite her at the Derby. Miss Richardson made it clear in the 1960 interview that there was no doubt whatsoever in her mind that Emily Davison had intentionally thrown herself under the King's horse.

Miss Edith ESKRIGGE was born in Liscard on the Wirral in 1872. By 1911 she was NUWSS Organiser for West Lancashire, West Cheshire and North Wales. During the war she worked for the Liverpool War Pensions Committee and the Soldiers and Sailors Families Association. Working with Eleanor Rathbone, Edith Eskrigge also established Invalid Childrens' Aid in Liverpool which became the Child Welfare Association and was also active in the Child Adoption Society in the city. After the war she became Secretary of the Liverpool Women Citizen's Organisation. Edith Eskrigge died in 1948.

Mrs Millicent GARRETT-FAWCETT (neé **Garrett**) was born in 1847 and was inspired to join the Suffrage Movement after hearing a speech by John Stuart Mill MP, an ardent supporter of women's suffrage. In 1867 she married Henry Fawcett, who although he was blind, was a Professor of Political Economy at Cambridge and Liberal MP for Brighton. In 1871 Mrs Fawcett undertook a speaking tour of the west Country and one of her lectures, *Electoral Disabilities of Women* was printed as a pamphlet and re-printed in *Before the Vote was Won*. Henry Fawcett died in 1884 and it was 1886 before his widow resumed her speaking tours. Most importantly, the same year, Mrs Fawcett was chosen to preside at the meeting of suffrage societies which resulted in the formation of the NUWSS. She became President in 1907 and one of her earliest engagements was leading the first-ever procession organised by the NUWSS, when 3,000 people joined the Mud March – presumably so named because it set off from Hyde Park on a cold, drizzly, February day. The thousands who turned out to watch and reporters from both Europe and the United States, were delighted by the unlikely sight of Mrs Fawcett pirouetting her way along the route! From that day until war was declared in 1914 Mrs Fawcett marched and spoke tirelessly for 'The Cause'. She was one of the founders of Newnham College, Cambridge, where her daughter Philippa later excelled, in 1890 scoring the highest marks in the Mathematical Tripos but as a woman was not allowed to append the letters of her degree after her name. However, she was honoured in poetry: 'Hail the triumph of the corset, Hail the fair Philippa Fawcett'.

After the war Mrs Fawcett was involved with the League of Nations and in 1925 was created a Dame of the British Empire. Unlike many of her contemporaries, Mrs Fawcett lived to see full women's suffrage achieved in 1928, sixty-one years after she was first inspired by John Stuart Mill and wrote in her diary that she counted herself fortunate to have seen 'The Cause' through to the very end. Millicent Fawcett died in 1929.

Miss (Susan) Ada FLATMAN was born in 1876. By 1908 she was working as a WSPU Organiser in the Midlands. In 1909 she moved to Liverpool and whilst there ran the most financially successful WSPU Shop in Britain, but when she asked to work in the London shop, she was refused. She then very successfully campaigned at by-elections against various Liberal candidates who refused to support women's suffrage. For undisclosed reasons Miss Flatman resigned from the WSPU in 1912. By 1922 she was living in South Africa where she offered to set up a militant suffrage organisation – but her offer was declined. By 1936 she had returned to Britain and settled in Eastbourne. Ada Flatman died in 1952. (She is mentioned in the memoirs of Mrs Annie Lawrence from Rhyl.)

Miss Helen FRASER was born in 1881. She joined the WSPU after having heard speeches by several Suffragettes including Mrs Pankhurst. Miss Fraser became Treasurer of the Glasgow WSPU and Organiser for Scotland. In the bitter winter of 1907, Mrs Pankhurst's daughter Adela was sent to Aberdeen to help her. Miss Fraser was horrified to see how ill Adela looked when she arrived and having installed her in lodgings, sent for a doctor who diagnosed pneumonia – a very serious condition then. Miss Fraser asked Adela if her mother had seen her before she left London and Adela admitted that she had. This may well have been the beginning of Miss Fraser's disillusionment with the WSPU. Adela recovered and worked with Miss Fraser to reduce the Liberal majority at the next by-election from 4,000 to less than 400. But not long afterwards Miss Fraser left the WSPU ostensibly as a protest against escalating violence. But she hinted that after a very complimentary article about her had been published in the *Daily Mail*, Mrs Pankhurst, always protective of her daughter Christabel's position in the organisation, had asked Miss Fraser not to take part in any more election campaigns.

Miss Fraser was invited to join the NUWSS and became

one of their most effective speakers. During the war she worked on the National War Savings Committee and then the Board of Agriculture, where she was employed to try to persuade women to work on the land. In 1917 she was sent to inform the Americans about the British War Effort; she visited forty states and spoke 332 times in 312 days. In 1918 Miss Fraser returned to England and concentrated on trying to get women elected to parliament. She herself was the first woman to stand for election in Scotland but was unsuccessful on three occasions.

She later married and in 1939 emigrated to Australia where she was able to renew her friendship with Adela Pankhurst. Helen Fraser is known to have been alive as late as 1964.

Miss Mary GAWTHORPE led an interesting life. She was born in 1881 and completed her education by passing the government Teacher's Certificate with a First Class degree. At twenty she won a scholarship in singing to the Leeds School of Music and was awarded honours in her examinations there. She also played the piano and later put both musical skills to good use at suffrage rallies.

She was an active member of the National Union of Teachers and through her fiancé, Tom Garrs, joined the ILP, edited the women's page of *The Labour News* and became Vice-Chairman of the Leeds branch of the ILP. Miss Gawthorpe also joined Leeds Arts Club, where she was first encouraged to speak in public. She went on to speak at the Leeds Labour Church, Labour Churches having been formed in response to members of the clergy supporting other political parties.

It was whilst she was a member of the Leeds Lord Mayor's Committee for Feeding School Children that she realised the importance of women having the vote and joined the NUWSS in Leeds where she was invited onto the Executive Committee.

In 1906 Miss Gawthorpe moved to London and became an official Organiser for the WSPU. She was involved in militant action, being arrested for the first time in the autumn of 1906 and imprisoned for two months in Holloway. Although he visited her in prison, it was about this time that her engagement to Tom Garrs ended.

In 1908 she was one of the main speakers at 'Women's Sunday' in Hyde Park and was described as 'A splendid speaker, full of humour, lucid and brilliant'. Greatly encouraged by the success of the Hyde Park Rally the WSPU wanted to continue the momentum in major towns and cities and Miss Gawthorpe was sent to Manchester to act as Lancashire Organiser, a post she held until late 1910, when continuing ill-health forced her to withdraw.

In 1912 she was arrested after breaking a window at the Home Office in protest against the forcible feeding in prison of a member of the Men's Political Union, who was subsequently moved to a lunatic asylum. In Holloway Miss Gawthorpe went on a hunger and thirst strike and was released into medical care after thirty-six hours. She continued to campaign against forcible feeding, until in 1916 along with her mother she emigrated to the USA and joined the struggle for women's rights there. In 1921 she married John Sanders and became an American citizen. She died in 1973.

Miss Vida GOLDSTEIN was born in New South Wales in 1869 and by the age of thirty was leader of the United Council for Women's Suffrage in Australia. In 1900 she founded and edited the *Australian Women's Sphere* and after women got the vote in the State of Victoria in 1908 launched another title, *Woman Voter*. The same year she founded the Women's Federal Association of Victoria, attended the International Women's Suffrage Alliance Conference in Washington DC and was elected Secretary.

In 1903 Miss Goldstein became the first woman in the British Empire to stand for parliament in the Australian Federal Elections and although unsuccessful, she did poll a not inconsiderable 51,500 votes. In 1911 she visited Britain for eight months to support the WSPU and during her stay she represented Australia in the Coronation Procession. The Men's League for Women's Suffrage gave a dinner in her honour.

It was Miss Goldstein who gave Adela Pankhurst the opportunity to emigrate to Australia to become Organiser of the Australian Women's Political Association. During WWI they jointly founded the Australian Women's Peace Army and after war ended Miss Goldstein spent the rest of her life campaigning for disarmament and birth control. She died in 1949.

Miss Leslie HALL – see **Selina MARTIN**

Dr Helena JONES was born in Conwy in 1870, orphaned at the age of six and brought up in Caernarfon. She studied at the Royal Free Hospital in London and qualified as a doctor in 1901. She was the first School's Medical Officer in Yorkshire and later transferred to the same post in Birmingham.

She was a passionate Suffragette and well respected within the WSPU. An able speaker in her own right, she chaired meetings here in north Wales addressed by Mrs Pankurst and Mary Gawthorpe – whom she regarded as a friend.

At the beginning of the First World War Dr Jones worked with Serbian refugees in Corsica.

In 1916 she returned to Wales where she was appointed Assistant Medical Officer for the Rhondda Valley in charge of maternity and child welfare services.

Also in 1916 she wrote in *The Suffragettes' News Sheet* 'Now is the psychological moment for demanding the admission of women to the franchise. The political machine during the war may be likened to sealing wax to which heat has been applied – it is in a condition to receive new impressions. After the war it will harden again and the old difficulties with party shibboleths will be revived.'

She remained in her post in the Rhondda until her retirement in 1935. She was described as 'having a forceful nature, thoroughly honest and forthright'.

At the outbreak of the Second World War Dr Jones voluntarily came out of retirement and worked as a Medical Lecturer to St John's Ambulance and the Red Cross in Cwmparc and Treorchy. During the blitz she was frequently the first doctor on the scene and despite being seventy years of age, she worked with willingness, energy and toughness, completely unconcerned about any danger to herself.

She died at the home of a colleague in 1946 and her obituary said 'Her memory will be cherished for all time in the Rhondda Valley'.

Mr Frederick PETHICK-LAWRENCE (neé **Lawrence**) was born in 1871. In 1901 he married Emmeline Pethick, unusually joining her name to his, so that they became Mr and Mrs Pethick-Lawrence. Through their friendship with Keir Hardie MP (Leader of the Labour Party in the House of Commons) Mr and Mrs Pethick-Lawrence met many officers of the WSPU and he was instrumental in obtaining the Clement's Inn Office for the WSPU.

After his wife's arrest, imprisonment and subsequent breakdown, he temporarily took over her post as WSPU

Treasurer. During this time he introduced the Literature Department which became The Women's Press – selling all manner of 'purple, white and green' WSPU merchandise. When his wife was well enough to resume her Treasurer's duties, Mr Pethick-Lawrence remained as business adviser and as militancy increased, put up bail and acted as legal adviser to Suffragettes after their arrest.

After the women who formed the Women's Freedom League broke away from the WSPU, although Mrs Pankhurst was still the figurehead, the real power lay equally with Christabel Pankhurst and Mr and Mrs Pethick-Lawrence.

In 1907 with his wife as co-editor, he founded *Votes for Women* which considerably increased the WSPU's profile and was an effective vehicle to put their message across to women all over Britain. As well as his time, in 1908 Mr Pethick-Lawrence donated nearly £1,700 and in 1909 £1,300 to the WSPU – not inconsiderable sums!

On 5 March 1912, whilst reporting on the window smashing campaign for *Votes for Women*, Mr and Mrs Pethick-Lawrence were arrested for and charged with conspiracy. Mr Pethick-Lawrence conducted their defence – knowing they would be found guilty, as indeed they were, sentenced to nine month's imprisonment and ordered to pay the prosecution's costs. Due to lobbying on their behalf, the Pethick-Lawrences and Mrs Pankhurst were granted first division status – i.e. political prisoners, not common criminals. But once Mr Pethick-Lawrence discovered that this status was not being accorded to other WSPU members he went on hunger strike and was forcibly fed.

Soon after their release the Pethick-Lawrences travelled to France to visit Christabel Pankhurst and were dismayed to hear that not only did she intend to continue the campaign of attacks on private property, but she intended to direct it from the safety of Paris and had no intention of returning to England in the foreseeable future. But Christabel also feared that her continued exile would give the Pethick-Lawrence's too much power in England and so she announced that forthwith the WSPU would have women members only.

Votes for Women reverted to Mr Pethick-Lawrence's ownership and he continued to campaign for women's suffrage through the Votes for Women Fellowship and later United Suffragists. He was also responsible for re-naming the Temporary Discharge for Health Act as 'The Cat and Mouse Act' – and even the Home Office subsequently referred to it as such.

To enable the government to recover the costs they had been awarded in the conspiracy case and to allow shop-keepers whose windows had been damaged to recover their expenses, the Pethick-Lawrences were declared bankrupt.

Some time after his first wife's death, Frederick married Helen Craggs, another WSPU supporter.

Despite her treatment of him, Mr Pethick-Lawrence remained loyal to Christabel Pankhurst to the very end, arranging for her book on the history of the WSPU – to which he gave the title *Unshackled*, to be published and for her name to be engraved on her mother's statue.

Frederick Pethick-Lawrence died in 1961 at the age of ninety and the WSPU flag which Emily Wilding Davison had carried during her encounter with the King's horse was paraded at his funeral.

Miss Marjory LEES was born in 1878, the daughter of Charles Lees and Sarah. Her father was Chairman of the company founded by his father, Eli Lees and Company (Cotton Maufacturers) and a director of several other businesses.

In 1897 Marjory and her mother, Sarah, attended the inaugural meeting of the proposed Oldham Branch of the National Council of Women, of which Sarah became the first President and Marjory later became Secretary.

In 1900 Marjory attended the University Settlement in Manchester to gain experience in social work and in 1902 was elected onto Oldham's Board of Guardians.

In 1910 she became a founder-member of Oldham NUWSS, about 130 women joined that night after attending a meeting at the Unity Hall. The first meeting of the newly-formed society was held in the Music Room at Werneth Hall, the Lees' home and Marjory was elected President. One woman who attended the meeting described the Music Room as 'beautiful' and remembered a Conservatory filled with tropical flowers and extensive collections of birds' eggs and fossils on display.

At that time Marjory's mother, Sarah, employed a lady's maid, a cook, a housemaid, a kitchen maid and a waitress and we know from Marjory's account of the Pilgrimage that her mother also employed at least four male outdoor staff.

On Friday 11 July, Marjory mysteriously left the Pilgrimage and travelled from Wolverhampton back to Oldham by train. She certainly had a good reason – she was due to be presented, along with her mother, to King George V and Queen Mary the following day, on their Royal Tour of Lancashire. After the ceremony at the Town Hall, Marjory and her mother had to hot-foot it back to Werneth Park where all the town's school-children had assembled to see the King and Queen. On Sunday Marjory re-joined the pilgrims in Birmingham.

When women got the vote in 1918 Oldham NUWSS was disbanded, but Marjory's contribution was recognised in a book documenting the history of the group, presented to her in 1919. She then took an active role in the town's

Women Citizen's Association and the Oldham Council of Social Service. She was a member of Oldham Council until 1934 and on her retirement was awarded the Freedom of the Borough. She retained her interest in the Women's Citizenship Association and Social Services until her death in 1970.

Lady Constance LYTTON was to have spoken at Rhyl in November 1910, but was too ill to attend. She. was born in 1869, her father being Viceroy of India and Constance lived there until she was eleven. After meeting the Pethick-Lawrences and other Suffragettes, she joined the WSPU in 1909. She was soon arrested and after refusing to be bound over was sentenced to one month's imprisonment, most of which she spent in Holloway's Hospital Wing, well aware that she was being accorded special treatment due to her social status and known heart condition.

The next time she was arrested the authorities bent over backwards not to convict her, but given that she, together with Emily Wilding Davison had thrown a stone at a car which she believed contained Mr Lloyd George and kept repeating that she had intended to be disorderly, they had no option but to imprison her. This time she went on hunger strike but prison doctors forewarned of her heart condition, declined to forcibly feed her and she was released.

Lady Lytton was deeply ashamed of receiving 'special treatment' and resolved that in future she would disguise herself. Further, she was horrified at the treatment meted out to Selina Martin (see next biography) whilst on remand. And so, whilst working on the General Election Campaign in Liverpool in 1910, Lady Lytton disguised as a seamstress and under the name 'Jane Wharton' took part in a demonstration outside Walton Gaol organised by Ada

Flatman. As a 'first-time offender' Jane Wharton, seamstress, was sentenced to two weeks imprisonment, went on hunger strike, was brutally forcibly fed and released on medical grounds due to weight loss.

In 1910 Lady Lytton was appointed as a WSPU Organiser.

Her brother, the Earl of Lytton was Chairman of the Conciliation Committee but after the failure of the bill, Lady Lytton, despite having suffered a stroke, resumed her militancy and took part in the shop-window-smashing campaign. On her return to Holloway she thought it considerably improved, but her fine was paid anonymously almost immediately and she was released. A further stroke in 1912 ended her physical militancy, but she taught herself to write with her left hand and her book *Prisons and Prisoners* had a huge effect on the WSPU.

Ethel Smyth (composer of 'The March of the Women') wrote to Lady Lytton's sister, Lady Balfour, that 'The adoration of the Suffragettes for 'Lady Conny' (Constance) is a thing to see – tho' not to wonder at'. Lady Lytton died in 1923.

Miss Selina MARTIN was arrested, together with Miss Leslie Hall for throwing a ginger-beer bottle into Mr Asquith's car after he had got out of it; no damage resulted. Miss Martin was arrested, charged, denied bail and imprisoned in Walton Gaol, Liverpool. Once there she was kept in solitary confinement against prison rules and as an unconvicted prisoner she refused to submit to prison discipline, barricaded herself in her cell and refused to eat prison food. As a result, despite the fact that she was still on remand and not convicted, her cell was broken into and she was threatened with forcible feeding, hand-cuffed, dragged to a punishment cell and flung down onto the stone floor.

It was as a direct result of this incident that Lady Lytton disguised herself as a seamstress and got herself arrested to prove how working-class Suffragettes were being treated in prison.

Miss Dora MASON was born in 1882. She was a lecturer in Classics at Liverpool University 1907-1912 but resigned to become an NUWSS Organiser. In 1913 she ran the NUWSS Conwy Valley Summer School. After the war she went on to train in medicine and worked as a GP in Bedford 1922-1936. She died in 1978.

Miss Muriel MATTERS was born in Australia in 1877 and trained in music and drama. She arrived in England in 1905 to further her musical career and soon started attending WSPU meetings. She was particularly impressed with Charlotte Despard and joined her when she broke away from the WSPU to form the Women's Freedom League (WFL).

There was extensive press coverage when Miss Matters chained herself to the front of a grille in the Ladies Gallery of the House of Commons behind which women were required to sit and the grille was wrenched out and removed with Miss Matters still attached! She was imprisoned for one month for disorderly conduct and later received a specially commissioned badge to honour her protest. She could often be found travelling around in the WFL caravan.

For the Opening of Parliament in February 1909 Miss Matters hired an airship sporting the logo 'Votes for Women' and a pilot and 'flew' from Hendon (despite being refused insurance) to the House of Commons. At 3,500 feet she thought it unlikely that the logo could be seen and so ejected 6 lbs weight of WFL leaflets over the side! The distribution of the leaflets was tracked by two fellow WFL members in a car.

During the 1910 Election Campaign she worked in Mr Lloyd George's constituency. At some time during 1913 she joined the NUWSS and under their auspices addressed the Durham Miner's Gala.

She married in 1914 becoming Mrs Matters-Porter, commenting that her husband didn't understand her commitment to women's suffrage and she wouldn't have married him had not the war put an end to her campaigning. She died in England in 1969.

Mrs Emmeline PANKHURST (neé **Goulden**) was born in Manchester in 1858 and was taken to her first suffrage meeting at the age of fourteen by her mother, a passionate feminist. In 1879 Emmeline married Dr Richard Pankhurst, a lawyer and strong advocate of women's suffrage. They had three daughters: Christabel, (Estelle) Sylvia and Adela and two sons (Henry Francis) Frank and Harry, both of whom pre-deceased her.

After Dr Pankhurst, who stood as an Independent, was defeated at the 1883 Election, the family moved to London and Mrs Pankhurst opened firstly a stationer's shop and secondly an art furniture shop – intended to rival Liberty's (opposite which it was situated). Neither venture was very successful.

In 1888 Mrs Pankhurst supported the Bryant and May's Match Girls' Strike. Apart from their appalling conditions – working fourteen hours per day for less than 5/- per week, they were fined for being late, talking, dropping matches and going to the lavatory without permission. Worse still, as a result of their contact with Phosphorous many of them suffered the terrible 'Phossy Jaw' – a virulent form of bone cancer which inevitably resulted in death.

In 1893 the family returned to Manchester and Dr and Mrs Pankhurst formed a branch of the ILP. In 1894 Mrs

Pankhurst became a Poor Law Guardian at Chorlton Workhouse and was deeply shocked and disturbed by the utter misery and suffering of the inmates. She was particularly concerned about the way women were treated and became even more convinced that women's suffrage was the only solution to the problem.

At the 1895 Election Dr Pankhurst stood for the ILP but was defeated. When her husband died in 1898, Mrs Pankhurst was forced to move to a smaller house and take up employment as a Registrar of Births and Deaths. Her husband's testimonial raised £1,000 for the family – a tribute to the affection and respect in which he was held.

Mrs. Pankhurst became increasingly disillusioned with existing women's suffrage organisations and when, in 1903, she discovered that a Memorial Hall named in her husband's honour would not admit women, (bearing in mind that he had always fully supported women's suffrage) she was inspired, together with her daughters, to form the WSPU with the battle-cry 'Deeds not Words'.

By 1905 the newspapers had lost interest in women's suffrage – they rarely reported on meetings and actively refused to publish articles by and letters from, supporters. The WSPU therefore decided to ensure their activities did get reported! Christabel Pankhurst and Annie Kenney attended a meeting at Manchester Free Trade Hall and constantly interrupted a government minister's speech by shouting 'When will the Liberal Government give women the vote?' When they refused to be quiet the police were called to evict them and when they refused to be evicted a struggle ensued during which the arresting officer claimed he had been kicked and spat at by the women. The women were found guilty of assault and each fined 5/-, when they refused to pay they were sent to prison and gained the publicity desired.

By 1907 the Chief Registrar had decided that Mrs Pankhurst's WSPU activities were no longer compatible with her position and informed her of this. With little hesitation Mrs Pankhurst left her Registrar's post, moved back to London and spent the rest of her life staying in hotels, particularly The Inns of Court Hotel, or with supporters of 'The Cause'. But around this time, several women who were unhappy with the undemocratic way in which Mrs Pankhurst and Christabel operated (never consulting members) broke away and founded the WFL. In 1908 the WSPU resorted to increased militancy and started breaking the windows of government buildings.

Mrs Pankhurst was imprisoned on countless occasions but her imperious demeanour seemed to paralyse even the most hardened prison officials and what she wanted, e.g. her watch, books, writing materials etc she usually got. Although she did threaten to go on hunger strike and thirst strike it is not clear whether she was ever forcibly fed and on occasions her own food was brought in, including half pints of Château Lafite!

Towards the end of 1909 she embarked on her first lecture tour of the US despite knowing that her only remaining son, Harry, was critically ill with polio – he died early in 1910. By now both Adela and Sylvia Pankhurst were convinced that increasing militancy was losing the WSPU support, but Mrs Pankhurst and Christabel would have none of it.

Around this time a wealthy WSPU supporter donated a car to Mrs Pankhurst to allow her to travel in comfort and Miss Vera Holme was appointed her chauffeur. This was almost certainly the car in which Mrs Pankhurst visited north Wales.

By 1912 the window-breaking campaign had escalated to include shops and wishing to avoid arrest in order to continue to direct operations, Christabel escaped to Paris. The campaign continued with attempts to burn down the houses of several government ministers who did not support women's suffrage, including a house being built for Mr Lloyd George. Cricket pavilions, golf club-houses and race-stands suffered the same fate and creases, greens and racecourses were burned with acid. At the end of the year pillar-boxes were added to the list of legitimate targets.

One of the most dramatic episodes of Mrs Pankhurst's extraordinary life occurred in 1913. When she set out for her third lecture tour of the United States, the British Embassy in Washington offered to advise the American Government not to allow Mrs Pankhurst to enter America, if the British Government feared the financial support she would receive. However, the American Government opted to leave the decision to their Immigration Authorities – Mrs Pankhurst was detained on Ellis Island and appeared before a Board of Special Inquiry before being allowed to continue her visit, on the direct authority of the President. The resulting publicity helped raise £4,000 for WSPU funds.

However, Mrs Pankhurst's arrival in the US had nothing on her return to Britain! The police had obviously been in close contact with the White Star Line and Scotland Yard sent no less than five members of Special Branch to assist the Chief Constable of Plymouth to arrest her. Typically Mrs Pankhurst refused to co-operate and had to be carried off the *Majestic* before being transported to Exeter Gaol.

When war was declared in 1914 the WSPU agreed to suspend all militant activity and support the war effort in return for any remaining WSPU prisoners being immediately released. And in July 1915 Mrs Pankhurst was responsible for the WSPU's staging of a March through Hyde Park entitled 'Women's Right to Serve' to support the war effort, at the request of their long-time adversary, Mr Lloyd George. The government was having difficulty recruiting sufficient women to staff the munitions factories – which was highly dangerous work, but Mrs Pankhurst agreed to take responsibility for female mobilisation, so long as women received equal pay for equal work. In fact it's not clear if equal pay was achieved but the Mutionettes certainly earned well in excess of the wage of domestic servants. Mrs Pankhurst also changed the name of the WSPU newspaper from *The Suffragette* to *Britannia – for King, for Country, for Freedom.*

Emmeline Pankhurst died in 1928 and was buried in Brompton Cemetery. Her statue was unveiled in Victoria Tower Gardens in 1930 and was moved to a more prominent position close to the entrance to the House of Lords in 1955.

Miss Eleanor RATHBONE was born in 1872, daughter of William Rathbone IV, Liberal MP and member of the philanthropic Liverpool Shipping and Anti-Slavery Dynasty, who had actually been present when Abraham Lincoln delivered his Gettysburg Address.

Miss Rathbone completed her education at Oxford, where she was a contemporary of Maude Royden (see below). On graduating she immediately went to Liverpool where she produced *A Report on Conditions of Labour at Liverpool Docks*, worked at the Liverpool Central Relief Centre, became Secretary of the Liverpool Society for Women's Suffrage and Chairman of the West Lancashire, West Cheshire and North Wales NUWSS. She was the first woman to be elected to Liverpool City Council. In 1929 Miss Rathbone was elected to parliament as Independent MP for the Combined Universities and remained there until the time of her death. She was known for her strong, clear voice and ability to clarify even the most difficult discussions.

Miss Rathbone was one of the first to recognise the threat from the Nazi Party and in the early 1930's worked to prevent the export of aero-engines to Germany to foil their being put to military use.

Her most important campaign in parliament was for the Family Allowance Act, which was introduced in 1945 despite strong opposition. Eleanor Rathone died in 1946.

Mrs Edith RIGBY (neé **Rayner**) didn't speak in north Wales but retired to Llanrhos (just outside Llandudno). She was born in 1872, the daughter of a Preston doctor. She married Charles Rigby, also a doctor, in 1893 and having no children of their own, they adopted a little boy. Shortly after her marriage Mrs Rigby set up a night-school for Preston mill-girls. It was her interest in the welfare of poorly paid and oppressed women that caused her to join the NUWSS but she later defected to the WSPU. She was also a member of the Women's Labour League. She served many prison sentences for her activities, most notably for her part in organising the 'Pantechnicon Raid' (also referred to as the 'Trojan Horse Incident') where Suffragettes were transported to the House of Commons in two pantechnicons and were successful on this occasion, in gaining entry. She set fire to Sir William Lever's bungalow (later Lord Leverhulme) and attempted to put a bomb in Liverpool Cotton Exchange.

She disagreed with the abandonment of the fight for women's suffrage at the outbreak of the war and formed the Preston branch of the Independent WSPU, but also joined the Land Army and after the war, ran a small-holding near Southport. She became a devoted follower of Steiner and the Anthroposophy Movement seeking spiritual reality.

Her niece Phoebe Hesketh, in her book *My Aunt Edith,* described Mrs Rigby's love of colour, how she dressed predominantly in azure blue and painted her house in Llanrhos in orange and purple.

Edith Rigby died in 1950 and her ashes were scattered on her husband's grave in Preston.

Miss (Agnes) Maude ROYDEN was born in 1876, daughter of a Liverpool ship-owner. At Oxford she was a contemporary of Eleanor Rathbone. She was a committed Christian and on graduating initially worked in Christian outreach in Liverpool. From 1905 she lectured in Oxford and became involved in women's suffrage. From its launch in 1909 she contributed to the NUWSS newspaper *The Common Cause.* Her ability as a lecturer made her one of the NUWSS's most accomplished speakers and she gave classes to would-be public speakers at 2/- for one class or 3/- for two. Miss Royden also supported the Tax Resistance League and was first Chairman of the Church League for Women's Suffrage. In 1911 she joined the Executive Committee of the NUWSS and that autumn undertook a speaking tour in the US. In 1912 she spoke at 267 suffrage meetings in Britain.

In 1913 Miss Royden became Editor of *The Common Cause,* President of the Chester NUWSS and Vice-President of the Oxford Women Student's NUWSS. But as a Christian pacifist she resigned the following year, feeling unable to support the war effort. In 1915 she became Vice-President of the Women's International League for Peace and Freedom. Despite her resignation from the NUWSS, after the war she spoke at a meeting at the Queen's Hall to celebrate the granting of the limited franchise to women. Subsequently she became a renowned preacher and campaigned tirelessly for the ordination of women. She also actively supported campaigns for birth control and family allowances. Maude Royden died in 1956.

Mrs Ethel SNOWDEN (neé **Annakin**) was born in 1880. She was a pupil-teacher with Mary Gawthorpe and completed her formal Teacher Training at Liverpool Training College. She became a lecturer for the ILP and in 1905 married the Chairman of the party, Philip Snowden. She joined the NUWSS and spoke on women's suffrage both in Britain and the US. She converted her husband to 'The Cause' and after his election in 1906 as MP for Blackburn he became a valuable supporter inside parliament and Vice-President of the Men's League for Women's Suffrage.

In 1913 Mrs Snowden was one of the speakers in Hyde Park at the end of the Pilgrimage. During the war she was a pacifist and a member of the British Section of the Women's International League for Peace and Freedom. Ethel Snowden died in 1951.

Mrs Gladstone SOLOMON was the most prominent Anti-Suffragist to visit north Wales, but try as I might, I have been unable to find any information about her.

Although **Violet TILLARD** did not speak in north Wales, she was responsible for running the WFL Committee Rooms at Caernarfon during the 1910 Election Campaign. She was born in India in 1874, where her father was serving in the Indian Army. 'Till' or 'Tilly' as most people knew her (because she so disliked 'Violet') trained as a nurse at Great Ormond Street and subsequently spent three years in the US looking after a paralysed child who needed special care.

She joined the WFL and with her friend, Muriel Matters, chained herself to the grille in the Ladies Gallery of the

House of Commons and like Muriel, she was removed – still attached to the grille and sentenced to one month's imprisonment. Muriel described her thus: 'Tall, slender, delicate, reticent ... even in prison clothes ... and I see her now that first awful day in Holloway – with rough boots, long unshapely dress, check apron and harshly pointed prison cap – yet 'Till' managed to look graceful. How cheerful she was, how philosophic, when many were either edgy or weepy with the strain, or rebellious'.

During the First World War Miss Tillard was a member of the No Conscription Fellowship (NCF). Predictably, members were constantly harassed and the office of their weekly news-sheet *The Tribunal* frequently raided; in fact two of their printers had their presses wrecked. Having refused to disclose the name of their current printer to the police, she was charged and sentenced to two months in prison.

Violet joined The Society of Friends and at the end of 1920 or early 1921 went to work at a Quaker Mission in Berlin. However, the Quaker's War Victim's Relief Committee was still operational in Russia and on hearing of the severity of the famine there, she asked to be transferred.

On 10 January 1922 Violet wrote to her sister from Buzuluk:

> I was today in one of the receiving homes where children are brought from the streets. 415 children (only you forget they are children) and there are no beds. In their misery and lousy clothes they wait, weak as they are, or huddle on the ground, for there is not even room to lie down. When the door was opened a crowd of crying children surged forward much as a cage full of animals might. One wonders how children can suffer so much

and yet live? Some are alive enough to be lonely and frightened, others are perfectly apathetic. Outside in the streets you see them falling from weakness and sometimes lying dead in the snow.

I also went to a home for orphans from one – three years of age. There was a kind of long wooden bed running down the room. Babies up to two years lay on little quilts all along it. Most of them just lay still, whimpering a bit and suffering from stomach and eye trouble.

So they cannot get out to get fresh air and generally too cold to walk about, just crouch against the wall or on their beds hour after hour, day after day. Clothes and bedclothes are almost as necessary as food. The pile of unburied bodies grows higher and higher. You cannot conceive of how everybody is down to their lowest level. You cannot get clothes altered for children because there is no cotton. There are no thermometers, no drugs, often no spoons – everyone is hungry, even if they are not dying.

Violet's sister received this letter by courier. Two days after it was published and barely three months after she had arrived in Russia, Violet Tillard died of Typhus at the age of forty-five. Among the many tributes published after her death was one from a colleague at the NCF: 'Her ability and courage, proved already in loyalty to another cause, were devoted unsparingly in ours'. It seemed appropriate to include her letter, as I think it shows so eloquently these women's courage and dedication.

In the next five Appendices I have looked in detail at the known Committee Members and Supporters along the north Wales coast. Each society is listed separately in the order in which the groups were formed.

The basic information has been gleaned from the 1911 Census and where ages are given, they are the ages in that year. I have included this information because it does give an idea of the backgrounds the activists and supporters came from. In some cases I have been able to find further details from newspapers and in a very few cases, books (see Bibliography).

Where I have been unable to trace people by the Census, I have referred to the *Llandudno and Colwyn Bay Directory*, which was published circa 1912.

Unfortunately there are some people with common surnames and no forenames or even initials, whom it has been impossible to identify. In other cases there are two people with the same Surname and initial, so I have included both possibilities. I have to say it isn't an 'exact science'!

Double-barrelled Surnames:
In the Appendices, double-barrelled Surnames (including St) will be found under the second name.

Appendix B

Llandudno
Founded January 1907

Officers and Committee Members:

Miss Lucy Dorothea CHAMPNEYS (fifty-four) was Llandudno's first Secretary. She lived with her sister **(Susan) Edith CHAMPNEYS** (forty-eight) a committee member at Epperstone, Abbey Road. Both were described as having private means.

They employed a cook and housemaid.

Miss Edith Champneys rose to become Chief Inspector of the Women's Auxilliary Police, which was formed during the First World War. Their main task was to 'prevent immorality' and to take a hard line with prostitutes, also to keep order in munitions factories and amongst Land Army girls. Although uniformed, they were volunteers and unpaid. Despite her strict demeanour, Miss Champney's obituary stated that: 'she was a leader of rescue and preventative work all over the country and a pioneer of this work in north Wales. She was known personally by thousands of fallen women and many who were saved by her showed their appreciation during her last days. One girl travelled all night from north Wales to Surrey with a bunch of grapes and a leg of mutton and another watched by her bedside in the last week of her illness'.

Edith Champneys died at the age of sixty-five in 1928. Women police from all over the country attended her funeral at her home village of Epperstone, Nottinghamshire, where her father had been Rector for thirty-seven years. Members of the Women's Auxilliary Police acted as bearers and her coffin was lowered into a grave lined with ivy and flowers. Her portrait hangs in the National Portrait Gallery.

Miss Barbara CRAIG (forty-eight) was a committee member and lived at 13 Mostyn Crescent, with her brother **James** (fifty-six) a doctor and sister **Isabel Primrose** (fifty). Barbara Craig was described as having private means.

They employed a sick nurse, cook and valet.

Mrs Isabella DEARDEN (fifty-two) lodging-house keeper, of Sea Bank, Penrhyn Bay, was a committee member. Her palm readings were extremely popular!

Miss Emmie DREYER (forty-two) and **Miss Jane FAWCETT** (forty-five) were both committee members. They lived at Dulnain, Roumania Crescent, Craig y Don, and were described as having private means.

They employed one servant.

Miss Marie-Louise EAKIN was a committee member. She and her sister **Rose** (thirty) both teachers, owned Bodlondeb (Castle) School for the Daughters of Gentlemen, on Church Walks. They lived with their widowed mother **Mrs Anne-Marie EAKIN** (sixty-one) and sister **Olive** (twenty-five) also a teacher.

They employed another teacher and two housemaids.

The first President of the Llandudno Cell was **Mrs Annie WALTON-EVANS** (sixty-four) wife of **Rev. David EVANS**, Archdeacon of St Asaph and Vicar of Abergele (1891 Census). The 1901 Census (when David Evans was still alive) gives their address as The Cloisters, Curzon Road, Llandudno.

By the time of the 1911 Census Mr Evans had died and his widow, eldest daughter **Annie Beatrice** (thirty-nine) and younger daughter **Ana Decima Dorothy** (twenty-six) were living in Westminster, London.

Although both Mrs Evans and her elder daughter used the surname 'Walton-Evans' whilst involved with the Suffragists, she and her family appear on Censuses as just 'Evans'. This is particularly strange as there is a splendid memorial in Abergele Church to Rev. and Mrs Evans' son, Private Herbert Walton-Evans of the Australian Commonwealth Forces who died in action just a few months before the end of the First World War.

Miss Annie Beatrice WALTON-EVANS (thirty-nine) was the third Secretary. According to Elizabeth Crawford's *The Women's Suffrage Movement* she lived at 4 Abbey Road. By 1911 she was employed as an Inspector of Establishments run by Boards of Guardians in London.

Miss Jane FAWCETT (see Miss Emmie **DREYER**)

Mrs Mary GOODDY (forty-five) was the first Treasurer and became the second Secretary. She lived at Glenthorn, Trinity Square, with her husband **Dr Edward GOODDY** (forty-seven) (see Supporters) and their adopted daughter **Dorothy Grace** (three).

They employed a child's nurse and one servant.

Dr Edith GUEST (thirty-seven) was the fourth Secretary. She lived at Asgard, Lloyd Street. It's possible that Rev. Thomas Hill Guest and his wife Mary Susannah, who lived at Cartrefle, Abbey Road, were her parents.

Dr Guest employed one servant.

Mrs Jessie KEEBLE (thirty-six) wife of **Rev. Samuel KEEBLE** (see Supporters) was a committee member. At the time of the Census in April 1911 Rev. and Mrs Keeble were resident in Southport and obviously moved to

Llandudno in August for the beginning of the new Methodist year in September.

They employed one servant.

Mrs Elsie May MARKS (thirty-eight) a committee member, lived at Plas Gwyn, Abbey Road, with her husband **James** (forty-two) a Solicitor (see Supporters) and daughter **Sara** (eleven).

They employed one general servant.

Alfred PUGH (fifty-four) became the second Treasurer. He was a chartered accountant and lived at Pen y Lan, Carmen Sylva Road, with his wife **Maude Mary** (forty-seven), daughter **Faith Margaret** (sixteen) and son **George** (thirteen).

They employed one servant.

Miss Florence Helena WRIGHT (forty-two) was the fifth Secretary and lived at Preswylfa, Abbey Road, with her widowed mother **Frances Ann Maria** (seventy-seven) and sister **Myra** (thirty-four). All were described as having private means.

They employed a cook and parlourmaid.

At the time of the 1911 Census two married sisters, Laura James (forty-five) and Lilian Margaret Tipping (thirty-eight), were also present.

Llandudno Supporters:

Miss Alice BAMFORD (fifty-five) headteacher of Shirecliffe, Clifton Road.

Ernest Edgar BONE – this could have been father (fifty-five) or son (twenty-two) – they shared the same name and both were solicitors. They lived at Ivanhoe, Fferm Bach Road, Craig y Don, and the solicitor's business was conducted from Llewellyn Chambers, Llewellyn Street. In addition, the family comprised **Mrs Bessie Frances Bone** (fifty-two), and two further sons **Philip Charles Llewelyn** (twenty-one) a shipping merchant's clerk, and **Victor Arnold** (fourteen), and two daughters, **Margery Frances** (twenty-six) and **Cicely Bessie** (twelve).

They employed two servants.

William Robert BROOKES (forty-four) was a draper, whose premises were at 25-27 Mostyn Street. He lived at Bryn Eglwys, Trinity Square, with his wife **Katharine** (thirty-eight), sons **Arthur Kynnersley** (eleven), **Robert Wakefield** (nine), **Gordon William** (seven) and daughter **Phyllis Mary** (three).

They employed one servant.

Reginald CHAMBERLAIN (sixty-three) solicitor, lived at Plas Brith, Church Walks, with his wife **Mary** (sixty-four) and daughter **Lucy Gwendoline** (thirty-seven). He appears to have worked from this address.

They employed a cook and housemaid.

As a result of giving a talk on the Llandudno Suffragists to the local History Society, I learned from her relatives that **Emily DAVIES** (neé **LUNT**) had almost certainly been a supporter. She lived in Llanrhos and married at Bethel Chapel, Overlea Avenue in 1910 into the Davies family, who owned Davies and Sons Bakery and General Store in Somerset Street. Sadly Emily died, aged thirty-three, in the 1918 flu epidemic and is buried in Llanrhos Churchyard. But when the family cleared out the shop after it had been sold in 1977 a handmade paper 'Votes for Women' badge was found.

John Roger DAWSON (forty-eight) journalist, lived at Tower View, Cwlach Road, with his widowed mother **Mary** (eighty).

They employed a household assistant, cook and housemaid.

Ralph FISHER (forty-seven) retired house furnisher, lived at Penarvon, Albert Drive, Deganwy, with his sister **Anne HAIGH** (forty-nine).

They employed one servant.

Dr Edward GOODDY (see **Mrs Margaret GOODDY** Officers).

John HORNSBY (forty-six) headteacher, lived at Ormiston, Morfa Road, with his wife **Florence Eveline** (fifty-seven), son **John Philip Skipworth** (twenty-one) a book-keeper and daughter **Julie** (twenty).

Hugh (forty-six) and **Sarah-Annie REEVES-HUGHES** (fifty-six) owned the Cocoa House.

They employed four servants.

George Alfred HUMPHREYS (forty-six) lived at Ardwy Orme, Ty Gwyn Road, with his wife **Jeannie** (forty-nine), two daughters **Merle Roden** (fourteen) and **Hilary Eirian** (twelve).

They employed a cook and housemaid.

George Humphreys was a pupil of Abraham Foulkes, Architect and when Mr Foulkes retired George Humphreys took over the firm. He was also assistant surveyor to the Mostyn Estate. In 1900 he designed Llandudno Post Office and The Mostyn Gallery and in 1907 Llandudno Library. In 1921 he became the Chief Agent of the Mostyn Estate. It is said that his vision prevented the destruction of Llandudno as a high-class resort in the period between the two World Wars.

Mr Humphreys was described as a non-smoker and teetotaller with strong evangelical beliefs and not a lot of humour! One of the Mostyn Estate's tenants said, 'He was a hard man – but just' and no doubt it was that sense of justice which enabled him to support the Suffragists.

Mrs HUNTER – there are two possibilities:
Mrs Louise HUNTER (forty-five) widow with private means of Holmwood, Conwy, or
Mrs Caroline HUNTER (forty-two) widow, housekeeper to Rev. Robert Williams, Llanbedr-y-Cennin Rectory.

Rev. Samuel KEEBLE (fifty-seven) Minister of St John's Methodist Church, Mostyn Street, lived at the Manse with his second wife, **Jessie** (thirty-six). In 1891 the Rev. Keeble was married to **Lucy** and living in Chester with their sons **Leslie** and **George**. By the time of the 1901 Census both the Rev. Keeble and Lucy had disappeared, but Leslie and George were living in Broughton, by that time Leslie was seventeen and employed as a shipping office clerk and George was twelve. By the time of the 1911 Census Samuel was married to Jessie and living in Southport. They moved to Llandudno in August 1911.

James MARKS (see **Mrs Elsie May MARKS** Officers)

Mrs Mary (sixty-two) or **Miss Minnie MARSDEN** (twenty-six) – both lived at East Clyne, Fferm Bach Road, with **Sarah WALLWORK** (fifty-three) (Mary's sister), all described as having private means. Their brother Thomas (thirty) a biscuit salesman, also lived at this address.

Mrs Emma MEREDITH (forty-three) lodging-house keeper, lived at Artro Villa, Trinity Street, with her husband **Thomas Head** (fifty-four), twin daughters **Gwladys** and **Eunice** (nineteen) and daughter **Elsie** (seventeen).

Miss Edith MIDDLETON (fifty) owned the Craig y Don Boarding Establishment.

She employed an assistant-manager, a cook, kitchen maid, pantry maid, laundry maid, waiter and two waitresses, five assistants, three housemaid/waitresses, head boots, porter and even a billiard marker!

So at least eighteen people were dependent on Miss Middleton for their livelihoods and there may well have been additional staff who didn't 'live in'; no wonder she felt aggrieved at not being considered fit to vote!

Charles MONTGOMERY (thirty-nine) private schoolmaster, of Tan y Bryn School, Fferm Bach Road.

Mrs Emily Kate OLDMAN (forty-seven) lived at 7 Clifton Villas, Deganwy, with her husband **Albert John** (forty-one) an auctioneer, and sons **Albert John** (ten) and **Philip Arthur** (eight). Mrs Oldman was the first woman to serve on the Conwy Board of Guardians.

Long before the formation of the Llandudno Cell **Henry POCHIN** and his wife **Agnes** were supporters of the Women's Suffrage Movement.

Henry was the son of a Leicestershire farmer and became an industrial chemist.He was also involved in the coal, iron and steel industries and by 1868 was MP for Stafford. He owned Nant Hall, Prestatyn; before moving on to Haulfre, Llandudno and finally Bodnant in the Conwy Valley. At Haulfre and Bodnant he designed the extensive gardens.

Agnes wrote an article entitled '*The Right of Women to Exercise the Elective Franchise*' which was published under the pseudonym 'Justitia' in *The Westminster Review* as early as 1855. 10,000 copies of the article were printed as pamphlets for the NUWSS in 1873. Agnes also ran classes for working-class girls to try to help them improve their employment prospects and Henry ran similar courses for working-class boys.

At the time of the 1891 Census they were living at Bodnant and employed a butler, housekeeper, cook, two servants, housemaid, kitchen maid, seamstress and page.

Henry died in 1895 and Agnes in 1908, but I've included them because they were such important supporters of 'The Cause'.

Their daughter, **Laura**, **Lady McLaren** became President of Rhyl NUWSS.

Harold Stewart RATHBONE (fifty three) was part of the Liverpool merchant shipping dynasty and founder of the world famous Della Robia Pottery in Birkenhead. When it closed down he opened a gallery on the corner of Bodhyfryd Road and Gloddaeth Street, Llandudno. Sadly the pillars topped by golden bears at the entrance have long since disappeared. Harold later bought, at a London auction, a painting that he believed to be the *Mona Lisa*, stolen from the Louvre some three years earlier. He took it to Paris to get it authenticated and was arrested on arrival – but released when French art experts declared it a fake!

Harold lived at Elwy Villa, Cwlach Road, with his wife **Alice Maude** (thirty-one), daughter **Lorna Louise** (eleven) and son **Gabriel Della Robia** (six).

They employed an Italian mother's help.

Harold's uncle was William Rathbone, Liberal MP, anti-slavery campaigner and philanthropist and his cousin was Eleanor Rathbone, a keen Suffragist.

Caroline RAW (forty-two) was joint principal of Lansdowne School, Abbey Road, with **Mabel BENNETT** (thirty-two).

They employed an art teacher, two English teachers, a music teacher and a Parisienne French teacher.

Lieutenant Colonel Edwin William REILLY (fifty-one) (Indian Army, retired), lived at Tantabin, Church Walks, with his wife of three years **Grace** (twenty-nine), three daughters from a previous marriage: **Nora** (eleven) and twins **Doris** and **Lilith** (eight) and son **Edwin Alan** (two).

They employed a nursemaid and housemaid.

William SEVER (fifty-five) printer, lived at Glan Morfa, Conwy, with his wife **Rosa** (forty-four) and daughter **Beatrice** (seventeen).

They employed a chauffeur/groom, cook and housemaid.

Charles SKELMERDINE (forty-five) retired cotton manufacturer, lived at Norwood, Abbey Road, with his wife **Charlotte** (forty-two) and daughter **Margaret** (nine).

They employed a cook, nursemaid and housemaid.

Henry SQUIRRELL (forty-five) retired stationer, currently poultry farmer, lived in Albert Drive Gardens, Deganwy, with his wife **Alice Mary** (forty-nine) and daughter **Marjorie** (eighteen).

Morris WARTSKI (fifty-five) jeweller, lived at Drinwood, Abbey Road, with his sons **Charles** (thirty-one) and **Harry**

(twenty-six), daughters **Sara** (eighteen) and **Rosie Snowman** (twenty-four) and grand-daughter **Freda Grace Snowman** (three months).

Mr Wartski employed a valet, nursemaid, housemaid and general servant.

It's interesting that as many as eleven officers/committee members and supporters lived in a single location – Abbey Road; and nearby were a further four in Church Walks, two in Cwlach Road and one in Ty Gwyn Road – giving a total of eighteen out of forty-three.

Appendix C

Rhyl and Abergele
founded February 1909

Officers:

Rhyl's first President was **Lady Laura McLAREN** (neé **Pochin**) of Bodnant Hall, Eglwysbach. She had inherited the Bodnant Estate from her father, Henry Pochin. (see Appendix A – Llandudno) and married **Charles McLaren MP**, who was created Lord Aberconwy in 1911 by Mr Lloyd George. Neither Lord nor Lady McLaren appear on the 1911 Census, but their son **Henry** is listed at Bodnant on Census night, although an undergraduate of Balliol College, Oxford.

Miss Florence Catherine PERKS (thirty-one) of Dolanog, Russell Road, was one of Rhyl's Secretaries (probably the third). She lived with her widowed father **Samuel** (seventy-two), sister **Annie** (thirty) a nurse and brother **Samuel Francis** (twenty-nine) an electrical contractor.

They employed a cook and two housemaids.

According to Elizabeth Crawford's *The Women's Suffrage Movement*, Rhyl's first Secretary was **Miss Margaret WILLIAMS** (forty-five) a Boarding House Manageress of Mor Afon, 75 West Parade. She lived with her sister **Eleanor** (fifty-eight) and brother **John** (forty-eight) a joiner.

They employed one general servant.

And the second Secretary was **Mrs WILLIAMS** of The Studio, High Street.

Rhyl Supporters:

Miss Jessie Madeline BEST (thirty-nine) Principal of Elwy Vale School, Grange Road.

She employed a governess, two student governesses (one French and one German), a cook/housekeeper, housemaid and parlourmaid.

Mrs Edith Maud BROMLEY (thirty-six) of Annerley, Russell Road, lived with her husband **Richard** (forty-six) Clerk to the County Council and daughter **Beryl Rose** (seven).

They employed a cook, nursemaid and housemaid.

Miss Sarah CHERRY (seventeen) from Ireland, a pupil at the Misses Marion and Maud Trousdell's and Miss Isabella Alexander's Ladies School, Blaencathra, Marine Drive.

There are two possibilities for the next supporter:
Mrs Annie CLOUGH (thirty-one) widow, of Plas Clough, who lived with her daughter **Constance May Willis Clough** (eight), widowed mother **Annie Willis** (sixty-one) and brother **John Willis** (thirty-five) biscuit salesman, or
Mrs Catherine Hannah CLOUGH (thirty-nine) of Pant Glas, Abergele, who lived with her husband **Frederick Norman** (forty-five) (private means).

They employed a cook.

Dr Wycliffe GOODWIN (forty-three) physician, born in Shanghai, China, lived in Russell Road with his wife **Olivia Adeline** (forty), their son **Charles Wycliffe** (fourteen) and daughter **Violet** (eight).

They employed two servants.

Charles HUBBARD (forty-one) tailor's cutter, and his wife **Thyrza Georgina** (thirty-three) of 1 Emlyn Grove, lived with their daughter **Louisa** (seventeen) an apprentice tailoress, and four sons **Charles** (thirteen), **John Wilson** (twelve), **Thomas Edwin** (eleven) and **James Leslie** (eight months).

On first reading this I thought Thyrza must have had her hands full with four boys and no help and then I noticed that she had been married for only a year. Curious, I went back to the 1901 Census and found Charles Hubbard living not at No.1 but at No.2 Emlyn Grove, with his wife Louisa and all the children mentioned above except obviously, the youngest, plus another daughter **Henrietta**, aged nine in 1901.

I then looked at deaths and found that Louisa died in the last quarter of 1906, leaving Charles with five children between the ages of five and fourteen.

Next I looked at marriages and found that Charles married Thyrza Georgina BOLWELL in her birthplace, Chippenham, Wiltshire in the third quarter of 1909, less than three years after Louisa died.

I then returned to the 1901 Census and looked for Thyrza and found that at that time she was employed as a housemaid by Morris Thomas CASE, a Colliery Manager of The Grange, Upton-by-Chester. I wonder how she came to meet Charles? Did she come to Rhyl on her day off and go into the shop where he worked … ?

For the final piece of the jigsaw puzzle I returned to the 1911 Census and found that the 'missing' daughter, Henrietta, by then aged eighteen, was employed as a housemaid at Howell's School, Denbigh.

Mrs Beatrice HUTTON (thirty) lived at Fernleigh, Seabank Road, with her husband **Dr Eustace** (thirty-six) medical practitioner, their daughters **Barbara** (nine) and **Gwynedd** (six), and sons **Horace** (seven) and **Wilfred** (four).

They employed a governess and cook.

Joseph LLOYD (thirty-seven) solicitor, lived at Bryndedwydd, St Asaph, with his wife **Margaret Ellen** (thirty-nine), daughters **Daisy Mandeville** (seventeen), **Phyllis Mandeville** (thirteen), son **Russell Llewelyn Mandeville** (fourteen), widowed mother-in-law **Catherine YOUNG** (seventy-nine) and niece **Olive Blanche Manley POWER** (eighteen) a student of music.

They employed one general servant.

Mrs Annie RANCE (sixty-two) widow, appears on the Census as plain 'Rance', but is always referred to in newspaper reports as 'Mrs de Rance'. She lived at Stonehurst, Bath Street.

She employed a lady's maid and general servant.

James Boyd ROBERTSON (thirty-four) assistant secondary school master of 1 Brownlow Villas, St Asaph, lived with his wife **Ada Margaret** (thirty-six), daughter **Morag** (seven) and son **James Ritchie** (three).

They employed one general servant.

Mrs Frances Susannah SUTTON (fifty-eight) lodging-house keeper, of 31 West Parade, lived with her husband **Arthur** (forty-four).

They employed a 'useful help – domestic'.

Henry TILBY (forty-four) political agent, of 1 Regent Villas, Paradise Street, lived with his wife **Elizabeth** (forty-nine) and daughter **Madge** (seven).

They employed one servant.

Rhyl also had the distinction of having the only known **Suffragette** supporter in north Wales. **Mrs Annie LAWRENCE** (thirty-six) of Medlock Villa, lived with her husband **Arthur** (thirty-nine) a meat purveyor, daughter **Florence Gertrude** (eleven) and son **Arthur Jack** (nine).

They employed a governess and cook.

Annie Lawrence is the only person from Rhyl about whom I have been able to find more detailed information, because her daughter, Gertrude Shannon, was one of the Suffragettes' relatives interviewed by Sir Brian Harrison in the 1970's.

Annie was born in West Bromwich in 1875. After her mother died she was put into a childrens' home for a short time, before being taken by her aunt to the US. After returning to Britain she married Arthur Lawrence about 1900 and became a well-respected cattle dealer, whilst her husband ran their butcher's shop, at 13 High Street, Rhyl.

The *London Gazette* of 5 February 1901 informs us that:

the partnership heretofore subsisting between Thomas Newman of High Street, West Bromwich, Butcher and Arthur Lawrence of 13 High Street, Rhyl, Butcher and Annie Lawrence, the wife of the said Arthur Lawrence carrying on the trade or business of Butchers and Meat Salesmen at Rhyl aforesaid, under the style or firm of 'T. Newman and Co.' has this day been dissolved by mutual consent. The business will in future be carried out under the style or firm of Arthur Lawrence.

I'm intrigued by the West Bromwich connection – was Thomas Newman a relative of Annie's and did she meet her future husband through him? Mrs Lawrence always considered herself the equal of her husband, was a forceful character and was also keen for her children, daughter Gertrude and son Arthur, to be treated equally.

Although business commitments prevented her from being an active Suffragette she certainly supported them and entertained both Mrs Pankhurst and Miss Ada Flatman when they visited Rhyl. As we have seen, Miss Flatman was responsible for opening the first WSPU Shop in Liverpool and Gertrude Shannon remembered being taken there as a little girl by her mother. Mrs Lawrence was very enthusiastic and active in amateur dramatics in Rhyl. After her husband died in 1945, she spent the remaining years of her life living sociably in a Rhyl hotel.

Abergele Supporters:

Miss Ada Bessie GITTINS (forty-two) head mistress, of Abergele Elementary School

Appendix D

COLWYN BAY
founded December 1909

Officers and Committee Members:

Colwyn Bay nominated Mrs Fawcett, National NUWSS President as their President, but they had numerous Vice-Presidents:

Miss ANDREWS was a committee member, possibly of Erin, 22 Hawarden Road or Wynncote, 9 Wynnstay Road.

Miss Alice Emma AYLES (fifty) was a committee member. She lived at Glyn View, Abergele Road, with **Miss Elizabeth SELBIE** who was a partner with Miss Ayles in a private school.

Miss Amy BARFIELD (forty) of Haslingden, was Assistant Treasurer and lived at 7 Victoria Park, where she was companion to Mrs Rose Kettlewell (fifty-five) who lived with her husband George (sixty) a retired corn merchant and son Norman Harold (twenty-two) a dental student.

The family employed one general servant.

Mrs Sarah BARKER (forty-seven) a committee member, was a hairdresser and lived at 2 Station Road, with her husband **John** (fifty-two) (see Supporters) and her father John Fielden (sixty-nine) retired draper.

Dr Lilian BLAKE (thirty-nine), a Vice President, was a

medical practitioner who lived at Netherhurst, Conwy Road.

She employed a housekeeper and servant.

Miss CHARNLEY – Ethel May (twenty-four) or her sister **Daisy Evelyn** (twenty) – of Cranford was a committee member. They lived with their parents **George William** (sixty-six) optologist and **Emily Ann** (sixty-one).

They employed one general servant.

A **Miss CONNOLLY** was a committee member, either of Norwood, The Promenade or 15 Mostyn Road.

Miss CROSFIELD, Bryn Eithin, was a Vice-President of Colwyn Bay NUWSS and member of the West Lancashire, West Cheshire and North Wales Federation Committee.

I know from newspapers that Miss Crosfield and her mother lived at Bryn Eithin, Upper Colwyn Bay. Indeed, there is even a description of the house from July 1907, when the gardens were open to the public to raise money for St Trillo's Church tower:

> The mansion stands at an eminence just underneath The Flagstaff, is splendidly situated and commands grand views of the surrounding area. It would be impossible to find a more charming environment. The grounds themselves are worthy of a visit and the flowers now in their full summer glory would alone constitute a delightful flower show. Wherever one turned and there were very many turns in the grounds, the eye was pleased with some beauty or other, the wealth of rare flowers being exceptionally fine. We understand that Mr Gibbs, the head gardener to Mrs Crosfield, deserves great praise for his work in this direction. The sun was blazing hot but

there were several cool and shady nooks, where one could hear the cheerful strains of Mr Underwood's string band.

It has proved impossible to trace either Mrs or Miss Crosfield through Census records.

However, on 29 May 1908 the *North Wales Weekly News* published a paragraph informing their readers that 'Mr A.H. Crosfield MP accompanied by Mrs Crosfield presided at the first Warrington Music Festival' and I can think of no reason why the paper would have published this information had Mr Crosfield not had a local connection.

And further, in September 1908 the same paper published a couple of paragraphs referring to the success of Messrs Crosfields and Sons, Soap Manufacturers, Warrington, in being awarded the 'Grand Prix' at the Franco British Exhibition, where their products were advertised by 'a fountain of bubbles'.

Crosfields also held the Royal Warrant for soap products.

In his book *Enterprise in Soap and Chemicals: Joseph Crosfield & Sons Limited 1815-1965*, A. E. Musson said that John Crosfield's obituary stated that he 'earned for himself the reputation of a kind and considerate employer of labour. To him, his workpeople were not so many 'hands' – he knew most of them by name, he freely conversed with them and those who had grown grey in his service retired on a pension'. And in 1892, John's son Arthur was presented with an illuminated address 'as a token of the respect and esteem in which he is held by his workmen'. It referred to his 'kindness and consideration, his sense of fairness and his warm interest in the welfare of his workmen'.

As early as 1868 there was mention of a 'Sick Club' for Crosfield's employees, managed by the firm's cashier and a comprehensive welfare scheme was introduced in 1903. Day trips were organised for employees and their families – 250 went to Llangollen in 1869 and 1,000 to Blackpool in 1883 and social evenings were held locally. The Crosfields also contributed generously to charitable and particularly educational schemes in Warrington.

In 1909 Miss Crosfield undertook an extensive tour of India and spoke about it to the local Liberal women when she returned. She landed at Calcutta and visited Cawnpore, Nepal, Benares, Lucknow, Delhi, Lahore, Amritsar and Agra before travelling home from Bombay. In her talk Miss Crosfield referred to the history of India, the mutiny and massacre at Cawnpore, the bathing ghatts or steps on the sacred river Ganges at Benares, the magnificent views of the Himalayan peaks from Darjeeling and many fine buildings which remained as monuments to great rulers long since dead. Miss Crosfield had seen what the Civil Service was doing particularly in relation to agriculture and had also visited schools and historic Raja's homes.

Dr Mary DEACON was a Vice-President.

Mrs Agnes ElCOCK (twenty-six) was the Literature and *The Common Cause* Secretary (*The Common Cause* being a Suffragist magazine). She lived at Swarthmoor, Conwy Road, with her husband **Charles Ernest** (thirty-two) (see Supporters), and their daughters **Jean Margaret** (four) and **Elizabeth** (one).

They employed a nurse/housemaid and general servant.

A **Mrs GUEST** was a committee member and a **Miss GUEST** was the Assistant Secretary, thought to be the wife and daughter of **Mr Edwin GUEST**, Lynton, Woodhill Road.

Hammersley HEENAN (sixty-four) was a Vice-President. He was a civil engineer, founder and chairman of Heenan Engineering and lived at Uwch y Don, Old Colwyn, with his wife **Ada** (forty-six) (also a supporter), and sons **Richard Edward** (nineteen) and **John Nelson Dundas** (eighteen) both engineering students, and **Robert Lawrence** (six) and daughters **Olivia Violet** (sixteen) and **Kathleen Ada** (eleven).

They employed a cook, nursemaid, parlourmaid, housemaid, sewing-maid and kitchenmaid.

Hammersley Heenan was once described as one of Manchester's most cosmopolitan citizens. Born in Ireland, on leaving Bootham Friends' (Quaker) School, York, he worked for the Indian Government, mainly on the construction of railways. On returning to Britain the business he set up was diverse – as well as supplying the steelwork for the Austin factory at Longbridge, the grandstand at Epsom Racecourse, Folkstone Pier and Pavilion, Wembley Tower, Whitby Swing-Bridge, a 1,600 foot Chilean Railway Bridge and Refuse Destructors which were eventually installed at 300 locations worldwide, Heenan's also patented the Tower Spherical Engine and built a steerable torpedo.

But perhaps closest to the heart of the inhabitants of north Wales, in 1892 his company was responsible for manufacturing all the steelwork used in the construction of Blackpool Tower and also won the contract for the electric lighting in the fish tanks in the Tower Aquarium.

Mr Heenan always ensured that any machinery he bought in had been made in Britain and tried whenever possible to export his goods through Manchester.

When he retired to Colwyn Bay he served on the Urban District Council.

Either **Miss Ethel** or **Miss Rosa HOVEY** was a Vice President and as **Ethel** was Treasurer it seems likely that **Rosa** was a Vice President. Ethel and Rosa were the seventh and ninth children of George Henry and Frances Hovey of Sheffield and there were two further children after Rosa. Their father was a draper, upholsterer and cabinet maker, at the time of the 1881 Census employing forty men, eighteen boys and forty-six women – so obviously a man of some substance and standing in the community. Both parents were staunch Methodists.

Miss Ethel HOVEY (forty-five) was Matron/Bursar at Penrhos College 1894-1928 and Colwyn Bay Suffragists' first Treasurer.

In 1919 Ethel Hovey was the first woman to be elected to the old Urban District Council, her bid being enthusiastically supported by the National Council of Women and her success was celebrated by a torchlight procession. From the outset she was eager to help to establish Child Welfare Committees and Clinics. Under her supervision, clinics in Colwyn Bay increased from one per fortnight to five per week. She was a member of the National Council of Maternity and Child Welfare and was highly influential in the establishment of Colwyn Bay's Maternity Home. She was a member of Denbighshire Education Committee and a governor of several local schools. She was active in the NSPCC and also a JP.

In 1926 Ethel Hovey became the first woman Chairman of an Urban District Council in Wales. When the town received its Charter in 1934 she became the first woman Alderman and was Mayor 1945-46.

It is known in her family that during the 1930's Ethel was responsible for a fountain being installed in Queen's Gardens with a plaque commemorating a women's organisation – possibly the National Council of Women. The fountain was removed to prevent vandalism, but it is believed that there are plans to reinstate it.

In 1952 Ethel Hovey was awarded the Honorary Freedom of the Borough 'in recognition of the public work she has so unostentatiously carried out locally and over a wide area of north Wales in a period of thirty-three years'. Councillor Gwilym Hughes said that there could be no more appropriate time to confer the honour on a woman than during the first year of the Queen's reign and no woman more worthy of it than Miss Hovey and described her as 'a gentle and gracious leader, who inspired others to give their best'. Typically, in her acceptance speech Ethel Hovey paid tribute to all the women she had worked with over the years.

She was involved in the formation of the Heaton Place Housing Trust in Rhos on Sea and is also remembered for introducing a bus service which ran along the Prom from Penrhyn Bay to Old Colwyn.

Due to the length of the guest list for her eightieth birthday party in 1951, Ethel instructed her Secretary to set a stop-watch so that each family member and friend was allotted only forty seconds to greet her!

Ethel Hovey died in 1953 and her ashes were buried in the family grave in Sheffield.

Miss Rosa HOVEY (forty) was Principal of Penrhos College, Colwyn Bay, 1894-1928. Rosa had actually been a pupil at the school, but completed her education at Jersey Ladies College. She studied at London University when it had been open to women for only five years and gained a BA First Class Honours degree.

When Rosa and Ethel arrived in Colwyn Bay in 1894 the school was still accommodated in the house, which became known as Gilbertville on The Promenade, but with the purchase of the old Hydro in 1895, massive expansion began. The development of the college is covered in fascinating detail in *Penrhos: 1880-1930*, which was actually written by Rosa at the request of the governors.

By the time of the 1911 Census the College employed fourteen assistant mistresses, a secretary, nurse, housekeeper, two cooks, eight housemaids, scullerymaid, groom, gardener and farm labourer.

Rosa treated every girl in her care as an individual. She believed that to offer girls anything less than the very best education would be a betrayal of their trust in her.

As mentioned in Chapter 9 a collection was made to mark the completion of Rosa's twenty-first year as Principal. As well as the £600 for the ambulance, a further £50 was raised – to be spent on an engraved tablet or window which would be a permanent record of Rosa Hovey's 'long, beneficial and successful connection with the school'. She was also presented with an album of the names of subscribers, the most distant being as far away as India and China.

She was President of the Old Penrhosians which even in the 1920's had members worldwide and at the 1928 Speech Day, held shortly after her retirement, she was presented with a cheque for £500 for the Provident Fund for old girls. Ethel was presented with a personal cheque – as an expression of the love and gratitude of past and present staff and students. And after Rosa had spoken at the 1931 Jubilee, she was presented with a motor-car.

Rosa died suddenly in October 1932 just a few days after her sixty-seventh birthday. The funeral was held at St John's Methodist Church and the Rev. A. J. Costain, Headmaster of Rydal, who conducted the service, described Rosa as: 'A good woman with a big heart, the human touch and a sense of humour; kindly, sympathetic and generous. She had striven to learn Welsh and had become fluent in the language. She had worked tirelessly to have poor families decently housed; to set up reasonably-priced housing for business girls and women and to provide a place for recreation for underprivileged boys and girls in the town and she had given generously of both her time and her money to achieve these aims. Right to the end she was young in spirit with a faith in the future that burned with a clear flame'. Mr Costain said her work would live on after her. Rosa Hovey's ashes were buried in the family grave in Sheffield.

Penrhos's Hovey House was named in Ethel and Rosa's honour. In 1954, a few days after overseeing the installation of a memorial window to his two sisters in the College Chapel, their brother (Arthur) Clement, a Penrhos governor, died. This window is now preserved at Rydal-Penrhos. Rosa's work does indeed live on after her – the Rosa Hovey Memorial Scholarship still provides funds for a local female student studying at Bangor University and the Rosa Hovey Housing Trust provides affordable housing for working people on low incomes and for the elderly.

Miss Elizabeth KENYON (forty-eight) was Colwyn Bay's first Secretary. She was a retired music teacher and lived at Kelmscott, Coed Coch Road, Old Colwyn.

Mrs Edith MOULD (fifty-four) was a Vice President and lived at Halstead, Coed Pella Road with her husband **George William** (seventy-five) physician and surgeon.

They employed a cook, nurse and parlourmaid.

Francis NUNN (fifty-one) was a Vice President and a solicitor. He lived at Coed Helyg, Brackley Avenue, with his wife **Margaret** (fifty-three) an Anti-Suffragist, son **Ronald Lloyd** (twenty-four) a law clerk and daughters **Theodora** (twenty-two) and **Anita** (twenty).

They employed a housemaid and general servant.

Miss Mildred SPENCER (forty-one) of Farlands, Penrhyn Bay, and later Longmead, Rhos Road, Rhos on Sea, was the second Secretary.

She employed a cook and housemaid.

Miss WOOD, possibly the daughter of **Stanley Wood**, Dinglewood School for Boys, Lawson Road, was a committee member.

Colwyn Bay Supporters:

Miss Daisy ALLEN (seventeen) schoolgirl, Penrhos College lived at 28 Victoria Park, with her widowed mother **Hannah** (sixty-five) (private means).

Her mother employed a companion, Emmie Chadderton (thirty-two) of Manchester.

Edward ALLEN (forty-three) cabinet maker, lived at 12 Woodhill Road with his wife **Alice** (forty-five).

Miss Alice ANDRESS (thirty-six) assistant mistress, Penrhos College.

John BARKER (fifty-two) hairdresser, of 2 Station Road, lived with his wife **Sarah** (forty-seven) and Sarah's father, John Fielden (sixty-nine) retired draper.

Miss BATES of Holmdale, 4 Wynnstay Road.

Miss Mabel BEST (thirty-eight) lived at Shawlands, with her widowed mother **Edith Mary** (sixty-nine).

They employed a nurse attendant and general servant.

George BEVAN (fifty) ironmonger, of 15 Coed Pella Road, lived with his wife **Mary** (forty-six), daughter **Ellen Elsie** (twenty-two) and son **George Herbert** (seventeen) an assistant in the family business.

They employed one general servant.

Mrs Sarah BROCK (fifty-five) lived at of Gwern Tyno, with her husband **John** (seventy-six) a chemical manufacturer.

They employed a cook, parlour maid and general maid.

Mrs CROSFIELD, Bryn Eithin. All I have been able to discover about Mrs Crosfield is that she supported the Ada Leigh Homes for British Girls in Paris, founded by Ada Leigh, who became Mrs Travers Lewis. Ada Leigh worked in Paris for forty years and recognised the difficulties and dangers which faced English-speaking girls who went to work in the city. There were four homes – for governesses, for companions, for students and an orphanage for children of English or Anglo-French parents.

Colonel EALES

Charles Ernest ELCOCK (thirty-two) and his wife **Agnes** (twenty-six) (see Officers), lived at Swarthmoor, Conwy Road, with their daughters **Jean Margaret** (four) and **Elizabeth** (one).

They employed a nurse/housemaid and general servant.

Charles Elcock was born in Belfast, educated at Bootham Friends' (Quaker) School, York and then served his articles with an architect back in Belfast, before moving to Glasgow where he worked on the design for the British Museum extension. Next he came to Liverpool where he worked on the Cotton Exchange (bombed by Suffragette, Edith Rigby!).

Mr Elcock then joined J. M. Porter, Architect and Surveyor of Colwyn Bay and they jointly undertook a special study of hospitals and sanatoriums, Mr Elcock being conversant with American and Continental practice. He spent six years at Colwyn Bay and during that time worked on Denbigh Municipal Buildings – as a result of winning a design competition; the Liverpool and District Bank on Conwy Road, Parr's Bank, Station Road, Colwyn Bay and the Congregational Church, Rhos on Sea

Mr Elcock was also a founder of Colwyn Bay Art Exhibition, supporter of Colwyn Bay 1910 Eisteddfod, Colwyn Bay Liberal Association and the YMCA.

The family moved to Manchester in 1912.

Mrs Margaret FLEET (forty-seven) lived with her husband **Arthur James** (fifty) a piano and music dealer, of Penrhyn Road, and son **Ernest** (twenty-one) an assistant in the family business.

They employed one servant.

Miss HALL opened The Swedish Gymnasium on Princes Drive in 1908. (Prior to this she had worked from premises in Penrhyn Road for five years). She engaged local architect William Earp of Wynnstay Road, to design the building and local builder Evan Owen of Belgrave Road, to construct it. The main hall was 59'x 34' x 24' high and there were eight large windows, each pane opening individually. Damp-proof material lined the floor and there were ventilators in the roof. Swedish apparatus for educational and medical gymnastics had been installed and the whole project was 'state of the art'. Miss Hall ran classes for both adults and children and carried out medical gym work in Colwyn Bay, Bangor and Rhyl on a weekly basis.

Miss Hall had trained at Southport for two years supervised by Mr Alexander of 'Alexander Technique' fame ('the skilful use of self'), studying anatomy, physiology, hygiene, first aid and medical and educational gymnastics. She passed her final examinations First Class and won the gold medal. She gained the Diploma of South Kensington College (also First Class) for advanced hygiene and advanced physiology and won medals for horse-work, jumping, ladder-work, rope-climbing, swimming and vaulting. She had spent six weeks in the summer of 1907 studying at Dr Aveson's Institute in Stockholm, Sweden and was granted a private certificate by Dr Aveson for massage and medical gymnastics.

Mrs Florence Susan HARSENT (thirty-seven) lived at 22 Park Road, and later at Brynhyfryd, Upper Colwyn Bay, with her husband **Alfred Thomas** (forty-two) a camp proprietor and daughter **Winifred** (fourteen).

Mrs Harsent wrote a strongly-worded letter to the *North Wales Weekly News* in defence of Mrs Pankhurst and the WSPU after a male reader had criticised them at great length.

Miss Alice JACKSON (forty-seven) assistant mistress, Penrhos College.

Cyril Francis KEEBLE (twenty-six) assistant master at Rydal School.

Mrs Clara Elizabeth LEGER (forty-six) appears on the Census as plain 'Leger', but is always referred to in newspaper reports as 'St Leger'. She was a masseuse and lived at Bay View, Penrhynside, with her mother **Elizabeth Mary Blackburn** (seventy-one) and sister **Margaret Eliza Blackburn** (fifty-one).

Mrs Thomas LLOYD, wife of **Rev. Thomas Lloyd** Congregational Minister, of Rhiw Grange, Rhiw Road.

Mrs Bernard LUCAS, wife of **William Bernard Lucas** of Highclere, Woodland Park.

The **Misses Edith** (forty-five) and **Margaret** (forty-three) **MORRIS**, proprietors of Wilton House School, Alexander Road, who lived with their widowed mother **Annie** (sixty-six).

They employed another teacher, a cook and housemaid.

Norman OLDHAM (twenty-one) who lived at Bryngraig, Rhos-on-Sea, with his mother **Mary** (fifty-four).

They employed Mrs Oldham's niece, Ida TONKIN (twenty-five) as a companion and a cook and housemaid.

John PORTER (forty-seven) estate agent and surveyor (and partner of **Charles Elcock**), lived at Braeside, Upper Colwyn Bay, with his wife who was away on Census night and twin sons **Graham** and **John Lawrence** (seventeen).

They employed a cook and housemaid.

The Porter family business was of great significance to development of Colwyn Bay.

Miss Winifred RAMSEY (thirty-two) assistant mistress, Penrhos College.

Arthur SARSON (forty) dental surgeon, lived at Haulfre, Rhos on Sea, with his wife **Ethel** (thirty-five) and two daughters **Ethel Nora** (eleven) and **Margaret** (eight).

They employed a cook and charwoman.

Miss Elizabeth SELBIE was a partner in a private school with **Miss AYLES** (see Officers). They lived at Glyn View, Abergele Road.

One or all of the **Misses SUGDEN: Caroline** (fifty), **Mary Ellen** (forty-seven), and **Annie Maud** (thirty-nine), who lived at Hayfield House, with their mother **Martha** (eighty).

They employed one servant.

Herbert TAYLOR (thirty-four) a farmer, lived at Cardigan Villa, Mochdre, with his wife **Elizabeth** (thirty-five), four daughters, **Phyllis** (eight), **Enid** (five), **Margaret** (two), **Frieda** (eight months) and son **John** (seven).

They employed a general servant.

Miss Kathleen THOMAS (twenty-five) assistant mistress, Penrhos College.

Mrs Beatrice WILKS (forty-nine) lived at 2 Meirion Gardens, with her husband **Stephen** (forty-three) a medical practitioner and daughters **Heather** (sixteen) and **Mary** (fourteen).

They employed one servant.

Miss Lucy Anne WOODHEAD (sixty-five) of 22 Erskine Road.

She employed one general servant.

Appendix E

Bangor
founded December 1909

Officers and Committee Members:

Mrs Edith MILNER-BARRY (forty-four) wife of **Edward Leopold** (forty-four) lecturer at Bangor (see Supporters). They had a daughter **Alea** (seventeen) and sons **Edward** (fourteen) and **John O'Brian** (twelve).

Miss Edith Maud WITTON DAVIES (twenty-four) of Bryn Haul, Victoria Drive, was the daughter of **Rev. Thomas William WITTON DAVIES** (sixty) widower and professor of Hebrew at Bangor (see Supporters).

Mrs Annie Eliza GAUNT (fifty-five) widow (independent means) lived at Bryn Mair, Callepa, with her daughter **Ethel Mary** (twenty-five).

Miss Mary Gertrude HARTLEY (thirty-four) a daily governess, or possibly her sister **Miss Ruth Olwen HARTLEY** (twenty-eight) was Bangor's first Secretary. They lived at Wylfa with their father **Lewis** (seventy) a commercial traveller in drapery and mother **Mary Elizabeth** (sixty-five).
They employed one servant.

Miss Evelyn LAMPORT (fifty) (private means) was Bangor's President. At the time of the 1911 census she was staying with a branch of the Rathone family – Hugh and Evelyn, in Liverpool.

Miss Nora LEWIS (twenty-six) daughter of **Sir Henry** and **Lady LEWIS** of Belmont (see Supporters) undertook some secretarial duties.

Miss Evelyn Hodgson MATTHEWS (twenty-four) daughter of **William** and **Margaret MATTHEWS** (see Supporters).

Miss Kate PINKERTON (thirty-four) lived with her parents **Thomas** (sixty-one) a novelist, and **Ophelia** (fifty-seven) and sisters **Evelyn** (thirty-two) and **Ethel** (twenty-four) a schoolmistress.

Mrs Emma Jane PRICE (forty-six) lived at 286 High Street, with her husband **Dr Emyr Owen PRICE** (fifty-three) a medical practitioner and daughters **Gwen** (twenty-two), **Iola** (eighteen), **Eltrud** (thirteen) and son **Emyr Ivor** (eight). The committee often met at this address.

They employed a cook.

Miss Gertrude RIGBY (twenty-three) lived at 3 Friar's Terrace, with her father **Thomas** (forty-nine) widower, book binder, and sisters **Dorothy** (eighteen), laundry packer, **Marion** (fifteen) and **Gwendoline** (thirteen).

Mrs (Charlotte) Price WHITE (thirty-eight) of Rockleigh was Bangor's second Secretary. She lived with her husband **Price Ffoulkes** (thirty-eight) Manager of Bangor's first Electricity Station, son **David Archibald** (four) and daughter **Margaret** (three). She was always referred to by her husband's name of Price White (not hyphenated).

They employed one general servant.

Charlotte was the daughter of Mr and Mrs James Bell of Briggart, Scotland. She completed her education at

University College, Bangor and went on to teach in London.

In 1902 she returned to Bangor and married Price Ffoulkes White. Mrs Price White was an active worker in education and Liberal politics as well as women's suffrage. She was keenly interested in disarmament and once the vote had been won, became Chairman of the North Wales Women's Peace Council.

In 1926 she became the first woman to serve on Caernarfonshre County Council and was described as being diligent, an accomplished speaker and highly respected. She was a member of the North Wales Colleges and Bangor Local Governing Body, having been appointed chairman of the Committee of the County School for Girls shortly before her death. She died in 1932 and her obituary said 'By her untimely death, the city of Bangor has lost a vigorous and interesting personality'.

The family had intended her funeral to be private, but were so besieged with pleas to be allowed to attend, that the service was opened to the public and the English Presbyterian Chapel was packed. Such was the regard in which she was held that there were nearly 100 floral tributes and flags were at half-mast throughout the city.

Her son David qualified as a solicitor and later followed his mother into politics, being the Conservative MP for the Caernarfon Boroughs 1945-1950.

Mrs Gwladys HUDSON WILLIAMS (thirty-two) lived at Plas Tirion, College Road, with her husband **Thomas Andrew** (thirty-eight) professor of Greek (see Supporters) and their daughter **Ilid Hudson** (four) and sons **Alun** (three) and **Harri Llwyd** (one month).

They employed a nursemaid and general servant.

Miss Winifred H. WORTHAM (twenty-seven) could not

be found on the 1911 Census, but in 1901 she was living at 47 Rathbone Place, Marylebone, London, with her parents **Hale** (commercial clerk) and **Caroline**, sisters **Katharine** and **Ada** and brother **Hale**.

A Miss Winifred H. Wortham of Bangor's Department of Botany wrote an unpublished MA thesis relating to a Long Hut on Anglesey, which can now be found on the internet .

Bangor Supporters:

I couldn't find the **MILNER-BARRY**'s on the 1911 Census, but in 1901 they were at Mill Hill School, Hendon, Middlesex. (The ages given in Mrs Milner-Barry's entry are their ages in 1911). From the Mill Hill School Roll of Honour 1914-1919 I learned that **Edward Leopold MILNER-BARRY** gained a First Class Honours degree in modern languages at Cambridge and an MA at Bangor. From 1891-1907 he was a master and housemaster at Mill Hill School. Subsequently he was professor of German and Teutonic Philology at Bangor. During WW1 he was a Commissioned Royal Navy Volunteer Reserve Lieutenant-Commander and served on the east coast as an interpreter and naval intelligence officer. During his service he developed bronchitis and died in 1917.

Mrs Margaret BAYNE (fifty-five) or one of her daughters **Jenny** (thirty-two) or **Fanny** (eighteen) who lived at 8 Menai View Terrace, with her husband **William** (sixty-two) retired clothier and youngest daughter **Elsie** (fifteen).

They employed one general servant.

Miss CARTER, Normal College

Albert CHAPMAN (twenty-six) lecturer in Philosophy at Bangor, lived at Cooldaragh, with his wife **Gertrude** (twenty-eight) and son **Robert** (eight months).

Miss Dorothy CHAPMAN (thirty-two) warden of the Women's College Hostel.

Miss COLQUITT from Liverpool.

Rev. Thomas William WITTON DAVIES (sixty), widower, (father of Edith Maud) (see Officers) and professor of Hebrew at Bangor. In 1911 he married **Hilda Mabel Everett** and later had a son and another daughter.

Thomas Witton Davies was a remarkable man, born in 1851 to Edmund and Elisabeth Davis who, early in the 1850's moved their family from Nantyglo, Glamorgan, to the village of Witton near Bishop Auckland in order for Thomas's father and older brothers to find work. Edmund, who was a 'heater of an iron forge' could neither read nor write and Elisabeth had learned to read at Sunday School but had not learned to write. The only books in their home were *The Bible* and *Pilgrim's Progress*. By the time of the 1871 Census the Davis's had acquired an 'e' and become the Davies's and Thomas was listed as an ironworks labourer.

But Thomas had attended Sunday School, the Band of Hope and the Mutual Improvement Society and borrowed books from the Mechanic's Institute Library, as well as listening to his mother read out loud from the *Christian World* and the *British Worker*. Thomas had been baptised in the river Wear in 1863 and returned to Wales in 1872 to enrol at Haverfordwest Baptist College. He gained a BA from London, a PhD from Leipzig and became the first non-Anglican to be awarded a Doctorate of Divinity by Durham University.

He joined the staff of the South Wales Baptist College when the principal was also Dr Thomas Davies and so changed his name to Witton Davies, thus honouring the village and ironworks where he had been brought up and worked as a young man.

His son **Carlyle** Witton-Davies acquired a hyphen after his father's death, because, as his mother explained, 'there were a lot of Davies's in Bangor'. Carlyle was also a Hebrew scholar and archdeacon of Oxford for twenty-six years, noted for his flamboyance – wearing gaiters well into the 1960's.

Miss GADSBY, dancing teacher.

Miss Helen Winifred GASQUOINE (thirty-six) lived at St Oswald's, Victoria Drive, with her father **Thomas** (seventy-seven) Congregational Minister, mother **Helen Eliza** (sixty-two) and brother **Roland Hartley** (thirty-three) a solicitor.

They employed a cook and housemaid.

Mrs Margaret Beatrice GIBSON (forty-seven) was boarding at Plas Helig, Cricieth, with her husband **James** (forty-six) professor of Philosophy at Bangor.

Miss GODWIN/GOODWIN of Bryn Menai.

George GRIERSON (thirty-eight) laundry proprietor, and his wife **Anna** (thirty-four) lived at 42 College Road, with their daughter **Ethel Shorbridge** (eight) and son **Colin McKay** (four).

They employed one general servant.

Ethel JARVIS (thirty) a masseuse, of Glyn Menai.

Mrs Florence Lilian JARVIS (thirty-six) lived at 1 Gambier Terrace, with her husband **John Ivor** (thirty-eight) bookseller and stationer, and sons **Reginald Ivor** (thirteen), **Percival Hastings** (twelve) and **Leonard Alan** (two).

Sir Henry LEWIS (sixty-three) corn merchant and his wife **Lady Annie** (sixty) of Belmont, lived with their daughter **Nora** (twenty-six) (see Committee) and son **Roger** (twenty-four) a solicitor's clerk.

They employed a cook and housemaid.

Sir Henry Lewis was the son of Thomas Lewis, MP for Anglesey 1886-94 and founder of the corn business that Henry continued. Henry was educated at Friar's School and Bala Calvinistic Methodist College. He was a prominent Calvinistic Methodist and an influential supporter of the University.

Sir Henry and Lady Lewis entertained Mrs Pankhurst at Belmont in August 1910 after she had spoken at Caernarfon, on her tour of Wales. Sir Henry was reported to have 'much enjoyed her company'.

Mrs Margaret Anne MATTHEWS (fifty-six) lived with her husband **William Peter** (fifty-one) a flour agent, her son **William Henry Edward** (fifteen) and daughters **Mary May** (twenty-six) and **Evelyn Hodgson** (twenty-four).

Mrs Edith MCKIE (forty-six) lived at Castlebank, with her husband **William** (fifty-two) quarry clerk and daughters **Phyllis Violet** (seventeen) and **Muriel** (eight).

They employed one general servant.

Mrs Mary MUIR (forty-five) lived at 20 College Road, with her husband **Thomas** (forty-five) a draper's traveller, daughters **Madge** (twenty-one) and **Ivy** (fourteen), and sons **Richard** (eighteen) and **Thomas** (seventeen) – both draper's assistants, and **Norman** (sixteen), **Campbell** (five), Thomas's brother **Richard** (forty-three) a tailor, and aunt **Agnes Fleming** (seventy-one).

Mrs Annie ORTON (forty-two) lived at Llwyn Eithin Villa, with her husband **Kennedy Joseph** (thirty-nine) professor of Chemistry, daughters **Edith Mary** (twelve) and **Dilys Kathleen** (four) and son **William Kennedy** (nine).

They employed a Swiss governess, cook and two housemaids.

Miss Gaynor PHILLIPS (twenty) a student, lived at 2 Snowden Villas, with her parents **Reginald William** (fifty-six) professor of Botany and **Esther Lizzie** (fifty-two), and sisters **Gwendolen** (twenty-two) also a student and **Vera** (fourteen).

The family employed one general servant.

Miss Elizabeth Ann PRICE (fifty) a draper's shopkeeper, lived at 235 High Street, with her sister **Margaret** (sixty-nine) also a draper's shopkeeper.

Mrs Grace Louisa ROWLAND (forty) lived at Hafodunos, with her husband **John Owen** (forty-five) retired petroleum traveller, son **Glyn Venmore** (eighteen) a student and daughter **Enid** (sixteen).

They employed one general servant.

Mrs Mary ROWLAND (forty-nine) lived at 3 Arvonia Buildings, High Street, with her husband **William Huw** (forty-seven) solicitor, and sons **Peredur** (twenty) a student, **Glyn** (eighteen) electrical apprentice and **Ronald** (twelve).

Mrs Flora Annie STEEL (neé **WEBSTER**) (sixty-four) authoress, lived at Talgarth Hall, Pennal, Machynlleth, with her husband **Henry** (seventy-one) retired civil servant (India), and grandsons **Patrick** (seven) and **Neil Webster** (four).

They employed a housemaid, parlourmaid, kitchenmaid, laundrymaid and general maid.

Flora was born in 1847 in Harrow, daughter of George Webster, a Scottish MP based in London, later Sheriff Clerk of Forfarshire and Isabella MacCallum Webster, an heiress to property in Jamaica.

Flora and her ten siblings were educated at home. At the age of ten she and her family moved back to Scotland – but not before she had met her future husband, Henry William Steel, who went on to join the Indian Civil Service.

After her marriage Flora lived in India for twenty-two years, mainly in the Punjab. Her husband was not very strong and whenever he was ill she took over some of his responsibilities – as a schools inspector and mediator in local disputes.

From the outset Mrs Steel was interested in all classes of Indian society and the birth of her daughter gave her the opportunity to interact with local women and learn their language. In 1884 she published a collection of their folk tales which she had avidly collected. She also encouraged the production of local handicrafts. Mrs Steel was a prolific writer and produced some thirty books: five volumes of short stories set in India and one volume set in Scotland; numerous novels about life in India and a few with a background in Britain; five historical novels set in India – probably the best-known being *On the Face of the Waters*, set at the time of the Indian Mutiny and Cawnpore Massacre and numerous children's books illustrated by no less a personage than Arthur Rackham. Her writing was favourably compared with that of Rudyard Kipling.

Several of her titles are still available, most notably *The Complete Indian Housekeeper and Cook*, which she co-authored with Grace Gardiner. Originally published in 1888, this volume was intended to provide practical advice to young memsahibs and was reissued as recently as 2010!

Although Mrs Steel could justifiably be considered part of 'The Raj', she had nothing but contempt for those English women who refused to adapt to the Indian way of life and was deeply troubled when she saw Indians being influenced by English customs.

Mrs Steel also published a pamphlet on women's rights and what is described as a 'vivid' unfinished autobiography *The Garden of Fidelity*, started when she was eighty – and published posthumously.

Flora Steel died at her daughter's home in Gloucestershire in 1928.

Mrs Gwendoline Chenevix TRENCH (forty-one) lived in Lime Grove, with her husband **Richard** (forty-nine) estate agent and son **Hugo** (twenty) a land agency student.

They employed a cook, housemaid, parlourmaid and kitchenmaid.

Mrs Bronwen Adelaide VINCENT (forty-one) lived at Bronwydd, with her husband **Hugh Corbet** (forty-eight) a solicitor and three times Mayor of Bangor, and daughters **Margaret Althea** (ten), **Mary Lilian** (seven), **Caroline Elizabeth** (five) and **Pamela Olive** (three).

They employed a cook, two nursemaids and a housemaid.

or **Miss Mary VINCENT** (fifty-one) (private means), lived at Treborth Uchaf, with her brother **Augustus** (forty-one) (also private means).

Professor Thomas Andrew HUDSON WILLIAMS (thirty-eight) professor of Greek at Bangor (see **Mrs Gwladys Hudson Williams**, Committee)

Harry Almond Saille WORTLEY (twenty-five) lecturer in Education at Bangor, boarding at Plas Menai.

Appendix F

Penmaenmawr
founded March 1911

Officers:

Miss Annie HARKER (forty-six) (private means) was Secretary and lived at Glanafon, with her widowed mother **Ann** (seventy-four) (private means) and sister **Catherine** (forty-eight) (also private means).

They employed a cook and housemaid.

Mrs Margaret Wood JENKINS (thirty-seven) President, lived at Tan y Berllan, Dwygyfylchi, with her husband **Dr Herbert Thomas Jenkins**, physician and surgeon.

They employed a cook and housemaid.

Penmaenmawr Supporters:

Mrs Augusta COXON (forty-one) lived at Winthrop Villa, Llanfairfechan, with her husband **Guy** (forty-five) (private means).

Charles DARBISHIRE (sixty-six) managing director of the family's quarry, lived at Plas Mawr, with his wife **Mary Lilian** (fifty-eight), daughter **Ada** (twenty-seven), son **Henry Watkin** (thirty-one), daughter-in-law **Muriel Bertha** (thirty-two) and grandsons **Donald Watkin** (eight), **Roy Levers** (five) and **Anthony** (two).

They employed a nursemaid, cook, waitress and two housemaids.

Mrs Laura Mary HELBY (sixty-one) purser on mail steamers and boarding-house keeper, lived at Plas y Glyn, with her husband **William** (sixty-three) also purser on mail steamers and boarding-house keeper, or one of her twin daughters **Laura** or **Ellen** (twenty-three).

They employed one general servant.

Miss Mabel POLLARD (thirty-two) art mistress at Vonhenlof School.

Miss Annie POTTER (forty-nine) companion to Miss Agnes Darbishire (seventy-one) (private means) of Plas Celyn.

Mrs Mary RHODES (fifty-six) matron at Merton House School, owned by her husband **William** (sixty-four). They lived their with their son **John Edgar** (twenty-nine) a tutor and **Mrs Helen McLaine** (fifty-five) (private means), Mary's widowed sister.

They employed a cook and housemaid.

Miss Hilda Myfanwy ROBERTS (twenty-one) lived at Glan Eigion, The Esplanade, with her father **David** (fifty-eight) quarry company clerk and mother *Mary Louisa* (forty-nine).

Appendix G

Caernarfon
founded 1909

Officers:

Secretary: **Miss Louisa REES** (forty-two) lived at Plas Brereton, with her father **Griffith Roberts** (sixty) retired bank manager, mother **Elizabeth Rumsey** (seventy-one), sisters **Margaret Elizabeth** (forty-three), **Annie Jane** (forty-one), **Isabella** (forty) and **Nesta Beatrix** (twenty-seven).

They employed a cook, waitress and housemaid.

She was followed by **Mrs Mary EVANS** (thirty-six) who lived at Brynafon, with her husband **David** (thirty-eight) an electrical engineer and two daughters **Margaret Davies** (six) and **Joan Lloyd** (one).

They employed one servant.

Mrs Evans held the post jointly with:

Miss Ryle DAVIES of Cartrefle, Segontium Road (whom I've not been able to trace on the census).

Bethesda – founded circa 1911

Officer:

In 1913 **Miss Agnes Marian HUWS** (twenty-five) of 17 Ogwen Terrace, was the Secretary. She was the daughter of **Rev. J. Rhys Huws** and his wife **Anne** (fifty-five). Rhys

Hughes does not appear on the 1911 Census, but it is not known whether he was simply away from home on Census night, or deceased.

Cricieth – founded 1911

Officers:

Secretary: **Mrs Annie JONES** (twenty-nine) lived at Emu, Llanystumdwy, with her husband **Walter** (thirty-five) an Estate Agent.

They employed one servant.

Pwllheli – founded 1911

Officers:

Secretary: **Mrs D. H. WILLIAMS** of Arden, Cardiff Road (whom I've been unable to trace on the Census).

The March of the Women

Sung by the north Wales Suffragists at their meetings and frequently on their 1913 Pilgrimage.

Shout, shout, up with your song!
Cry with the wind, for the dawn is breaking;
March, march, swing you along,
Wide blows our banner, and hope is waking.
Song with its story, dreams with their glory
Lo! They call, and glad is their word!
Loud and louder it swells
Thunder of freedom, the voice of the Lord!

Long, long – we in the past
Cowered in dread from the light of heaven,
Strong, strong – stand we at last,
Fearless in faith and with sight new given.
Strength with its beauty, Life with its duty,
(Hear the voice, oh hear and obey!)
These, these – beckon us on!
Open your eyes to the blaze of day.

Comrades – ye who have dared
First in the battle to strive and sorrow!
Scorned, spurned – nought have ye cared,
Raising your eyes to a wider morrow,
Ways that are weary, days that are dreary,
Toil and pain by faith ye have borne;
Hail, hail – victors ye stand,
Wearing the wreath that the brave have worn.

Life, strife – those two are one,
Naught can ye win but by faith and daring.
On, on – ye that have done
But for the work of today preparing.
Firm in reliance, laugh a defiance,
(Laugh in hope, for sure is the end)
March, march – many as one,
Shoulder to shoulder and friend to friend.

Words: Cicely Hamilton   Music: Ethel Smyth

Postscript

For those of you who are 'on the net', please go to 'YouTube', type in 'March of the Women' and look at the tribute to the Women's Movement by American, Professor Mark Lause, Lecturer at the University of Cincinatti.

You'll see Ethel Smyth, herself a Suffragette (and close friend of Mrs Pankhurst) who wrote the music for 'The March of the Women' and Cicely Hamilton who wrote the words.

In the early 1960's Sir Brian Harrison recorded the memories of as many Suffragettes as he could find. In 2012, fifty years after he completed his work, some of the tapes were included in a Radio 4 programme about his project. One of the most moving was by a woman who described walking up to Holloway with her friends in the evenings, carrying lanterns, standing outside the prison singing: 'March, march, many as one; shoulder to shoulder and friend to friend' and seeing Ethel Smyth appear at the high window of her cell, having climbed up onto a chair to conduct them with her toothbrush!

Acknowledgements:

I wish to thank the following:

My husband John, for his patience, encouragement, proof reading and preparation of the photographs.

Myrddin ap Dafydd at Carreg Gwalch for his enthusiasm
for this project.
Dr Jen Llywelyn for her 'light touch' with editing.
Mererid Jones for her skill in typesetting the book exactly
as I'd hoped.

Gaynor Davies for her help and information re Agnes Huws.
Michael Hovey for his help and the information re Ethel
and Rosa Hovey.
David Price for his help and information re Bangor.
Angharad Rhys Williams for her help and information
re Dr Helena Jones.
Ros Dudley at Colwyn Town Council and Sarah Ritchie at
Rydal-Penrhos for their help with locating photographs of
the Misses Hovey.

Susan Ellis, Leila Fillingham, Gary Jones, Oliver Tickner
and volunteer, Haydn Mather at Conwy Archives
for their interest and repeatedly bringing out large, heavy,
bound volumes of newspapers for me.

The Staff at
Bangor University Archives
Gwynedd Archives, Caernarfon
and Rhyl Library.

Photographic Credits:

I wish to thank the following:

Peter Brindley for his kind permission to print the
photograph of the Queen's Head Café, Bangor

Colwyn Bay Council for permission to print the
photograph of Ethel Hovey

Conwy County Archives at Llandudno for permission
to print the photograph of
Llandudno Ladies' Temperance Society

Liverpool University for permission to print the
photograph of Eleanor Rathbone.

The Museum of London for permission to print the
photographs of Welsh Suffragettes in traditional costume,
Photographic Portrait of Emmeline Pankhurst
and
the Funeral of Emily Wilding Davison

Llyfrgell Genedlaethol Cymru – The National Library of
Wales for permission to print the photograph of
a Suffragette at Llanystumdwy

The National Portrait Gallery for permission to print the
photograph of
(Susan) Edith Champneys

Rydal-Penrhos for permission to print the photograph of
Rosa Hovey

Bibliography:

Local newspapers 1907-1914:
The Bangor and Denbigh Herald
The Llandudno Advertiser
The North Wales Chronicle and Advertiser
The North Wales Coast Pioneer
The North Wales Weekly News
The Rhyl Record

The Minute Book of the Bangor NUWSS
held at Bangor University Archives

The Women's Suffrage Movement – a Reference Guide 1866-1928 Elizabeth Crawford
The Women's Suffrage Movement in Britain and Ireland Elizabeth Crawford

Bangor 1883-1982 A Study in Municipal Government Peter Ellis Jones
Colwyn Bay 1934-1974 Geoffrey Edwards
Enterprise in Soap and Chemicals – Joseph Crosfield & Sons Ltd. 1815-1965 A. E. Musson
My Aunt Edith – The Story of a Preston Suffragette Phoebe Hesketh
Penrhos 1880-1930 Rosa Hovey
Penrhos College-the Second Fifty Years M. Beardsworth
'Your Obedient Servant' – The History of an Historic Welsh Estate George Hiller

Article: *The Women's Suffrage Movement in Caernarfonshire* Peter Ellis Jones, published in *Caernarfonshire Historical Society Transactions No 48*, 1987

Index

Double-barrelled names are indexed under the 2nd part of the name.

ABERCONWY, Lady 125
ABERGELE 141, App C
ADABAN, Miss 161
ALLEN, Miss Daisy (*Colwyn Bay*) 64, 242
ALLEN, Mr Daniel (*Colwyn Bay*) 64
ALLEN, Mr Edward (*Colwyn Bay*) 242
ANDRESS, Miss Alice (*Colwyn Bay*) 64, 91, 242
ANDREWS, Miss (*Colwyn Bay*) 233
ANKERS, Mrs Fru 133, 136, 137, 138, 186
ANTI-SUFFRAGE LEAGUE 22, 27, 118, 122, 127, 153
CORBETT-**ASHBY**, Mrs Margery 119, 129, 186
ASHTON, Councillor Miss Margaret 24, 25, 70, 115, 142, 144, 145, 146, 147, 186-7
ASQUITH, Mr Herbert MP 18, 21, 29, 41, 60, 84, 85, 89, 90, 91, 106, 147, 189, 203
AYLES, Miss Alice (*Colwyn Bay*) 233

BAKER, Miss (*Bangor*) 156
BAKER, Mr E. (*Bangor*) 74
BALFOUR, Lady Frances 43, 44, 45, 137, 187, 203
BAMFORD, Miss Alice (*Llandudno*) 219
BANGOR 15, 41, 42, 47, 53, 55, 56, 57, 60, 62, 63, 66, 67, 68, 69, 71, 72, 74, 80, 88, 91, 92, 93, 97, 98, 100, 103, 104, 107, 110, 111, 112, 116, 118, 123, 124, 125, 127, 129, 130, 133, 137, 138, 153, 154, 155, 156, 159, 160, 164, 168, 169, 170, 171, 172, 173, 174, 175, 185, App E
BANGOR MEN'S SOCIETY FOR WOMEN'S SUFFRAGE 63
BARBRIDGE 142
BARFIELD, Miss Amy (*Colwyn Bay*) 233
BARKER, Miss (*Llandudno*) 16
BARKER, Mr John (*Colwyn Bay*) 64, 242
BARKER, Mrs Sarah (*Colwyn Bay*) 233
BARLOW, Lady 53, 78
BARRETT, Miss Rachel 72, 81, 82, 83, 85, 187-8
BARRY, Miss 34
MILNER-**BARRY**, Prof. E. (*Bangor*) 74, 93, 137, 251
MILNER-**BARRY**, Mrs Edith (*Bangor*) 116, 129, 159, 248
MILNER-**BARRY**, Master Walter (*Bangor*) 74
BATES, Miss (*Colwyn Bay*) 243
BAYNE, Mrs Margaret/Misses Jennie/Fanny (*Bangor*) 251
BEAVAN, Miss (*Bangor*) 129
BELL, Mr Fred (*Rhyl*) 65
BENNETT, Miss Mabel (*Llandudno*) 88, 225
BESANT, Miss Annie 81
BEST, Miss Jessie (*Rhyl*) 228
BEST, Miss Mabel (*Colwyn Bay*) 243
BETHESDA 69, 71, 92, 93, 130, 261, App G

BEVAN, Mr George (*Colwyn Bay*) 243
BEVINGTON, Mr E. (*Rhyl*) 65
BIRKENHEAD NUWSS 144
BIRMINGHAM 145
BLAKE, Dr. Lilian (*Colwyn Bay*) 53, 57, 62, 64, 95, 96, 101, 102, 134, 137, 233-4
BONE, Councillor Ernest (*Llandudno*) 17, 18, 96, 219-20
BOWES, Miss (*Llandudno*) 38
BRAILSFORD, Mr Henry 57, 60
BREESE, Mr C. (*Porthmadog*) 81
BRITISH WOMEN'S TEMPERANCE ASSOCIATION 11, 103, 117, 118, 161
BROCK, Mrs Sarah (*Colwyn Bay*) 94, 243
de BROKE, Lord & Lady Willoughby 146
BROMLEY, Mrs Edith (*Rhyl*) 74, 142, 228
BROOKES, Mr William (*Llandudno*) 18, 220
BROWN, Miss 65
LEADLEY-BROWN, Miss Cicely 145
BROWNE, Miss Millicent 36, 38, 188
BRYANT & MAY'S MATCH GIRLS 205
BURSLEM 143, 144
BURTON, Mr Richard 191

CAERNARFON 34, 41, 42, 45, 47, 55, 56, 63, 66, 92, 104, 110, 127, 138, 153, App G
CAFÉ ROYAL, COLWYN BAY 46, 95, 106, 115, 116

CARSON, Sir Edward MP & Lady 171
CARTER, Miss (*Bangor*) 151
CAT & MOUSE ACT 188, 189, 200
CHAD, Miss 100
CHAMBERLAIN, Mr Reginald (*Llandudno*) 220
CHAMPNEYS, Miss Lucy (*Llandudno*) 14, 24, 216
CHAMPNEYS, Miss (Susan) Edith (*Llandudno*) 13, 17, 216
CHAPMAN, Mr Albert (*Bangor*) 74, 252
CHAPMAN, Miss Dorothy (*Bangor*) 74, 252
CHARNLEY, Miss Ethel/Miss Daisy (*Colwyn Bay*) 234
CHEETHAM, Councillor (*Rhyl*) 108
CHERRY, Miss Sarah (*Rhyl*) 228
CHESTER 142
CHURCH LEAGUE FOR WOMEN' SUFFRAGE (*CLWS*) 145, 173,, 211
CHURCHILL, Lord Randolph 122
CHURCHILL, Mr Winston MP 41, 67, 122
CLAPHAM, Mr 144, 150
CLARK, Dr Gordon 53
CLARKSON, Miss 39
CLAYTON, Miss (*Colwyn Bay*) 120
CLOUGH, Mrs Annie/Mrs Catherine (*Rhyl*) 228
COCOA HOUSE, LLANDUDNO 10, 12, 221
COHEN, Mrs Leonora 125, 126, 128, 189-90
COLWYN BAY 33, 34, 35, 36, 37, 46, 51, 52, 53, 54, 57, 62,

64, 65, 67, 79, 81, 85, 87, 89, 90, 92, 94, 95, 96, 100, 101, 102, 104, 106, 111, 115, 116, 117, 119, 121, 123, 128, 134, 136, 137, 153, 154, 155, 158, 159, 161, 165, 166, 176, 177, 179, 180, 181, 182, 183, App D

COLWYN BAY SUFFRAGE SHOP 96, 101

COMPTON VERNEY 146

CONWY 26, 28, 29, 30, 32, 33, 35, 37, 38, 47, 132, 140, 172

COULTER, Miss Dorothy (*Colwyn Bay*) 57

COXON, Mrs Augusta (*Llanfairfechan/Penmaenmawr*) 160, 259

CRAGGS, Miss Helen 200

CRAIG, Miss Barbara (*Llandudno*) 217

CRAIG-Y-DON BOARDING ESTABLISHMENT, LLANDUDNO 15, 23, 51, 64, 223

CRICIETH 55, 56, 92, 113, 138, App G

CROMER, Lord 58, 85

CROSFIELD, Miss (*Colwyn Bay*) 87, 90, 91, 94, 100, 101, 120, 154, 169, 234, 235, 236

CROSFIELD, Mrs (*Colwyn Bay*) 87, 136, 234, 235

CROSFIELD'S SOAP MANUFACTURERS, WARRINGTON 87, 235

CURZON, Lord 158

CYMRIC UNION, LONDON 30

DARBISHIRE, Colonel Charles (*Penmaenmawr*) 68, 160, 163, 259

DAVIES, Mrs Conan (*Bangor*) 159

DAVIES, Mrs Dingad (*Bangor*) 159

DAVIES, Mrs Emily (*Llandudno*) 220

DAVIES, Mr Henry (*Tal-y-Bont*) 153

DAVIES, Mr J. O. (*Colwyn Bay*) 52

DAVIES, Mrs N. (*Caernarfon*) 55

DAVIES, Councillor Percy (*Abergele*) 134

RYLE-**DAVIES**, Miss (*Caernarfon*) 261

VAUGHAN-**DAVIES**, Mrs (*Bangor*) 88

WITTON-**DAVIES**, Miss Edith (*Bangor*) 155, 156, 165, 170, 248

WITTON-**DAVIES**, Prof. Rev. Thomas (*Bangor*) 93, 252-3

WILDING-**DAVISON**, Miss Emily 131, 134, 190

DAWSON, Mr J. Roger (*Llandudno*) 24, 221

DEACON, Dr Mary (*Colwyn Bay*) 121, 161, 236

DEAKIN, Miss Evelyn 87, 116

DEARDEN, Mrs Isabella (*Llandudno*) 88, 217

DEGANWY 177, 178

DESPARD, Mrs Charlotte 84, 204

DREYER, Miss Emmie (*Llandudno*) 217

DRIFFIELD, Mr (*Colwyn Bay*) 101

DUFF, Dr (*Colwyn Bay*) 102

DUNDONALD, Earl & Countess 131

EAKIN, Miss Marie-Louise (*Llandudno*) 13, 24, 57, 217
EALES, Colonel (*Colwyn Bay*) 243
EARP, Mrs 142
EARP, William (*Colwyn Bay*) 244
EDGELL, Mrs (*Llandudno*) 13
EDWARDS, Miss Alice (*Rhyl*) 74
EDWARDS, Bishop of St. Asaph 43, 45 & Mrs 43
EDWARDS, Miss Gwalyn (*Bangor*) 156
ELCOCK Mrs Agnes (*Colwyn Bay*) 101, 236
ELCOCK Mr Charles (*Colwyn Bay*) 102, 115, 116, 243-4, 246
ELLIOTT, Miss 40
WOLSTENHOLME-ELMY, Mrs Elizabeth 80
ESKRIGGE, Miss Edith 65, 67, 68, 71-2, 73, 98, 101, 102, 129, 130, 134, 136, 145, 192
EVANS, Mr Evan William (*Dolgellau*) 114-15
EVANS, Councillor Llew (*Rhyl*) 108
EVANS, Mrs Mary (*Caernarfon*) 261
EVANS, W. Police Constable (*Colwyn Bay*) 179
WALTON-EVANS, Miss Ana Decima (*Llandudno*) 24
WALTON-EVANS, Mrs Annie (*St Asaph*) 12, 14, 19, 20, 28, 43, 50, 51, 136, 217
WALTON-EVANS, Miss Annie Beatrice (*Llandudno*) 14, 20, 21, 22, 23, 24, 218
(WALTON)-EVANS Archdeacon David (*St Asaph*) 12, 217, 218

FAIRBROTHER, Mr 149, 150
FAWCETT, Mr Henry MP 192, 193
FAWCETT, Miss Jane (*Llandudno*) 217, 218
GARRETT-FAWCETT, Mrs Millicent 15, 51, 52, 70, 81, 90, 105, 125, 157, 158, 192, 193, 233
GARRETT-FAWCETT, Miss Philippa 193
FELL, Mr (*Rhyl*) 65
FISHER, Mr Ralph (*Deganwy*) 221
FLATMAN, Miss (Susan) Ada 60, 61, 193, 194, 203, 221, 232
FLEET, Mrs Margaret (*Colwyn Bay*) 64, 244
FRANCIS, Miss (*Rhyl*) 39
FRASER, Miss Helen 157, 163, 164, 165, 172, 173, 194, 195
FRIMSTON, Mr J. (*Rhyl*) 43

GADSBY, Miss (*Bangor*) 130, 133, 253
GARRS, Mr Tom 195, 196
GASQUOINE, Miss Helen (*Bangor*) 253
GAUNT, Mrs Annie (*Bangor*) 124, 248
GAWTHORPE, Miss Mary 15, 28, 30, 31, 32, 33, 34, 35, 38, 47, 195-6, 197, 212
LLOYD-GEORGE, Mrs 73
LLOYD-GEORGE, Mr David MP 23, 29, 30, 32, 33, 38, 41, 42, 45, 48, 49, 50, 55, 56, 57, 60, 63, 66, 67, 81, 84, 85, 90, 99, 104, 106, 110, 111, 112, 113, 114, 117, 155, 182, 202, 205, 208, 209, 227
LLOYD-GEORGE, Miss Megan 185

GIBBS, Miss, 66
GIBSON, Prof. James (*Bangor*) 93
GIBSON, Mrs Margaret (*Bangor*) 253
GITTINS, Miss Ada (*Abergele*) 232
GLAN CONWY 174, 175, 177, 270
GODWIN/GOODWIN, Miss (*Bryn Menai, Anglesey*) 253
GOLDSTEIN, Miss Vida 86, 87, 196-7
GOODDY, Dr Edward (*Llandudno*) 21, 23, 24, 25, 43
GOODDY, Mrs Mary (*Llandudno*) 12, 14, 24, 50, 218
GOODWIN, Miss (*Bangor*) 156
GOODWIN, Dr Wycliffe (*Rhyl*) 24, 26, 228
GORNA, Barbara 191
GREAT ORME 177
GREY, Sir Edward MP 90, 111
GRIERSON, Mrs Anna (*Bangor*) 129, (253)
GRIERSON, Mr George (*Bangor*) 253
GUEST, Miss (*Colwyn Bay*) 101, 236-7
GUEST, Mrs (*Colwyn Bay*) 236-7
GUEST, Dr Edith (*Llandudno*) 14, 54, 55, 218

HALDANE, Lord 120
HALL, Miss E. (*Colwyn Bay*) 54, 244-5
HALL, Miss Leslie 61, 197, 203
HANLEY, 144
HARDIE, Mr Kier MP 198
HAREFIELD, Miss 164
HARKER, Miss Annie (*Penmaenmawr*) 109, 161, 163, 259

HARRISON, Sir Brian 119, 231, 264
HARSENT, Mrs Florence (*Colwyn Bay*) 245
HARTLEY, Miss Mary/Ruth (*Bangor*) 47, 248
HASLAM, Mrs Anna Maria 112, 140
HASLAM, Mr Thomas 112, 140
HAYES, Miss 37, 40, 41
HAYES, Police Inspector (*Rhyl*) 39
HAMMERSLEY-HEENAN, Mr (*Colwyn Bay*) 166, 237
HAMMERSLEY-HEENAN, Mrs Ada (*Colwyn Bay*) 94, (237)
HELBY, Mrs Laura (*Penmaenmawr*) 137, 259
HESSELL, Miss 117, 118
HEWITT, Miss 40
HIGH WYCOMBE 149
HIRAEL INFANT'S SCHOOL (*Bangor*) 173
HOLME, Miss Vera 86, 207
HORNSBY, Mr John (*Llandudno*) 221
HOVEY, Miss Ethel (*Colwyn Bay*) 46, 65, 121, 168, 184, 238-9
HOVEY, Miss Rosa (*Colwyn Bay*) 46, 52, 53, 57, 62, 65, 66, 115, 117, 136, 183, 238, 239-40-41
HOWARD, Colonel & Mrs (*Rhyl*) 43, 45
HUBBACK, Mrs Eva 186
HUBBARD, Rev. (*Conwy*) 31
HUBBARD, Mr Charles (*Rhyl*) 65, 229
HUBBARD, Miss Louie (*Rhyl*) 74
HUGHES, Miss (*Bangor*)
HUGHES, Miss 129

HUGHES, Mrs (*Bangor*) 113
HUGHES, Councillor Gwilym
(*Colwyn Bay*) 39
HUGHES, Miss H. (*Bangor*) 125
HUGHES, Miss H. (*Rhyl*) 74
HUGHES, Mrs H. O. (*Bangor*)
130, 164, 173
HUGHES, Mr John (*Conwy*) 32
HUGHES, Mr T. Arthur
(*Colwyn Bay*) 128
REEVES-HUGHES, Mrs Sarah
(*Llandudno*) 10, 12, 221
HUMPHREYS, Mr George
(*Llandudno*) 221-2
HUNTER, Mrs Caroline/Louie
(*Llandudno*) 222
HUTTON, Mrs Beatrice (*Rhyl*)
141, 229
HUWS, Miss Agnes (*Bethesda*)
92, 261
HUWS, Rev. J. Rhys (*Bethesda*)
92, 261

JACKSON, Miss Alice (*Colwyn
Bay*) 168, 245
JAMES, Mr (*Rhyl*) 65
JARVIS, Miss Ethel (*Bangor*)
253
JARVIS, Mrs Florence (*Bangor*)
254
JENKINS, Dr Herbert
(*Penmaenmawr*) 139, 259
JENKINS, Mrs Margaret
(*Penmaenmawr*) 139, 160,
161, 163, 259
JOHN, Miss 37
JOHN, Mr E. T. MP 171
JOHNSTONE, Miss M. (*Colwyn
Bay*) 64
FFOULKES-JONES, Mrs
(*Bangor*) 125, 129
JONES, Police Constable
(*Llanrwst*) 132

JONES, Mrs Annie (*Cricieth*)
262
JONES, Miss Bessie
(*Newborough*) 41, 42
JONES, Dr Helena 28, 41, 47,
55, 197
JONES, Iorwerth Police
Constable (*Colwyn Bay*) 179
JONES, Isgoed (*Llanrwst*) 41
JONES, Mrs J. D. (*Bangor*) 159,
173
JONES, Mr Jonathan (*St Asaph/
Rhyl*) 62
JONES, Prof. Lewis (*Bangor*) 93
JONES, Mr R. P. (*Anglesey*) 42
JONES, Rev. Verrier (*Rhyl*) 24,
25, 43
JONES, Mr William MP 68, 108
JONES, Miss Winnie (*Colwyn
Bay*) 57
PUGHE-JONES, Miss
(*Anglesey*) 98
ROWLAND-JONES, Mrs Hugh
(*Bangor*) 156, 159

KEEBLE, Mr Cyril (*Colwyn Bay*)
64, 245
KEEBLE, Mrs Jessie
(*Llandudno*) 88, 177, 218, 222
KEEBLE, Rev. Samuel
(*Llandudno*) 88, 97, 218, 222
KENNEY, Miss Annie 206
KENYON, Miss Elizabeth
(*Colwyn Bay*) 46, 57, 62, 64,
101, 102, 107, 116, 121, 154,
121
KING GEORGE V & QUEEN
MARY 201
KNOWLE 145

LAMPORT, Miss Evelyn
(*Bangor*) 95, 96, 97, 124, 130,
170, 248

LAWRENCE, Mrs Annie (*Rhyl Suffragette*) 194, 231, 232
PETHICK-LAWRENCE, Mrs Emmeline 29, 198, 199, 200, 202
PETHICK-LAWRENCE, Mr Frederick 61, 198, 199, 200, 202
LEAMINGTON 145
LEES, Miss Marjory 144, 145, 146, 148, 149, 150, 150, 151, 200, 201
LEES, Dame Sarah 150, 151, 200, 201
St LEGER, Mrs Clara (*Penrhynside/Colwyn Bay*) 57, 64, 246
LEONARD Mr (*Conwy/Llandudno*) 172
LEVER, Sir William *later* Lord LEVERHULME 210
LEWIS, Lady (*Bangor*) 56, 125, 129, 138, 254
LEWIS, Sir Henry (*Bangor*) 30, 56, 93, 110, 138, 254
LEWIS, Miss Nora (*Bangor*) 56, 164, 169, 170, 249
LINCOLN, Abraham 209
LIVERPOOL branch WOMEN'S FREEDOM LEAGUE 15, 35, 36, 40, 41, 42, 45, 47, 49, 55, 80, 212
LLANDUDNO 10, 11, 12, 14, 15, 16, 17, 19, 20, 22, 23, 24, 25, 26, 33, 34, 35, 38, 41, 43, 50, 51, 54, 58, 63, 64, 81, 85, 86, 88, 92, 93, 96, 100, 102, 104, 11, 124, 136, 137, 140, 156, 157, 172, 174, 176, 177, 210 App B
LLANDUDNO ANTI SUFFRAGE LEAGUE 22
LLANDUDNO LADIES TEMPERANCE SOCIETY 10

LLANRWST 40, 132
LLANYSTUMDWY 112, 114
LLOYD, Mr Joseph (*Rhyl*) 62, 230
LLOYD, Rev. Thomas (*Colwyn Bay*) 102, 246
LLOYD, Mrs Thomas (*Colwyn Bay*) 102, 121, 246
LLŶN 81
LLYSFAEN 141
LUCAS, Mrs Bernard (*Colwyn Bay*) 246
LYTTON, Earl of 203
LYTTON, Lady Constance - *aka Miss Jane Wharton* 60, 61, 62, 202, 203, 204

MANNING, Miss 35, 37, 40, 41
MARKS, Mrs Elsie (*Llandudno*) 17, 24, 111, 219
MARKS, Councillor James (*Llandudno*) 20, 81, 102, 219, 222
MARSDEN, Mrs Mary/Miss Minnie (*Llandudno*) 222
MARTIN, Miss Selina 61, 202, 203
MASON, Miss Dora 153, 204
MATCH GIRLS 81, 205
MATTERS, Miss Muriel 47, 49, 125, 128, 146, 154, 204-5, 212
MATTHEWS, Miss Evelyn (*Bangor*) 124, 130, 138, 155, 156, 159, 165, 169, 249
MATTHEWS, Mrs Margaret (*Bangor*) 254
McKIE, Mrs Edith (*Bangor*) 254
McLAREN, Lady Laura (*Eglwysbach*) 26, 224, 227
McPHERSON, Miss 89, 107
MEREDITH, Mrs Emma (*Llandudno*) 223

MEREDITH, Miss Gwladys (*Colwyn Bay*) 82
MIDDLETON, Miss Edith (*Llandudno*) 23, 52, 223
MILL, Mr John Stuart MP 192, 193
MOCHDRE 158, 177, 247, 270
MOIR, Miss Cordelia 119, 127, 128
MONTGOMERY, Mr Charles (*Llandudno*) 156, 223
MORRIS, Miss Edith (*Colwyn Bay*) 246
MORRIS, Miss Margaret (*Colwyn Bay*) 246
MOTTRAM, Mr 149, 150
MOULD, Mrs Edith (*Colwyn Bay*) 121, 241
MANSELL-MOULLIN, Mrs Edith 30
MUIR, Mrs Mary (*Bangor*) 254

NANTWICH 143
NATIONAL LEAGUE OPPOSING WOMEN'S SUFFRAGE (NLOWS) 93, 127, 129
NEFYN 81
NEWBOROUGH (*Anglesey*) 41
NUNN, Mr Francis (*Colwyn Bay*) 67, 158, 159, 242
NUNN, Mrs Margaret, Anti-Suffragist (*Colwyn Bay*) 158, 159, 242

OLD COLWYN 141, 177
OLDHAM, Mr Norman (*Colwyn Bay*) 246
OLDHAM NUWSS 144, 145, 147, 149, 150, 201
OLDMAN, Mrs Kate (*Deganwy*) 223

ORTON, Mrs Annie (*Bangor*) 74, 255
ORTON, Miss Edith (*Bangor*) 74
ORTON, Prof. Previte (*Bangor*) 93, 255
ORTON, Master Will (*Bangor*) 74
OWEN, Mr (*Colwyn Bay*) 36
OWEN, Evan (*Colwyn Bay*) 244
OXFORD 147, 148, 164

PANKHURST, Miss Adela 194, 195, 197, 205, 207
PANKHURST, Miss Christabel (Estelle) 187, 194, 199, 200, 205, 206, 207, 208
PANKHURST, Mrs Emmeline 15, 55, 56, 72, 73, 81, 82, 83, 84, 85, 86, 90, 123, 141, 182, 194, 199, 205-9, 232, 245, 254, 264
PANKHURST, Dr Richard 205-6
PANKHURST, Miss Sylvia 205, 207
PARRY, Mr Jacob (*Bethesda*) 92
PENMAENMAWR 35, 68, 69, 71, 86, 130, 137, 138, 163, 172, 176, 181, App F
PENRHYNSIDE 177, 270
PEN-Y-GROES 92, 138
PERKS, Miss Florence (*Rhyl*) 24, 43, 227
PHILIPPS, Mrs Leonora (Nora), Lady St David's 54
PHILLIPS, Mrs (*Penmaenmawr*) 68, 108, 109
PHILLIPS, Miss Gaynor (*Bangor*) 156, 255
PINKERTON, Miss Kate (*Bangor*) 124, 129, 156, 249
POCHIN, Mrs Agnes (*Bodnant*) 223

POCHIN, Mr Henry (*Bodnant*) 223, 227

POLLARD, Miss Mabel (*Penmaenmawr*) 47, 260

PORTER, Mr John (*Colwyn Bay*) 95, 244, 246

POTTER, Miss Annie (*Penmaenmawr*) 260

PRESTATYN 142

PRICE, Miss Elizabeth (*Bangor*) 255

PRICE, Mrs Emma (*Bangor*) 249

PRICE, Dr Emyr (*Bangor*) 74, 249

PRICE, Mrs G. O. (*Bangor*) 129, 130, 159, 164, 173

PRITCHARD, Councillor J. (*Llandudno*) 174

PUGH, Mr Alfred (*Llandudno*) 14, 26, 50, 219

PWLLHELI 50, 55, 81, 92, 104, 138, App G

QUEEN VICTORIA 27

QUEEN'S HEAD CAFÉ, BANGOR 47, 62, 93, 104, 107, 116, 155, 169

QUIMBY, Miss Harriet 105

de **QUINCEY**, Mr & Orchestra (*Rhyl*) 65

RAMSEY, Miss Winifed (*Colwyn Bay*) 52, 246

de **RANCE**, Mrs Annie (*Rhyl*) 24, 43, 62, 65, 230

RATHBONE, Miss Eleanor 20, 21, 46, 47, 68, 93, 100, 104, 129, 160, 192, 209-10, 211, 225

RATHBONE, Mr Harold (*Llandudno*) 16, 24, 26, 224-5

RATHBONE, Sir William MP 20, 93, 209, 224

RAW, Miss Caroline (*Llandudno*) 88, 124, 225

RAYMOND, Rev. J. (*Llandudno*) 100

REDMOND, Mr J. MP 105

REES, Miss Louisa (*Caernarfon*) 261

REILLY, Lt Col Edwin William (*Llandudno*) 225

RHODES, Mrs Mary (*Penmaenmawr*) 260

RHYL 24, 25, 26, 27, 35, 38, 39, 40, 43, 60, 62, 65, 67, 72, 73, 86, 92, 104, 108, 141, 142, 165, 202, App C

RICHARDSON, Miss Mary 'Slasher' 192

RIGBY, Dr Charles 210

RIGBY, Mrs Edith 18, 210, 211, 244

RIGBY, Miss Gertrude (*Bangor*) 164, 169, 249

JONES-**ROBERTS**, Mrs (*Bangor*) 159

ROBERTS, Mr (*Bangor*) 133

ROBERTS, Mr & Mrs Harold (*Rhyl*) 43

ROBERTS, Sir Herbert MP 54, 68, 107, 112, 115, 116, 121, 131

ROBERTS, Miss Hilda (*Penmaenmawr*) 160, 260

ROBERTS, Alderman J. (*Caernarfon*) 45

ROBERTSON, Mr James (*St Asaph/Rhyl*) 62, 74, 230

ROWLAND, Mrs Grace (*Bangor*) 255

ROWLAND, Mrs Huw (*Bangor*) 124, 125, 133, 164, 170, 173

ROWLAND, Mrs Mary (*Bangor*) 255

ROYDEN, Miss (Agnes) Maude 94, 106, 107, 108, 109, 123, 125, 152, 209, 211-12

SARSON, Colonel A. (*Colwyn Bay*) 120, 168
SARSON, Mr Arthur (*Colwyn Bay*) 247
SARSON, Mrs A. (*Rhyl*) 62, 65
SCHOLES, Mr 144, 146, 150
SEDGEWICK, Miss (*Bangor*) 138
SELBIE, Miss Elizabeth (*Colwyn Bay*) 247
SEVER, Mr William (*Conwy*) 225
SHACKLETON, Mr David MP 21
SHAW, Mr George Bernard 71
SHEFFIELD, Lord and Lady 153
SKELMERDINE, Mr Charles (*Llandudno*) 225
SMITH, Mona (*Bangor*) 74
SMYTH, Miss Ethel 203, 264
SNOWDEN, Mrs Ethel 47, 96, 97, 102, 103, 166, 167, 168, 212
SNOWDEN, Mr Philip MP 47, 212
GLADSTONE **SOLOMON**, Mrs 116, 127, 153, 212
SOMERVILLE, Mrs Mary 66
SPENCER, Miss Mildred (*Penrhyn Bay/Rhos on Sea/Colwyn Bay*) 4, 26, 27, 28, 54, 57, 58, 64, 77, 101, 105, 112, 120. 126, 128, 140, 141, 154, 155, 159, 166, 167, 177, 181, 182, 182, 242
SQUIRRELL, Mr Henry (*Deganwy*) 225
STAFFORD 144

STEAD, Mr William 124
STEEL, Mrs Flora (*Machynlleth/ Bangor*) 97, 125, 129, 256-7
STRATFORD ON AVON 145
SUGDEN, Misses Caroline/Mary/Annie (*Colwyn Bay*) 182, 247,
SUMMER SCHOOL (*Tal y Bont, Conwy Valley*) 153, 155
SUTTON, Mrs Frances (*Rhyl*) 230
SYKES, Mr (*Rhyl*) 65

TAL-Y-BONT 153
TAL-Y-SARN 92
TARPORLEY 142
TARVIN 142
TAYLOR, Mr Herbert (*Mochdre*) 158, 247
THAME 148
THOMAS, Miss Kathleen (*Colwyn Bay*) 247
THOMPSON, Mr R 120, 121
TILBY, Mr Henry (*Rhyl*) 24, 25, 230
TILLARD, Miss Violet 47, 48, 212-14
TITANIC 110,
CHENEVIX-**TRENCH**, Mrs Gwendoline (*Bangor*) 257
TURNPENNY, Police Inspector Victor (*Llandudno*) 19
TUTTON, Rev. (*Colwyn Bay*) 166

UXBRIDGE 149

VAUGHAN, Rev. T. (*Rhuddlan*) 43
VERNEY, Lady (*Bangor*) 174
VICKERY, Mr (*Rhyl*) 74
VINCENT, Mrs Bronwen (*Bangor*) 257

VINCENT, Councillor Hugh (*Bangor*) 107
VINCENT, Miss Mary (*Bangor*) 257

WARD, Mrs Humphrey 85
WARTSKI, Mr Charles (*Llandudno*) 225-6
WARTSKI, Mr Harry (*Llandudno*) 225-6
WARTSKI, Mr Isodore 99-100
WARTSKI, Mr Morris (*Llandudno*) 225-6
WARWICK 145
WATLING STREET PILGRIMS 144
WEDGWOOD, Major Cecil & Mrs 144
CORNWALLIS-WEST, Mrs Jennie 122
WHARTON, Miss Jane (Lady Constance Lytton) 61, 62, 202, 203
WHELDON, Rev. T. (*Bangor*) 15
PRICE-WHITE, Mrs Charlotte (*Bangor*) 4, 47, 56, 57, 58, 62, 69, 88, 93, 124, 125, 130, 137, 139, 140, 143, 152, 153, 155, 156, 159, 160, 164, 168, 169, 170, 171, 173, 174, 183, 185, 249-50
PRICE-WHITE, Mr Ffoulkes (*Bangor*) 74
WHITE, Miss Margery (*Bangor*) 74
WHITEHEAD, Mrs (*Bangor*) 156, 164, 169
WHITEHEAD, Mr J. (*Bangor*) 74
WILKS, Mrs Beatrice (*Colwyn Bay*) 247
HUDSON-WILLIAMS, Mrs Gwladys (*Bangor*) 97, 125, 129, 130, 133, 155, 156, 164, 168, 173, 250
HUDSON-WILLIAMS, Prof. Thomas (*Bangor*) 32, 93
PHILLIPS-WILLIAMS, Mrs (*Penmaenmawr*) 163
WILLIAMS, Miss (*Bangor – Llys Tirion*) 159
WILLIAMS, Mrs (*Bangor – The Palace*) 174
WILLIAMS, Mrs (*Bangor – Treflan*) 159
WILLIAMS, Mrs (*Rhyl – The Studio*) 227
WILLIAMS, Mrs D. (*Pwllheli*) 262
WILLIAMS, Rev. Dewi (*Penmaenmawr*) 68
WILLIAMS, Mr H. (*Penmaenmawr*) 35
WILLIAMS, Miss Margaret (*Rhyl*) 227
WILLIAMS, Mr Pentir (*Bangor*) 97, 104
WILLIAMS, Miss Selina (*Bangor*) 185
WILSON, Mrs (*Llandudno*) 16
WINCHESTER, Bishop of 158
WOLVERHAMPTON 145
WOMEN'S FREEDOM LEAGUE (WFL) 15, 35, 36, 40, 41, 42, 45, 47, 49, 55, 80, 81, 188, 199, 204, 207, 212
WOMEN'S SOCIAL & POLITICAL UNION (WSPU) 15, 20, 21, 30, 33, 41, 52, 60, 61, 72, 73, 80, 81, 85, 86. 91, 97, 98, 103, 134, 151, 155, 173, 181, 182, 187, 188, 189, 190, 193, 194, 196, 197, 198, 199, 200, 202, 203, 204, 206, 207, 208, 209, 210, 232, 245

WOMEN'S TAX RESISTANCE GROUP (WTRG) 151

WOOD, Miss (*Colwyn Bay*) 101, 242

WOODHEAD, Miss Lucy (*Colwyn Bay*) 247

WORTHAM, Miss Winifred (*Bangor*) 124, 125, 133, 250-51

WORTLEY, Mr Harry (*Bangor*) 74, 258

WRIGHT, Miss Florence (*Llandudno*) 14, 17, 24, 25, 219